Leading Work with Young People

Leading Work with Young People

This Reader forms part of the Open University course *Leading Work with Young People* (E132). This is a 30-point course and is part of the Foundation Degree in Working with Young People.

Details of this and other Open University courses can be obtained from the Student Registration and Enquiry Service, The Open University, PO Box 197, Milton Keynes MK7 6BJ, United Kingdom: tel. +44 (0)845 300 6090, e-mail general-enquiries@open.ac.uk

Alternatively, you may visit the Open University website at http://www.open.ac.uk where you can learn more about the wide range of courses and packs offered at all levels by The Open University.

Also available…

Working with Young People

Edited by Roger Harrison and Christine Wise both at The Open University

'A useful contribution to the development of resources for workers and students' – **Youth & Policy**

Working with Young People provides a selection of writing from a dynamic field of practice. The book draws together key readings reflecting the diversity of the field and covering core themes currently under discussion. These include practical guidelines for novice practitioners; policy texts from national bodies; theoretical and research based analyses; and debates about professional development.

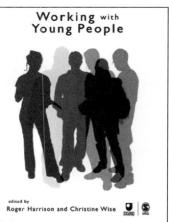

Included are chapters on:

- The ethical values and principles guiding practice
- Anti-discriminatory practice
- Concepts of youth
- Informal education
- Counselling and youth work.

This is a student-friendly and engaging text that is linked to the National Occupational Standards for Youth Work and also includes recent policy statements from the National Youth Agency and the DfES.

The book will be a core text for all those studying for foundation degrees and NVQ2 or 3 in youth work and youth studies, as well as being relevant across the undergraduate fields of social care and education. It is also an invaluable resource for experienced professionals and practice supervisors working with young people in statutory or voluntary organisations.

Working with Young People is a Course Reader for The Open University course E131: Introduction to Working with Young People.

2005 • 240 pages
Paperback (978-1-4129-1946-3)
Hardback (978-1-4129-1945-6)

Leading Work with Young People

Edited by
Roger Harrison, Cathy Benjamin,
Sheila Curran and Rob Hunter

The Open University

in association with

SAGE Publications
Los Angeles • London • New Delhi • Singapore

The Open University
Walton Hall
Milton Keynes
MK7 6AA
United Kingdom
www.open.ac.uk

First published 2007

SAGE Publications Ltd
1 Oliver's Yard
55 City Road
London EC1Y 1SP

SAGE Publications Inc.
2455 Teller Road
Thousand Oaks, California 91320

SAGE Publications India Pvt Ltd
B 1/I 1 Mohan Cooperative Industrial Area
Mathura Road, New Delhi 110 044
India

SAGE Publications Asia-Pacific Pte Ltd
33 Pekin Street #02-01
Far East Square
Singapore 048763

Library of Congress Control Number: 2007923292

British Library Cataloguing in Publication data

A catalogue record for this book is available from the British Library

ISBN 978-1-4129-4603-2
ISBN 978-1-4129-4604-9 (pbk)

Typeset by C&M Digitals (P) Ltd., Chennai, India
Printed on paper from sustainable resources
Printed in Great Britain by The Cromwell Press Ltd, Trowbridge, Wiltshire

Contents

CONTENTS

Acknowledgements

Chapter 1
This is an edited version of material first published as Chapters 1 and 2 from Doyle, M.E. and Smith, M.J. (1999) *Born and Bred: Leadership, Heart, and Informal Education*. London: YMCA George Williams College/The Rank Foundation. Reproduced by kind permission of the authors and YMCA George Williams College.

Chapter 3
Williamson, H., 'Youth work and the changing policy environment for young people'. Leicester: The National Youth Agency. Reproduced by permission of The National Youth Agency (www.nya.org.uk).

Chapter 4
This is a revised and updated version of a chapter previously published as McCulloch, K. and Tett, L., 'Ethics, accountability and the shaping of youth work practice', in S. Banks (ed.) (1999) *Ethical Issues in Youth Work*. London: Routledge. © 1999 Routledge. Reproduced by permission of Taylor & Francis UK.

Chapter 6
Figure 6.1: Roger Hart's Ladder of Participation is adapted from Arnstein, in Hart, R. (1992) *Children's Participation: From Tokenism to Citizenship*. Florence: UNICEF International Child Developement Centre (Innocenti Eassay 4). Reproduced by permission of UNICEF Innocenti Research Centre.

Figure 6.2: the *Hear by Right* framework is reprinted with the permission of Simon & Schuster Adult Publishing Group from *The Art of Japanese Management* by Richard Tanner Pascale and Anthony G. Athos.

Chapter 8
This is a revised and updated version of an article previously published as Thomas, P. (2006) 'The impact of community cohesion on youth work', *Youth and Policy*, 93. Reproduced by permission of The National Youth Agency (www.nya.org.uk).

Chapter 9

This is an edited version of material first published as Chapter 12 in Hudson, M. (2002) *Managing without Profit: The Art of Managing Third Sector Organizations*. London: Directory of Social Change. Published with permission of the author, Mike Hudson, Director of Compass Partnership (www.compasspartnership.co.uk). Compass Partnership is a management consultancy that works with Chairs and Chief Executives on the governance, strategy and management of voluntary and nonprofit organisations.

Chapter 10

This is an edited version of material first published as Chapter 12 in Hawkins, P. and Shohet, R. (2005) *Supervision in the Helping Professions: An Individual, Group and Organisational Approach*. Maidenhead: Open University Press. Reproduced with the kind permission of the Open University Press Publishing Company.

Figure 10.1: The five levels of organizational culture is after Schein, E.H. (1985) Organizational Culture and Leadership. San Francisco, CA: Jossey-Bass. Reproduced by permission of John Wiley & Sons, Inc.

Chapter 11

This is an edited version of material first published as Chapter 7 in Thompson, N. (2002) *People Skills*. New York: Palgrave Macmillan. Reproduced by permission of the author and publisher.

Chapter 13

This is an edited version of material first published as Chapter 10 in in Hudson, M. (2002) *Managing without Profit: The Art of Managing Third Sector Organizations*. London: Directory of Social Change. Published with permission of the author, Mike Hudson, Director of Compass Partnership (www.compasspartnership.co.uk). Compass Partnership is a management consultancy that works with Chairs and Chief Executives on the governance, strategy and management of voluntary and nonprofit organisations.

Chapter 14

This is an edited version of material first published as Chapter 14 in Thompson, N. (2002) *People Skills*. New York: Palgrave Macmillan. Reproduced by permission of the author and publisher.

Chapter 15

This is an edited version of material first published as Merton, B., Hunter, R. and Gore, H. (2006) *Getting Better all the Time*. Leicester: National Youth

Agency. Reproduced by permission of The National Youth Agency (www.nya.org.uk).

Chapter 17
Table 17.1: Approaches to partnership working is adapted from Orme, J., et al. (2003) *Public Health for the 21st Century: New Perspectives on Policy, Participation and Practice*. Maidenhead: Open University Press. Reproduced with the kind permission of the Open University Press Publishing Company.

Chapter 18
The *Hear by Right* framework is reprinted with the permission of Simon & Schuster Adult Publishing Group from *The Art of Japanese Management* by Richard Tanner Pascale and Anthony G. Athos.

Chapter 19
This is an edited version of a chapter first published in Smith, M. and Jeffs, T. (2005) *Informal Education: Conversation, Democracy and Learning, third edition*. Nottingham: Educational Heretics Press. Reproduced by kind permission of the publisher (www.edheretics.gn.apc.org).

Chapter 20
This is an edited version of material first published as Merton, B., Comfort, H. and Payne, M. (2005) *Recognising and Recording the Impact of Youth Work*. Leicester: The National Youth Agency. Reproduced by permission of The National Youth Agency (www.nya.org.uk).

Chapter 21
This is an edited version of Vipin Chauhan's chapter first published in Factor, F., Chauhan, V., and Pitts, J. (2001) *The RHP Companion to Working with Young People*. Lyme Regis: Russell House Publishing. Reproduced by permission of the publisher (www.russellhouse.co.uk).

Introduction

Roger Harrison, Cathy Benjamin, Sheila Curran and Rob Hunter

This book is relevant to anyone who works with, or has an interest in working with young people. It will be particularly useful to those who are working their way towards qualification or who have already qualified and want to develop a fuller understanding of the processes and policies which influence practice. The book forms a companion volume to *Working with Young People* (Harrison and Wise, 2005) and is similarly linked to The Open University's Foundation Degree. As we noted in the introduction to that book, we use the phrase 'work with young people' to indicate a wide range of practices, traditions, contexts and roles; taking account of the current breadth and diversity of this professional field. As a reader of this book you might be a youth worker, a learning mentor, a Scout or Guide leader, a sport or after-school club leader, or a specialist adviser working with young people at risk. You might be working in the voluntary or community sector, or within a local authority scheme; you might be based in an established centre or be part of a detached youth work team; you might be employed full time or giving a few hours a week as a volunteer worker. You might also be a tutor, course organiser or researcher in this or a related field of practice.

The focus of this book on 'leading' signals a shift from working directly with young people towards a broader examination of the ways in which this work is planned, developed and delivered. It represents a more strategic viewpoint, taking account of the context in which practice occurs, the teams and organisations through which it is developed, and the social and political environment in which it is both shaped and enacted. We understand leadership as linked not only with hierarchical position, but dispersed throughout the organisation, occurring at all levels, including that of the young people who are the 'clients' or 'users' of the services. In this sense we view leadership not simply in terms of leading, but as participating in making informed contributions to the work of a project or an organisation. The chapters we have selected and commissioned for inclusion in this book aim to develop understandings which will allow this more informed participation in decision making and the implementation of practice. They examine the meanings of leadership and how these play out in the current policy context (Part 1); the practical and ethical tensions which occur when different forms of practice are introduced into work with young people (Part 2); the role of supportive relationships and their effects on organisational culture and performance (Part 3); and the challenges presented by organisational change (Part 4); the potential of interagency partnerships in delivering the best outcomes for young people (Part 5); the place of evaluation and monitoring in improving the quality of services provided to young people (Part 6). In this sense leadership becomes the responsibility of all those working within organisations, not simply those of the manager or director. It aligns our concept of leadership with the view that 'leading is surely the act of working with a group of individuals to achieve communal goals' (Goddard, 2003).

We recognise that ideas of leadership and management are controversial across the helping professions. In many areas of the public and voluntary sectors discourses of leadership have become associated with 'managerialist' concerns with control, target setting and the measurement of performance, often at the expense of those outcomes which are more difficult to quantify but are nevertheless valuable. In addition to these negative associations, those who work with young people often see themselves as advocates for, and activists on behalf of, the young people they work with, taking their side against the forces of authority whether this is represented by the popular press, government agencies or their own organisation (Millar, 2003). So while some are enthusiastic about taking on leadership roles in order to promote the interests of young people, for others their suspicion of authority and their instinctive support for the less powerful make them uncomfortable about taking on the role of leader or manager.

The idea of leadership is also controversial and contested within the academic literature. Leadership is sometimes defined in contrast with management, where leadership is visionary and concerned with influencing and inspiring others, while management is concerned with the more mundane or practical activities of planning, co-ordinating, monitoring and controlling the activities of the organisation. Here leadership is creative, dynamic and overarching while management focuses on the day-to-day business of making sure the organisation runs smoothly and efficiently. Another perspective views management as the overarching concept, with leadership as a subset of management. We often hear about the 'management of change' or 'strategic management' both of which involve leadership concerns with vision, mission and direction. It can sometimes appear that the two terms are used interchangeably or simply spliced together in the single phrase 'leadership and management'. In the title of this book we have put the emphasis on leadership as this seems more appropriate to the nature of the work we are engaged in. Those who work with young people generally see themselves as 'people workers' rather than managers. However, the effective delivery of good quality services to young people is also dependent on the efficient management of organisations, and so you will find that many of the chapters refer to 'management' rather than 'leadership'.

The chapters included in this book are a mixture of edited pieces which have already been published in books, journals or on websites, and newly commissioned chapters. While the literature on work with young people is vibrant and diverse, one of the challenges in putting this book together has been the dearth of writing specifically on leadership in the field of work with young people. The opening chapter by Michele Erina Doyle and Mark K. Smith, taken from the INFED website, was one of the few. About half the chapters are therefore newly commissioned pieces, chosen because they bring new perspectives from practising leaders and managers, such as Michael Bracey's account of becoming an 'accidental leader', or Bill Badham and Tim Davies' chapter on involving young people in designing and implementing services. The chapters included here are not intended to provide comprehensive coverage of the subject matter. There is, for example, far more attention to English policies and practices than to those of Wales, Scotland and Northern Ireland, though we note that the different nation states are attempting to address similar themes and looking to each other for 'cautionary messages' (Davies, 2006). More attention is given to statutory youth work than to work in the voluntary or not-for-profit sector, though we recognise that these boundaries are becoming increasingly difficult to draw. What we have tried to do is represent a range of viewpoints and cover a number of themes and issues which seem particularly relevant at this time, and which we hope will be useful to anyone who wishes to develop their understanding of work with young people.

References

Davies, B. (2006) 'Cautionary messages from England', in F. Patrick (ed.) *Youth Work and Young People: Realising Potential*. Dundee: University of Dundee.

Goddard, J.T. (2003) 'Leadership in the (post) modern era', in N. Bennett and L. Anderson (eds) *Rethinking Educational Leadership*. London: Sage.

Harrison, R. and Wise C. (eds) (2005) *Working with Young People*. London: Sage.

Millar, G. (2003) 'Beyond managerialism: an exploration of the occupational culture of youth and community work', in *20 Years of Youth Policy: A Retrospective*. Leicester: National Youth Agency.

Leadership

Leadership has been studied over time, across cultures and from different theoretical positions, yet there remains no settled definition of what it means. In our everyday understandings we tend to fall back on what Michele Erina Doyle and Mark Smith refer to here as the 'classical' theories which focus on the traits, qualities and behaviours of individual leaders. What these theories suggest is that as long as we can learn how to behave and respond to situations in certain ways we will be able to exercise effective leadership in almost any setting. The consequences of this belief can be seen in the current fashion for identifying and rewarding exceptionally skilled individuals such as 'super-heads', who can move into a struggling organisation and 'turn it around'.

The observation that leaders who are effective in one organisation are not always effective when they transfer to another has contributed to the emergence of theories which move the focus away from the individual leader to the context or situation in which leadership occurs, where context includes the history and traditions of the organisation, the people who work for it and the social and political environment in which it operates. In the context of informal education with young people Doyle and Smith argue in Chapter 1 that values and ethics are a central part of this history and tradition and this leads them to a particular understanding of the forms of leadership which are therefore most appropriate. For them, democratic and shared forms of leadership with an emphasis on cooperation, participation and learning provide the best model for informal educators.

The preoccupation of research with the individual characteristics or traits of leaders has led to the idea that leaders are born, not made, and therefore the key to success lies in identifying those who were born to the role. Michael Bracey's account of his own career path forms a powerful antidote to that simplistic view. His chapter entitled, 'The Accidental Leader' introduces a key theme; the important role played by situation, by events and by timing in the development of individuals and organisations. Where opportunities are offered and when situations demand it, people are capable of developing into leadership roles. This is not to underplay the importance of individual agency. As Bracey's story indicates it is how people respond to situations and how they learn from events and from other people which determines the outcomes.

As we have seen, it is difficult to think about leadership outside of a particular context. In Chapter 3 Howard Williamson brings into focus the wider social policy context against which youth services have developed over the last decade and outlines the dramatic reorganisation of services to children and young people which follow in their wake. His account reminds us that the kind of work we do with young people is, and always has been, in transition. Williamson identifies the social policy priorities which youth work is seen as contributing towards: the development of personal responsibility, active citizenship, community involvement; and preparation for the labour market. He reviews the opportunities for youth work in moving from the margins to the mainstream of government policy, but also the dangers of losing sight of the values and principles which underpin this work.

What is leadership?

Michele Erina Doyle and Mark K. Smith

Classical leadership

Leadership is one of those qualities that you can recognize when you see it, but is nonetheless difficult to describe. There are almost as many definitions as there are commentators, however many associate leadership with one person leading. Four things stand out in this respect: (i) to lead involves influencing others; (ii) where there are leaders there are followers; (iii) leaders seem to come to the fore when there is a crisis or special problem, in other words, they often become visible when an innovative response is needed; and (iv) leaders are people who have a clear idea of what they want to achieve and why. Thus, leaders are people who are able to think and act creatively in non-routine situations – and who set out to influence the actions, beliefs and feelings of others. In this sense being a 'leader' is personal, it flows from an individual's qualities and actions, however, it is also often linked to some other role such as manager or expert. Here there can be a lot of confusion, for example, not all managers are leaders and not all leaders are managers.

In the recent literature of leadership (that is over the last 80 years or so) there have been four main 'generations' of theory:

1. Trait theories
2. Behavioural theories
3. Contingency theories
4. Transformational theories

This is an edited version of material first published as Chapters 1 and 2 from Doyle, M. E. and Smith, M. K., *Born and Bred? Leadership, Heart and Informal Education*, London: YMCA George Williams College/The Rank Foundation.

Traits

Leaders are people who are able to express themselves fully, says Warren Bennis. 'They also know what they want', he continues, 'why they want it, and how to communicate what they want to others, in order to gain their co-operation and support.' Lastly, 'they know how to achieve their goals' (Bennis, 1998: 3). But what is it that makes someone exceptional in this respect? As soon as we study the lives of people who have been labelled as great or effective leaders, it becomes clear that they have very different qualities. We only have to think of political figures like Nelson Mandela, Margaret Thatcher and Mao Zedong to confirm this.

Instead of starting with exceptional individuals many turned to setting out the general qualities or *traits* they believed should be present. Surveys of early trait research by Stogdill (1948) and Mann (1959) reported that many studies identified personality characteristics that appear to differentiate leaders from followers. However, as Peter Wright (1996: 34) has commented, 'others found no differences between leaders and followers with respect to these characteristics, or even found people who possessed them were less likely to become leaders'. Yet pick up almost any of the popular books on the subject today and you will still find a list of traits that are thought to be central to effective leadership. The basic idea remains that if a person possesses these she or he will be able to take the lead in very different situations. At first glance, the lists seem to be helpful (see, for example, Exhibit 1). But spend any time around them and they can leave a lot to be desired.

Exhibit 1: Gardner's (1989) leadership attributes

John Gardner studied a large number of North American organizations and leaders and came to the conclusion that there were some qualities or attributes that did appear to mean that a leader in one situation could lead in another. These included:

- Physical vitality and stamina
- Intelligence and action-oriented judgement
- Eagerness to accept responsibility
- Task competence
- Understanding of followers and their needs
- Skill in dealing with people
- Need for achievement

(Continued)

(Continued)
- Capacity to motivate people
- Courage and resolution
- Trustworthiness
- Decisiveness
- Self-confidence
- Assertiveness
- Adaptability/flexibility

The first problem is that the early searchers after traits often assumed that there was a definite set of characteristics that made a leader – whatever the situation. In other words, they thought the same traits would work on a battlefield and in the staff room of a school. They, and later writers, also tended to mix some very different qualities. Some of Gardner's qualities, for example, are aspects of a person's behaviour, some are skills, and others are to do with temperament and intellectual ability. Like other lists of this nature it is quite long – so what happens when someone has some but not all of the qualities? On the other hand, the list is not exhaustive and it is possible that someone might have other 'leadership qualities'. What of these?

Behaviours

As the early researchers ran out of steam in their search for traits, they turned to what leaders did – how they behaved (especially towards followers). They moved from leaders to leadership and this became the dominant way of approaching leadership within organizations in the 1950s and early 1960s. Different patterns of behaviour were grouped together and labelled as styles. Various schemes appeared, designed to diagnose and develop people's style of working. Despite different names, the basic ideas were very similar. The four main styles that appeared as described by Wright (1996: 36–7) are:

- **Concern for task**. Here leaders emphasize the achievement of concrete objectives. They look for high levels of productivity and ways to organize people and activities in order to meet those objectives.
- **Concern for people**. In this style, leaders look upon their followers as people – their needs, interests, problems, development, and so on. They are not simply units of production or means to an end.

- **Directive leadership**. This style is characterized by leaders taking decisions for others and expecting followers or subordinates to follow instructions.
- **Participative leadership**. Here leaders try to share decision making with others.

Often, we find two of these styles present in books and training materials. For example, concern for task is set against concern for people (after Blake and Mouton, 1964) and directive is contrasted with participative leadership (for example, McGregor's [1960] portrayal of managers as 'Theory X' or 'Theory Y'). If you have been on a teamwork or leadership development course then it is likely you will have come across some variant of this in an exercise or discussion.

Many of the early writers that looked to participative and people-centred leadership, argued that it brought about greater satisfaction among followers (subordinates). However, as Sadler (1997) reports, when researchers really got to work on this it didn't seem to stand up. There were lots of differences and inconsistencies between studies. It was difficult to say style of leadership was significant in enabling one group to work better than another. Perhaps the main problem, though, was one shared with those who looked for traits (Wright, 1996: 47). The researchers did not look properly at the context or setting in which the style was used. Is it possible that the same style would work as well in a gang or group of friends, and in a hospital emergency room? The styles that leaders can adopt are far more affected by those they are working with and the environment they are operating within, than had been thought originally.

Situations

Researchers began to turn to the contexts in which leadership is exercised and the idea that what is needed changes from situation to situation. Some looked to the processes by which leaders emerge in different circumstances, for example, at moments of great crisis or where there is a vacuum. Others turned to the ways in which leaders and followers viewed each other in various contexts, for example, in the army, political parties and in companies. The most extreme view was that just about everything was determined by the context. But most writers did not take this route. They brought the idea of style with them, believing that the style needed would change with the situation. Another way of putting this is that particular contexts would demand particular forms of leadership. This placed a premium on people who were able to develop an ability to work in different ways, and could change their style to suit the situation.

What began to develop was a *contingency* approach. The central idea was that effective leadership was dependent on a mix of factors. For example, Fred E. Fiedler argued that effectiveness depends on two interacting factors: leadership style and the degree to which the situation gives the leader control and influence. Three things are important here:

- **The relationship between the leaders and followers**. If leaders are liked and respected they are more likely to have the support of others.
- **The structure of the task**. If the task is clearly spelled out as to goals, methods and standards of performance then it is more likely that leaders will be able to exert influence.
- **Position power**. If an organization or group confers powers on the leader for the purpose of getting the job done, then this may well increase the influence of the leader. (Fiedler and Garcia, 1987: 51–67; see also Fiedler, 1997)

Models like this can help us to think about what we are doing in different situations. For example, we may be more directive where a quick response is needed, and where people are used to being told what to do, rather than having to work at it themselves. The models have found their way into various management training aids, such as Hersey and Blanchard's (1977) very influential discussion of choosing the appropriate style for the particular situation as shown in Exhibit 2.

Exhibit 2: Hersey and Blanchard (1977) on leadership style and situation

Hersey and Blanchard identified four different leadership styles that could be drawn upon to deal with contrasting situations:

Telling (high task/low relationship behaviour). This style or approach is characterized by giving a great deal of direction to subordinates and by giving considerable attention to defining roles and goals. The style was recommended for dealing with new staff, or where the work was menial or repetitive, or where things had to be completed within a short time span. Subordinates are viewed as being unable and unwilling to 'do a good job'.

Selling (high task/high relationship behaviour). Here, while most of the direction is given by the leader, there is an attempt at encouraging people to 'buy into' the task. Sometimes characterized as a 'coaching' approach, it is to be used when people are willing and motivated but lack the required 'maturity' or 'ability'.

(Continued)

(Continued)

Participating (high relationship/low task behaviour). Here decision making is shared between leaders and followers – the main role of the leader being to facilitate and communicate. It entails high support and low direction and is used when people are able, but are perhaps unwilling or insecure (they are of 'moderate to high maturity' (Hersey 1984).

Delegating (low relationship/low task behaviour). The leader still identifies the problem or issue, but the responsibility for carrying out the response is given to followers. It entails having a high degree of competence and maturity (people know what to do and are motivated to do it).

Aside from their very general nature, there are some issues with such models. First, much that has been written has a North American bias. There is considerable evidence to suggest cultural factors influence the way that people carry out, and respond to, different leadership styles. For example, some cultures are more individualistic, or value family as against bureaucratic models, or have very different expectations about how people address and talk with each other. All this impacts on the choice of style and approach.

Second, there may be different patterns of leadership linked with men and women. Some have argued that women may have leadership styles that are more nurturing, caring and sensitive. They look more to relationships. Men are said to look to task. However, there is a lot of debate about this. We can find plenty of examples of nurturing men and task-oriented women. Any contrasts between the style of men and women may be down to the situation. In management, for example, women are more likely to be in positions of authority in people-oriented sectors, so this aspect of style is likely to be emphasized.

Transformations

Burns (1978) argued that it was possible to distinguish between transactional and transforming leaders (Exhibit 3). The former, 'approach their followers with an eye to trading one thing for another' (1978: 4), while the latter are visionary leaders who seek to appeal to their followers' 'better nature and move them toward higher and more universal needs and purposes' (Bolman and Deal, 1997: 314). In other words, the leader is seen as a change agent.

Exhibit 3: Transactional and transformational leadership (Bass, 1985; Wright, 1996: 213)

Transactional

The transactional leader:

Recognizes what it is that we want to get from work and tries to ensure that we get it if our performance merits it.

Exchanges rewards and promises for our effort.

Is responsive to our immediate self-interests if they can be met by getting the work done.

Transformational

The transformational leader:

Raises our level of awareness, our level of consciousness about the significance and value of designated outcomes, and ways of reaching them.

Gets us to transcend our own self-interest for the sake of the team, organization or larger polity.

Alters our need level (after Maslow) and expands our range of wants and needs.

There is strong emphasis in the contemporary literature of management leadership on charismatic and related forms of leadership. However, whether there is a solid body of evidence to support its effectiveness is an open question. Indeed, Wright (1996: 221) concludes 'it is impossible to say how effective transformational leadership is with any degree of certainty'. We will return to some questions around charisma later, but first we need to briefly examine the nature of authority in organizations (and the relationship to leadership).

Authority

Frequently we confuse leadership with authority. To explore this we can turn to Heifetz's (1994) important discussion of the matter. Authority is often seen as the possession of powers based on formal role. In organizations, for example, we tend to focus on the manager or officer. They are seen as people who have the right to direct us. We obey them because we see their exercise of power as legitimate. It may also be that we fear the consequences of not following their orders or 'requests'. The possibility of them sacking, demoting or disadvantaging us may well secure our compliance. We may also follow them because they show leadership. As we have seen, the latter is generally something more informal – the ability to make sense of, and act in, situations that are out of the ordinary. In this way leaders don't simply influence, they have to show that crises or unexpected events and experiences do not faze them. Leaders may have formal authority, but they rely in large part on informal authority. This flows from their personal qualities and actions. They may be trusted, respected for their expertise, or followed because of their ability to persuade.

Leaders have authority as part of an exchange: if they fail to deliver the goods, to meet people's expectations, they run the risk of authority being removed and given to another. Those who have formal authority over them may take this action. However, we also need to consider the other side. Followers, knowingly or unknowingly, accept the right of the person to lead – and he or she is dependent on this. The leader also relies on 'followers' for feedback and contributions. Without these they will not have the information and resources to do their job. Leaders and followers are interdependent.

People who do not have formal positions of power can also enjoy informal authority. In a football team, for example, the manager may not be the most influential person. It could be an established player who can read the game and energise that colleagues turn to. In politics a classic example is Gandhi, who for much of the time held no relevant formal position but through his example and his thinking became an inspiration for others.

Having formal authority is both a resource and a constraint. On the one hand it can bring access to systems and resources. Handled well it can help people feel safe. On the other hand, formal authority carries a set of expectations and these can be quite unrealistic in times of crisis. Being outside the formal power structure, but within an organization, can be an advantage. You can have more freedom of movement, the chance of focusing on what you see as the issue (rather than the organization's focus), and there is a stronger chance of being in touch with what people are feeling 'at the frontline'.

Charisma

Before moving on it is important to look at the question of charisma. It is so much a part of how we look at leadership but it is a difficult quality to tie down. Charisma is, literally, a gift of grace or of God (Wright, 1996: 194). Max Weber, more than anyone, brought this idea into the realm of leadership. He used 'charisma' to talk about self-appointed leaders who are followed by those in distress. Such leaders gain influence because they are seen as having special talents or gifts that can help people escape the pain they are in (Gerth et al., 1991: 51–55).

When thinking about charisma we often look to the qualities of particular individuals – their skills, personality and presence. But this is only one side of things. We need to explore the situations in which charisma arises. When strong feelings of distress are around there does seem to be a tendency to turn to figures who seem to have answers. To make our lives easier we may want to put the burden of finding and making solutions on someone else. In this way we help to make the role for 'charismatic leaders' to step into. They in turn will seek to convince us of their special gifts and of their solution to the crisis or problem. When these things come together something very powerful can happen. It doesn't necessarily mean that the problem is dealt with, but we can come to believe it is. Regarding such leaders with awe, perhaps being inspired in different ways by them, we can begin to feel safer and directed. This can be a great resource. Someone like Martin Luther King used the belief that people had in him to take forward civil rights in the United States. He was able to contain a lot of the stress his supporters felt and give hope of renewal. He articulated a vision of what was possible and worked with people to develop strategies. But there are also considerable dangers.

Charisma involves dependency. It can mean giving up our responsibilities. Sadly, it is all too easy to let others who seem to know what they are doing get on with difficult matters. By placing people on a pedestal the distance between 'us' and 'them' widens. They seem so much more able or in control. Rather than facing up to situations and making our own solutions, we remain followers (and are often encouraged to do so). There may well come a point when the lie implicit in this confronts us. Just as we turned to charismatic leaders, we can turn against them. It could be we recognize that the 'solution' we signed up to has not made things better. It might be that some scandal or incident reveals the leader in what we see as a bad light. Whatever, we can end up blaming, and even destroying, the leader. Unfortunately, we may simply turn to another rather than looking to our own capacities.

In this part of the chapter, we have tried to set out some of the elements of a 'classical' view of leadership. We have seen how commentators have searched for special traits and behaviours and looked at the different situations where leaders work and emerge. Running through much of this is a set of beliefs that we can describe as a classical view of leadership where leaders:

- Tend to be identified by position; they are part of the hierarchy
- Become the focus for answers and solutions. We look to them when we don't know what to do or when we can't be bothered to work things out for ourselves
- Give direction and have vision
- Have special qualities setting them apart. These help to create the gap between leaders and followers.

This view of leadership sits quite comfortably with the forms of organization that are common in business, the armed forces and government. Where the desire is to get something done, to achieve a narrow range of objectives in a short period of time, then it may make sense to think in this way. However, this has its dangers. While some 'classical' leaders may have a more participative style, it is still just a style. A great deal of power remains in their hands and the opportunity for all to take responsibility and face larger questions is curtailed. It can also feed into a 'great-man' model of leadership and minimize our readiness to question those who present us with easy answers. As our awareness of our own place in the making of leadership grows, we may be less ready to hand our responsibilities to others. We may also come to realize our own power:

> I don't think it's actually possible to lead somebody. I think you can allow yourself to be led. It's a bit like other things – you can't teach, you can only learn – because you can only control yourself.

More inclusive and informal understandings of leadership offer some interesting possibilities, as we can see in our discussion of the next part of the discussion.

Shared leadership

> The group took over. There was a whole group leadership thing. I don't think leadership's necessarily about one person sometimes – everyone has the qualities of being a leader or taking some form of responsibility in their lives, and sometimes that's a whole group ethos.
> I want to work in a situation where people can take on roles and responsibilities, tasks, whatever they want to do. As long as I can assist in this, rather than being the forerunning force taking it over, then that's what I'm aiming for.

Everyday leadership

If we look at everyday life – the situations and groups we are involved in – then we soon find leadership. Friends deciding how they are going to spend an evening, families negotiating over housework – each involve influence and decision. However, such leadership often does not reside in a person. It may be shared and can move. In one situation an individual may be influential because of their expertise or position, in another it can be someone completely different. What these people may be able to do is to offer an idea or an action that helps to focus or restructure the situation and the way in which others see things.

Sometimes there may not even be one person we can readily label as leader – just a group working together to achieve what is wanted. Rather than people leading, it is ideals and ideas. We don't follow an individual; we follow the conversation. Through listening and contributing, thoughts and feelings emerge and develop. It is not the force of personality that leads us on but the rightness of what is said.

From this we can see that it is not our position that is necessarily important, but our behaviour. The question is whether or not our actions help groups and relationships to work and achieve. Actions that do this could be called leadership, and can come from any group member. Many writers – especially those looking at management – tend to talk about leadership as a person having a clear vision and the ability to make it real. However, as we have begun to discover, leadership lies not so much in one person having a clear vision as in our capacity to work with others in creating one.

We may also recognize the power of self-leadership, as one worker put it: 'me trying to get the most out of my own resources'. Some people have talked of this as the influence we exert on ourselves 'to achieve the self-motivation and self-direction we need to perform' (Manz et al., 1989). Such self-motivation and self-direction can impact on others. The worker continued:

> [It] then moves onto staff, for them to discover the self-resources that they have within themselves and then look for anything that needs developing ... For young people, it's about getting them to realise their self-leadership, to realise their own potential.

The leadership process is part of our daily experience. We may lead others, ourselves, or be led. We play our part in relationships and groups where it is always around. Sometimes there is an obvious 'leader', often there isn't. Nor are there always obvious followers. The world is not neatly divided in this respect. Part of our responsibility as partners in the process is to work so that those who may label themselves as followers come to see that they, too, are leaders.

> What I understand of leadership is encouraging, or getting, people to realise their own resources, what they've got within them.

As individuals we are part of the leadership process and, at times, receive the gift of being the leader from others.

Ethics

We also want to take things a stage further. For something to qualify as 'leadership' we must also make judgements about the quality of what happens. It should enrich the lives we all lead. Here we want to highlight two aspects. Leadership must be:

- **Inclusive** – we all share in the process.
- **Elevating** – we become wiser and better people by being involved (Heifetz, 1994).

We want to include these ethical qualities so that we can make proper judgements about leadership. For example, if we stay with a simple technical definition such as that offered by Bass (1990) (leadership as the exercise of influence in a group context) then we can look at a figure like Hitler and say he was, in many respects, a great leader. He had a vision, was able to energize a large number of people around it, and develop the effectiveness of the organizations he was responsible for. However, as soon as we ask whether his actions were inclusive and elevating we come to a very different judgement. He was partly responsible for the death and exclusion of millions of people. He focused people's attention on the actions of external enemies, internal scapegoats and false images of community while avoiding facing a deeper analysis of the country's ills.

Hopefully, the point is made. Leadership involves making ethical as well as technical judgements.

Craig E. Johnson (2001: 9–23) has usefully employed the metaphor of shadow and light in this respect. He argues that leaders 'have the power to illuminate the lives of followers or to cover them in darkness' (2001: 9) and they cast shadows when they:

- *Abuse power*. Power can have a corrosive effect on those who possess it. Large differentials in the relative power of leaders and followers can also contribute towards abuse. Power deprivation exerts its own corruptive influence. Followers can become fixated on what minimal influence they have, becoming cautious, defensive and critical of others and new ideas. They may even engage in sabotage (2001: 10–14).
- *Hoard privileges*. Leaders nearly always enjoy greater privileges (in the form of perks, pay and access). Leaders that hoard power are also likely to hoard wealth and status as well, and in so doing contribute to a growing gap between the haves and the have-nots. (2001: 14–15).
- *Encourage deceit*. Leaders have more access to information than others in an organisation. They are more likely to participate in the decision-making processes, network with those with power, have access to different information sources such as personnel files. Patterns of

deception, whether they take the form of outright lies or hiding or distorting information, destroy the trust that binds leaders and followers together (2001: 15–18).

- *Act inconsistently*. Diverse followers, varying levels of relationships and elements of situations make consistency an ethical burden of leadership. Shadows arise when leaders appear to act arbitrarily and unfairly (2001: 18–19).
- *Misplace or betray loyalties*. Leaders have to weigh a range of loyalties or duties when making choices. Leaders cast shadows when they violate the loyalty of followers and the community (2001: 19–20).
- *Fail to assume responsibilities*. Leaders act irresponsibly when they fail to make reasonable efforts to prevent followers' misdeeds; ignore or deny ethical problems; don't shoulder responsibility for the consequences of their directives; deny their duties to their followers; and hold followers to higher standards than themselves (2001: 21–22).

Democratic leadership and shared leadership

Aspects of the approach we are exploring here are sometimes called democratic leadership. It involves people, and can foster a belief in democratic principles and processes such as self-determination and participation. These are concerns that we share. However, we want to widen things out. We want to include everyday behaviour that is inclusive and looks to enriching all our lives, but that does not have an explicit democratic focus. We call this 'shared leadership'.

For such leadership to develop we need to pay special attention to three things. We need to encourage (after Gastil, 1997):

- **Ownership**. Problems and issues need to become a responsibility of all with proper chances for people to share and participate.
- **Learning**. An emphasis on learning and development is necessary so that people can share, understand and contribute to what's going on.
- **Sharing**. Open, respectful and informed conversation is central.

We want to look at each of these in turn.

Ownership

Leadership to me is around taking some form of responsibility in any given situation.

There are some very practical reasons for encouraging people to own the problems facing them. For example, where the problem is non-routine and needs an unusual response, it is important to have the right information. Involving those with a stake in the situation – especially those at the sharp end – gives a chance for insights to emerge. Further, the more people take on an issue or problem as theirs and involve themselves in thinking through responses, the more likely they are to act and to carry things through. They have an investment in making things happen. It is their solution, not somebody else's. When we own a problem it becomes our responsibility. If things go wrong when trying to find a solution, we cannot blame others. For these reasons alone we may be very resistant to shouldering responsibility.

We may also be frightened and lost. Sometimes the issue facing us is so complex or of such a scale that we don't know where to start. We may be worried about getting things wrong, of not understanding what the issues are, or adding to conflict. Faced by a crisis or an apparently insoluble problem, we may look for strong leadership. It may be through anxiety, hostility or helplessness (to name just a few emotions) that we are ready to turn to those who seem to have an answer.

We may also try to avoid taking responsibility for things because we are lazy or want others to do things for us. After all, if we own a problem then we will have to act at some point. Why bother exerting ourselves if we can sit back and let someone else take the strain? This takes us straight into the realm of ethical questions. Is it fair that someone should take a ride on the back of others? Is it right to benefit from belonging to a group, team or organization without making the fullest contribution we can?

Learning

> I don't think leadership is about being a manager and cracking the whip and getting people to do the job, but do I think it is about just keeping the learning on track, so there is some sort of agreed ... way forward.

To act for the best we need to be informed. Our actions have to be shaped by a good understanding of the situation and of the possibilities open to us. We also need to develop some very practical skills and to attend to our feelings. In short we need to deepen our understanding and develop and share in this with others. Leadership entails learning; it means becoming wiser and more knowledgeable.

Wisdom is not something that we possess like a book or computer. It is a quality that appears in action. The people we describe as wise do not necessarily know a lot of things. They are not encyclopedias. Rather, they are able to reflect on a situation and, as likely or not, encourage others to join with them. Crucially they are also able to relate this to the sorts of practical actions that are right for the situation (Kekes, 1995).

Yet there is something more at work here. Wisdom is wrapped up with morality. To be wise, we would argue, is also to have a care for people (including ourselves) and for how we may all live more fulfilling lives. If we are to think and to evaluate we must have standards by which to judge what we find. This means looking to what philosophers like Aristotle talked about as the good life. This involves having an understanding of the different things that need to come together if people are to flourish. Wisdom lies in not having fixed ideas, but in taking a position and modifying it in the light of experience. We must have some humility – to be open to others, to experiences and to criticism.

This is a theme picked up by writers like Ronald A. Heifetz. He argues that true leaders are educators. Their task is to work with communities to face problems and lead themselves rather than to influence people to agree to a particular position. They help to build environments in which people can reflect upon how they can help with solving problems and with achieving goals. Furthermore, there is a need to develop people's ability to make decisions, work together and think in ways that respect others.

Sharing

> I feel if there's openness and honest sharing, I think you can deal with (things). If the climate is not set, people won't share and (things) are harder to deal with.

Alongside spreading ownership and cultivating learning we need to develop open and productive ways of sharing our thoughts and feelings. This isn't just so that we can make better decisions, but also so we can talk and be with others. Through this we may learn about them, ourselves and find our place in the world. In short, this means developing conversations that involve people, deepen understanding and help us make sound judgements and decisions.

Good conversation involves us in cooperating, thinking of each other's feelings and experiences, and giving each room to talk. It is for this reason that Peter Senge (1990) accords dialogue a central role in the learning organization. The virtues it involves are central to building stronger and healthier communities and organizations:

- **Concern**. To be with people, engaging them in conversation involves commitment to each other. We feel something for the other person as well as the topic.

- **Trust**. We have to take what others are saying in good faith. This is not the same as being gullible. While we may take things on trust, we will be looking to check whether our trust is being abused.
- **Respect**. While there may be considerable differences between partners in conversation, the process can only continue if there is mutual regard.
- **Appreciation**. Linked to respect, this involves valuing the unique qualities that others bring.
- **Affection**. Conversation involves a feeling with, and for, those taking part.
- **Hope**. We engage in conversation in the belief that it holds possibility. Often it is not clear what we will gain or learn, but faith in the process carries us forward (Burbules, 1993).

In good conversation the topic takes over; it leads us, rather than us leading it. Where conversation has taken over, people run with the exchanges and gain learning from that. It turns into a journey of discovery rather than a route with a fixed destination. For leadership this can be liberating. It means that as individuals we don't have to know the answers. What we need is to develop ways of being in conversation (including silence) that allow those answers to surface.

Conclusion

We have seen some deeply contrasting views of leadership (and) we can see how easy it is for people to misunderstand each other. When we talk of leadership are we looking to position or process, individual activity or social interaction, orders or conversation? What one person means can be very different to another. It is also clear why many informal educators like youth workers are unhappy talking of leadership. Their understanding often leans to the classical. If it were the other way it might be a very different picture. 'Shared leadership' carries some familiar qualities for informal educators.

Both approaches have their pitfalls. We have already discussed some of the problems with classical approaches. Here we highlight four associated with shared leadership. First, the emphasis on process can lead to a lack of attention to product or outcome. It can provide an alibi for laziness and incompetence when little is achieved. Care needs to be taken not to lose sight of the question or problem that is the subject of decision making.

Second, the emphasis on group life within shared leadership approaches may mean that the excellence or flair of the individual is not rewarded. The person concerned can experience this as unfair and demotivating – and the group may lose out as a result. Resentment might grow, and innovative solutions to problems may not be forthcoming. There will be times when it makes sense to follow the lead of a gifted individual.

Third, the commitments, understandings and practices of shared leadership are sophisticated and it is easy to see why, at this level alone, people may shy away from it. It is an 'ideal model' and as such can easily mutate.

Fourth, all models of leadership are culturally specific. What may be viewed as appropriate in one society or group may not be so in another.

This said, thinking about leadership in these ways allows us to begin to get to the heart of what it may involve and how we may respond.

References

Bass, B. M. (1985) *Leadership and Performance Beyond Expectation*, New York: Free Press.

Bass, B. M. (1990) *Bass and Stogdill's Handbook of Leadership* (3rd edn), New York: Free Press.

Bennis, W. (1998) *On Becoming a Leader*, London: Arrow.

Blake, R. R. and Mouton, J. S. (1964) *The Managerial Grid*, Houston TX: Gulf.

Bolman, L. G. and Deal, T. E. (1997) *Reframing Organizations. Artistry, Choice and Leadership* (2nd edn). San Francisco: Jossey-Bass.

Burbules, N. C. (1993) *Dialogue in Teaching*. New York: Teachers College Press.

Burns, J. M. (1978) *Leadership*, New York: Harper Collins.

Fiedler, F. E. and Garcia, J. E. (1987) *New Approaches to Effective Leadership*, New York: John Wiley.

Fiedler, F. E. (1997) 'Situational control and a dynamic theory of leadership', in K. Grint (ed.) *Leadership: Classical, Contemporary and Critical Approaches*, Oxford: Oxford University Press.

Gardner, J. (1989) *On Leadership*, New York: Free Press.

Gastil, J. (1997) 'A definition and illustration of democratic leadership', in K. Grint (ed.) *Leadership*. Oxford: Oxford University Press.

Gerth, H. and Wright Mills, C. (eds) (1991) *From Max Weber. Essays in Sociology*, London: Routledge.

Heifetz, R. A. (1994) *Leadership Without Easy Answers*, Cambridge, MA: Belknap Press.

Hersey, P. (1984) *The Situational Leader*. New York: Warner.

Hersey, P. and Blanchard, K. H. (1977) *The Management of Organizational Behaviour* (3rd edn). Upper Saddle River, NJ: Prentice Hall.

Johnson, C. E. (2001) *Meeting the Ethical Challenges of Leadership. Casting Light or Shadow*. Thousand Oaks, CA.: Sage.

Kekes, J. (1995) *Moral Wisdom and Good Lives*, Ithaca, NY: Cornell University Press.

McGregor, D. (1960) *The Human Side of Enterprise*, New York: McGraw Hill.

Mann, R. D. (1959) 'A review of the relationship between personality and performance in small groups', *Psychological Bulletin* 66(4): 241–70.

Manz, C. C. and Sims, H. P. (1989) *Superleadership: Leading Others to Lead Themselves*. New York: Prentice Hall.

Reddin, W. J. (1987) *How to Make Management Style More Effective*, Maidenhead: McGraw Hill.

Sadler, P. (1997) *Leadership*, London: Kogan Page.

Senge, P. M. (1990) *The Fifth Discipline. The Art and Practice of the Learning Organization*, London: Random House.

Stogdill, R. M. (1948) 'Personal factors associated with leadership: a survey of the literature', *Journal of Psychology*, 25: 35–71.

Wright, P. (1996) *Managerial Leadership*, London: Routledge.

2

The accidental leader

Michael Bracey

Introduction

Youth services are full of accidental leaders. Very few people I've come across entered the profession because of a driving ambition to lead it. For many it 'just sort of happens'. This chapter offers a personal account of my experience of leadership within the context of a local authority youth service and how becoming a leader 'just sort of happened' to me. It describes the factors that have influenced me and contributed to my own development and attempts to highlight the opportunities that exist for leaders in youth services to be transformational.

Circumstance, confidence and self-interest

Accidental leaders do not have a clearly defined career path. They do not have access to significant structured professional development opportunities. Their appointment is not part of any succession plan or well ordered process. Instead they are created by a combination of circumstance, confidence and self-interest.

Circumstance

Wrong place, wrong time? Recruitment difficulties, particularly acute at middle management level, together with regular reorganisations, sickness and other long-term absence problems and the freezing of posts due to constant budget pressures have all contributed to creating an environment where competent and committed practitioners regularly take on leadership roles not because they necessarily want to, but because of a sense of responsibility and a feeling that they have to.

Take the recent experience of one county youth service. Following an inspection which highlighted unsatisfactory operational management, two new middle management posts were created. The posts were both graded well above the market rate in anticipation of the likely problems of recruiting quality staff.

The first recruitment round did not attract any suitable candidates. The second round resulted in the appointment of one candidate who later withdrew their application. On the third attempt one post was finally filled. In the absence of anyone to appoint to the other role, responsibilities were reallocated to other members of the Senior Management Team.

Youth workers and middle managers frequently take on additional responsibilities because of a deep rooted commitment to ensuring that young people are well supported and that they receive a good service. They want to support colleagues, and ensure that the service, and indeed the profession (or at least their little bit of it) doesn't fall apart.

Confidence

For many years now the structure and organisation of youth services have offered people at all levels the opportunity to gain real experience of leading teams. The expectation that practitioners will also be leaders, responsible for teams of sessional youth workers, developing good community relations and managing assets such as buildings or vehicles is increasingly particular to our sector. It certainly isn't a responsibility that other allied professionals, for example, social workers or education welfare officers are required to take on. And although at times these leadership responsibilities, however modest, can be hard work, they can also be incredibly empowering. They can increase the confidence and capacity of practitioners and enable them to develop important leadership skills.

Self-interest

Of course the decision to take on a senior leadership role is also driven by a certain amount of self-interest. Most of us invest considerable time and effort in our work and in contributing to an organisational culture that we feel comfortable with and that we can operate effectively in. Working with a new leader, or having no leader at all, can present difficulties and threaten the status quo. As a result, people who didn't necessarily set out with any leadership ambitions find themselves going forward for positions of responsibility.

I was an accidental leader. When my predecessor was seconded elsewhere within the authority I was asked to take on some additional responsibility for a few months. Looking back, circumstance, confidence and self-interest were certainly all key factors in my decision to take on the role. Six months later and I was offered the post of Principal Youth Officer. Six years on and I think I may have finally worked out what being a leader is all about. How did I find my way through? With considerable difficulty.

The vision thing

Every organisation needs a vision and so does every leader. Organisational visions are usually easy to work up. More often than not they are the result of a group of like-minded people spending a few hours together along with some flip chart paper and pens. But developing a more personal vision of what I wanted to achieve as a leader wasn't something I found so easy to do. Where should I start? How ambitious should I be? And most importantly, who was going to help me work all of this out? Certainly not my line manager. He had little or no interest in challenging me to be ambitious for the service I was now leading or for the young people we were there to work with. Instead I was encouraged to take a more managerialist approach, rewarding administrative efficiency and focusing on outputs rather than outcomes.

The environment I found myself in didn't make it any easier. For a start I was busy, responding to events, dealing with problems and generally getting drawn into the day-to-day detail. And then there was the inspection.

The impact of inspection

Inspection is a good thing. It drives up standards and focuses attention on achievement. But does it necessarily improve leadership?

Just a few months after taking up my new role as head of service I received notification from Ofsted that we were to be inspected. The experience was profound. At an important point in my own professional development, when I should have been taking stock of the service I was now leading and formulating my own approach to how I wanted to improve performance, I was presented with a diagnostic report that I was encouraged to think did the job for me.

Predictably my response to the inevitable 'areas for improvement' that were identified through the inspection was to continue to take a managerialist approach encouraged by my line manager. I incorrectly believed that a good post-inspection action plan, drafted up and submitted to our local government office for monitoring, would somehow be sufficient to enable the service to move forward.

Looking back, what was really needed was a clear vision and strong leadership and not another project management plan. Of course the plan did enable us to address those specific areas of weakness identified by the inspection and to move forward. But unfortunately it also distracted me from what I now consider to be the fundamental part of leadership – implementing significant structural and cultural change.

It was only when we had completed all the tasks set out in our post-inspection action plan that I realised that the sum of the parts would not be greater than the whole. We had made some progress in individual service areas but it was far from transformational. I knew that a new approach would be needed, one that focused more on whole system change. What I didn't know was how difficult this approach would be to develop.

Investing in leadership

Most organizations are over-managed and under-led (Bennis and Nanus, 1985).

Too little energy is invested in developing leaders. Local authorities may organise endless training on specific management competencies such as target setting or applying disciplinary processes but traditionally many do very little to develop the leadership abilities of their more senior staff.

There may be many reasons for this, but the result is that a 'command and control' culture flourishes in many authorities where the focus is firmly on transactional management as opposed to transformational leadership. Why does this matter? Of course a successful organisation needs transactional management. But as individuals we are far more likely to have deeper and more lasting influence on organisations if our focus extends beyond maintaining high standards (Fullan, 2002).

Table 2.1 is a helpful model adapted from Kotter (1990) in *Leading and Managing Youth Work and Services For Young People* (Ford et al., 2005) that sets out the difference in approaches:

Table 2.1 Differences in approaches to leading and managing

Leading Role (Transformation)	Managing Role (Transaction)
Sets direction; develops vision and strategies to achieve vision.	Plans and budgets; establishes detailed steps and timetables to achieve results; allocates resources.
Aligns people to do things; communicates vision and strategy to all those whose co-operation may be needed.	Organises and staffs; sets up structures; delegates authority for implementation; develops policies and procedures; creates monitoring systems.
Motivates and inspires people to overcome major political, bureaucratic and resource barriers to achieving the vision.	Controls and solves problems; monitors results against plans.
Produces change of dramatic nature; may create disorder but also new ideas, products, etc.	Key results expected by various stakeholders; predictability and order.

Youth services haven't done much better either. At the national level there has been a failure to invest significantly in the development of leadership skills, with the notable exception of the Transforming Youth Work Management Programme (YAU, 2004).

The programme, funded by the Department of Education and Skills, aimed to develop the ability of managers to lead effective modern services. I was one of the 451 managers who completed the programme between October 2002 and June 2003. Seventy-seven per cent (114) of 149 Principal Youth Officers or equivalents listed in September 2003 attended one of the 18 courses. An impressive achievement.

The formal evaluation report remarked that, 'such a national management development programme had never been offered before' (Youth Affairs Unit, 2004). It may have been popular and evaluated well, but unfortunately and rather predictably it's never been seen again in quite the same format.

External funding and benchmarks

The increasing levels of external funding and the inevitable demands for greater accountability that come with it has also led to more energy being focused on transactional management tasks. Most services and organisations now have a huge range of external funding streams, each with their own individual reporting and monitoring arrangements. Take for example a service level agreement that we currently have in place with another department of the council. The agreement is for the employment of a youth worker to support young carers and although the agreement is not for a particularly large sum of money, the condition placed upon us is to provide a quarterly written report and statistical data on a full set of indicators and to provide a weekly return on the number of carers reached by the worker. Of course reporting in this way is important, but it comes at a cost. Put simply, providing funders with performance reports on what's happened today means less time can be spent on working out what we want to do tomorrow.

So where does leadership live?

In the absence of any significant investment in leadership and the increasing focus on an 'inspection friendly' transactional management approach, I have had to find my own 'places and spaces' to develop and exercise leadership and bring about transformation. So far I have found three: partnerships, transition and learning from others.

Partnerships

Partnership must be one of the most overused words in both local government and the voluntary and community sectors. It has its champions as well as its critics, many of whom cynically describe it as nothing more than the suppression of mutual loathing in the pursuit of government funding. But partnership is about much more than just the money; it offers the opportunity for people to be leaders, to be transformational, free from the demands of the day-to-day business of service management. Table 2.2 uses one of our most successful partnerships, work with the Teenage Pregnancy Board, and relates it to elements of what Kotter (1990) sees as a transformational role. There are striking similarities between the two.

Through my involvement in partnerships I have been able to explore and reflect upon my own role as leader. Chairing a local partnership such as the Teenage Pregnancy Partnership Board demands a different set of skills than being a member of the Children and Young People's Strategic Partnership or the Local Safeguarding Children Board. But whichever role I am in or whatever the business of the partnership, effective partnership working requires:

- A positive 'can do' attitude, unrestricted by current performance and practice
- A determination to work with others, rather than trying to manage them

Table 2.2   Leading in the teenage pregnancy partnership

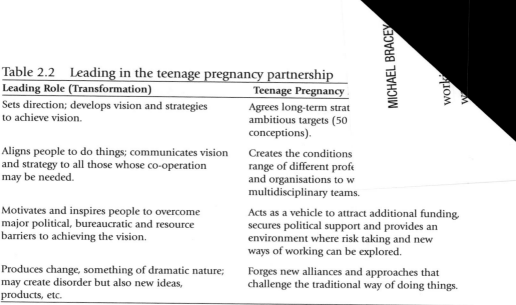

Leading Role (Transformation)	Teenage Pregnancy
Sets direction; develops vision and strategies to achieve vision.	Agrees long-term strat ambitious targets (50 conceptions).
Aligns people to do things; communicates vision and strategy to all those whose co-operation may be needed.	Creates the conditions range of different prof and organisations to w multidisciplinary teams.
Motivates and inspires people to overcome major political, bureaucratic and resource barriers to achieving the vision.	Acts as a vehicle to attract additional funding, secures political support and provides an environment where risk taking and new ways of working can be explored.
Produces change, something of dramatic nature; may create disorder but also new ideas, products, etc.	Forges new alliances and approaches that challenge the traditional way of doing things.

- A clear understanding of what I can bring to the table
- An approach to working with others that isn't based on traditional hierarchies.

Partnerships can provide a way though bureaucracy to a place when people can really be visionary. They can provide a laboratory for new ideas, a place where risk taking is acceptable and where alternative ways of working can be explored.

Transition

One of the few constants in local government is transition and change. It can be an unsettling and distracting process, however it also offers the opportunity to develop and apply transformational leadership.

For many people change is difficult. In fact they would much prefer things stayed as they are, something I'm regularly reminded of. But this view isn't necessarily a positive endorsement of the status quo, it's just as likely to be a negative response to the process of change itself.

During periods of transition, leaders have the opportunity to reflect on the strategy and revise the vision and the approach being taken. The challenge is to predict and prepare for these periods of change and to be in a position to take advantage of them.

Take *Every Child Matters* (DfES, 2003) and the *Change for Children* (DfES, 2004) agenda. Underpinning the Children Act 2004 is a commitment to integrated ing. For most local authorities this is leading to a wholesale reform in the way local services are organised and how professionals interact with each other. This change programme also includes the introduction of a Common Assessment Framework (CAF) and the development of the role of Lead Professional.

This present youth work manages with a number of challenges. Some focus on how the proposed new referral arrangements fit with those we currently have in place. Others express concerns about how people will be trained to carry out assessments. But, more importantly, this also presents us with an opportunity to explore much more fundamental questions about the way we work. Is youth work best delivered as part of a universal or targeted service? What should be the relationship between youth workers and other parts of the children's service workforce? Would a youth worker make a good Lead Professional? Do we need a youth service to deliver high quality youth work?

Youth workers may prefer not to think about some of these issues, hoping instead that they will simply go away. Transactional managers may think about the issues in terms of how they will affect operational delivery. But for leaders this period of transition offers the opportunity to consider some of the fundamentals and to be really transformational.

Learning from others

Ideally, there should be lots of opportunities for leaders to learn from positive role models around them and from their own experiences of being well led. In my own experience I have often learnt from more negative experiences – from poor and ineffective leadership – as I have tried to work out what it means to be a leader.

Nearly all youth workers must be able to recall at least one person they have met within the course of their professional practice who enabled them to reflect on the sort of practitioner they did *not* want to become. Mine was a particular practitioner who had hopelessly unclear professional boundaries between themselves and the young people they worked with.

The same principle can be applied to leadership. I recently spoke with a senior youth service manager at a regional event. He couldn't hide his delight that his local Connexions partnership was struggling. His perception that this was somehow not his problem provided a real reminder of what leadership of youth services is *not* about.

Unlike in the commercial sector where the failure of your competitor is likely to be regarded as something to celebrate, leadership of public services is about working with others to improve things for people and communities.

This isn't something that can be achieved by working alone, however comfortable that may feel.

To be most effective, leaders need to have moral purpose. They need to be concerned with the bigger picture and not just with how well their individual service is performing (Fullan, 2002).

Conclusion

I did not set out to be a leader. In that respect it was an accident. No one gave me a handbook or provided me with an induction, instead I had to find my way through and that has not always been an easy journey in an organisational culture that encourages managers to focus on day-to-day management, rather than real transformational leadership. In spite of these pressures, however, I have been able to identify the 'places and spaces' where I could learn what it means to be a leader.

As a result of this, I have three messages to share:

- Being a good manager just isn't enough to improve and strengthen services for young people. For that you need leadership.
- Partnerships and transitions offer the best opportunities for exercising leadership and bringing about transformation.
- Having a moral purpose and believing in what you are trying to achieve is absolutely essential.

References

Bennis, W. and Nanus, N. (1985) *Leaders: The Strategies for Taking Charge*, New York: Harper Row.

DfES (Department for Education and Skills) (2003) *Every Child Matters*, London: The Stationery Office.

DfES (Department for Education and Skills) (2004) *Every Child Matters: Change for Children*, London: The Stationery Office.

Fullan, M. (2002) 'The Change Leader', *Educational Leadership*, 59(8): 16–20.

Kotter, J.P. (1990) 'A force for change: how leadership differs from management' in Ford, K., Hunter, R., Merton, B. and Waller, D. (eds) *Leading and Managing Youth Work and Services For Young People* (2005), Leicester: National Youth Agency.

YAU (2004) *The Evaluation of the Transforming Youth Work Management Programme Final Report*, Leicester: Youth Affairs Unit, De Montfort University.

3

Youth work and the changing policy environment for young people

Howard Williamson

Introduction: policy goals

Just under a decade ago, when New Labour came to power, the political objectives around 'youth policy' could be distilled into four themes:

- Active citizenship ('rights and responsibilities')
- Lifelong learning ('education, education, education')
- Social inclusion ('a hand up, not a hand out')
- Community safety ('tough on crime, tough on the causes of crime').

These overarching goals have not changed dramatically in the intervening years, though the content and emphasis within them may have altered. This chapter explores what has been developed and established on these fronts, and the place of youth work (non-formal education) practice within those initiatives, an issue first considered and examined at the turn of the millennium (UK Youth Work Alliance 2000). New Labour's youth policy development and its commitment to youth work, especially under the emergent conditions of devolution and European-level initiatives, has been a mixed story. It is time

This is an edited version of a paper first published as Williamson, H., 'Youth work and the changing policy environment for young people', Leicester: The National Youth Agency.

once more to take stock of the contribution made by youth work and the 'youth service' to the contemporary policy agenda for young people.

A note on devolution

This paper is primarily about England. The devolved administrations of the United Kingdom have, since 1999, developed their youth, and youth work, policies in rather different ways. The landscape is complex. Some youth policy is UK-wide (such as youth employment programmes), some for England and Wales only (such as youth justice), while most is significantly at the discretion of each of the four constituent nations of the United Kingdom, allowing for differences in both policy and practice. Inevitably, there are also overlaps between what goes on in the different countries. Indeed, the confusion is compounded for, beyond there being quite separate initiatives (e.g. Connexions in England, Extending Entitlement in Wales), there are different interpretations of the same initiatives (youth crime prevention), or very similar policy and practice given different names (Relaunch/New Start, the Youth Access Initiative). It would require a lengthy chapter to unravel this web and this is not the place for that. Unless comparisons with the devolved administrations of Wales, Scotland and Northern Ireland serve a particular purpose, the trajectory of policy for young people in England will guide the subsequent discussion.

Youth transitions: individual complexities and challenges

It became apparent, by the end of the 1970s, that the 'traditional' (post-war) linear transitions that were typically followed and experienced by the vast majority of young people (leaving education, finding work, establishing a relationship, leaving home, having children) were fragmenting. Social and economic change at local, national and global levels was contributing to youth transitions that were becoming increasingly individualised, more challenging and complex, potentially reversible, and more prone to risk and vulnerability (see Furlong and Cartmel, 1997). The metaphor of a shift from train journeys to car journeys has often been invoked to capture these changes. Young people from different class backgrounds had previously travelled similar journeys with their peers from similar backgrounds. They were herded into 'trains' and unable to change course, arriving eventually at their occupational destination of the coalmine or steelworks, white-collar administrative work, the helping professions, or higher occupations in the civil service, the church or the law. In the late

20th century, young people benefiting from greater opportunity in education and employment (at least in theory) had to navigate their own way. That proclaimed equality of opportunity concealed the allocation (or acquisition) of 'cars' of different quality and reliability, access to different standards of 'road', the provision – for some – of maps, and a differential ability to read those maps amongst those who received them. The metaphor allows also for the fact that while many young people cope admirably, or sufficiently, well, a significant minority 'break down', have collisions, end up in cul-de-sacs or arrive at inappropriate destinations. These may take a variety of forms, not only in relation to the labour market, but also in the context of their personal relationships, and places in the housing market. Such differential outcomes speak to a range of policy concerns such as educational underachievement, youth unemployment, teenage pregnancy, youth homelessness, substance misuse, offending behaviour, family estrangement, and so on. These are the issues upon which the Labour government built its 'youth policy' agenda (Coles, 2001), though there is no reason to suppose that any other administration would depart dramatically from these priorities.

The last decade of youth policy initiatives: a brief résumé

These social issues were certainly sharply recognised – and responded to – during the first days of the new Labour administration. The Social Exclusion Unit (recently disbanded) was described by Coles (2001) as a *de facto* Ministry of Youth. While the distinctive contribution of *youth work* as a professional intervention was rarely made explicit, the range of initiatives established (see below) depended on the hidden hand of youth work practitioners applying various versions of youth work approaches. Even if the emphasis turned increasingly to results and outcomes, the processes invoked to achieve them were essentially about improving understanding by services of individual needs and responding through tailored individual interventions. Some of those initiatives are listed below:

- Youth Gateway
- e2e (Entry to Employment)
- New Start/Relaunch
- Connexions
- New Deal for Young People
- Alternative curriculum and school inclusion
- Health promotion
- Drugs education and prevention
- Sexual health awareness

- Youth justice and youth inclusion through positive activities
- Housing support
- Millennium Volunteers
- Anti-Social Behaviour Orders (ASBOs)

The workforce involved in the execution of these measures has been drawn significantly from those with youth work backgrounds and through the application of youth work approaches of building relationships, working with small groups, and so on. The nature of this professional engagement has been a source of intense ideological debate amongst the luminaries of youth work in the UK, though rarely policy-makers. The overall effect of these early initiatives was an apparent 'displacement' of youth work into more focused practice in a variety of policy areas with arguably, a diminution of youth work as an independent, autonomous service and practice.

The place of youth work and non-formal learning

At the turn of the millennium, however, youth work as a distinct professional practice received renewed political attention in the form of *Transforming Youth Work* (Department of Education and Employment, 2001), and *Transforming Youth Work – Resourcing Excellent Youth Services* (Department for Education and Skills, 2002). These placed new expectations on youth services, including in relation to the numbers of young people they would reach and the proportion of those who would gain at least recorded – preferably accredited – outcomes. In return, there were more explicit political commitments to increased resources and policy support. The Department for Education and Skills commissioned a major evaluation of the impact of youth work (Merton et al., 2004), which drew some positive conclusions about its contribution to the development of 'social capital'. In the subsequent development of policy, however, references by government ministers to this work have been limited: they have been more inclined to refer to a single critical evaluation based on an analysis of the 1970 Birth Cohort study. Indeed, early in 2005, the then youth minister Margaret Hodge – using 'evidence' from the latter study – was widely reported as saying that it was better to stay at home and watch TV than attend a youth club. (What was not specified was that the study cited was reporting on young people who had attended youth clubs in 1986!) Occasionally ministers have celebrated the contribution of youth work to effective practice in the policy domains of school inclusion or youth mental health (Department of Health,

2006) but have rarely mentioned the 'promising approaches' evident in other domains, including preparing young people for employment, youth crime prevention and youth homelessness. The width of youth work's contribution to different social agendas is often more evident in local communities than in high-level policy thinking.

As well as contributing to combating or forestalling some of the more negative aspects of vulnerable youth transitions, youth work also proclaims its contribution to positive youth development on such issues as personal responsibility, active citizenship, community involvement – and preparation for the labour market. Indeed, there is increasing support for the congruence between the skills and attributes acquired through non-formal learning experiences and those that are forecast to be needed for life and work in the future (see, for example, United Church Schools Trust, 2006). There is also a recognition that youth work contexts provide a platform for moving into more structured volunteering and community service, a point noted both in the development of Millennium Volunteers and, more recently, of 'v', the youth volunteering programme arising from the Russell Commission.

Youth work and non-formal education and learning is therefore, arguably, both a safety net for those young people who may have succumbed to the social and personal risks of 'modernity' and a trampoline to enable individuals to maximise their potential in complex and rapidly changing times.

But what is 'youth work'?

Youth work as both a concept and a practice is often little understood. Yet it is relatively simple to depict, if not to execute. It is about the building of a trusting and credible *relationship* with young people in order to support and broaden their learning experiences and thereby enhance their personal *development*. That the relationship is voluntary means that interaction and exchange between youth worker and young people is qualitatively different from relationships within more coercive or structured environments, such as teaching, the workplace or the youth justice system. On this basis, the essential idea of youth work is often portrayed as follows:

- Its *goals* relate to the personal and social development of young people.
- Its *methods* are embedded in personal relationships and experiential learning.
- Its *values* are based on voluntarism, working from the interests of young people and winning their consent rather than coercing their compliance.

Young people may enter, and exit, the relationship freely. Sustaining their engagement, interest and involvement – through the selective and differential application of a variety of methods at different times, in different places, on different issues – lies at the heart of the *skill* of youth work practice. Some young people are harder to engage than others; some methods more difficult to apply; some locations harder to use; and some issues more difficult to address. But this is the framework within which the practice of youth work takes place and outcomes, over time, are achieved.

The four pillars within which youth work practice is constructed

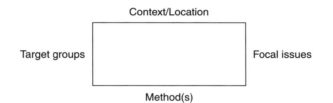

Figure 3.1   The framework of practice

As relationships are established with groups of young people, both reactively and proactively, and in different settings (through street work, in youth clubs, on youth projects), it becomes possible to invoke a range of methods (from individual counselling and support, to developmental group work) on a variety of issues, deriving from the expressed needs and wishes of the young people, and from the professional judgment of the youth worker. These issues – for example, health, learning, community involvement, responsibility – themselves invite different kinds of methodological interventions and suggest the use of different locations. While a photography project designed to heighten young people's awareness of the strengths and weaknesses of their neighbourhood has necessarily to be local community-based, young men's health issues might well be better addressed in the more framed and 'private' setting of a residential weekend.

The hidden hand of youth work can be found inside the 'effective practice' of youth justice and crime prevention, health promotion and health risk reduction. Youth workers have been asked to contribute to summer time Positive Activities for Young People and Youth Inclusion Programmes. They have been at the forefront of the delivery of teenage pregnancy initiatives.

Indeed, continuing with a trend over many years, the most recent National Youth Agency figures demonstrate that although 1,500 nationally qualified youth workers are being trained each year, only 60 per cent enter clearly identifiable youth work occupations. Although some were lost completely to immediate work with young people, most of the remainder find work in areas such as youth justice, housing support, substance misuse, outdoor activities and counselling. Youth work is explicitly none of those things but is indisputably a close relation, bringing its particular approach to relationships with young people and to non-formal learning.

At academic, policy and practice levels, the idea of youth work is subject to shifts and drift, but that should not devalue the distinctive contribution it can make to the lives of young people – through good quality intervention and support, appropriate processes and a proportionate focus on outcomes. To develop successfully it needs to find its place within the framework of wider public policy aspirations, as well as ensuring that its practice responds to the expressed needs of young people while still adhering to its core principles and values. Managing these pulls and tensions is critical.

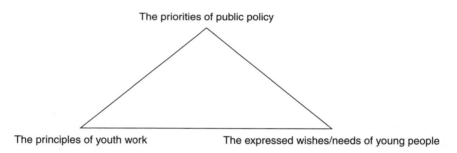

Figure 3.2   Policy, principles and needs

Youth work and youth workers have to negotiate a position in between the three corners of this triangle: slavish attachment to any one corner is a recipe for paralysis, inertia or ineffectiveness.

Every Child Matters, *Youth Matters*, 'Even yobs matter', and v

The central goals of England's children and youth policy were set out in *Every Child Matters* (Department for Education and Skills, 2003), followed by *Youth Matters* (Department for Education and Skills, 2005). Both are concerned with establishing services that contribute to the production of five concrete outcomes; there is less concern about the process by which these are achieved. For youth work, the five outcomes (see below) were foreshadowed by the expectation in *Transforming Youth Work* (Department for Education and Employment, 2001) that youth services were about helping to keep young people 'in good shape'. This is the intermediary stage between the 'safety and development' priorities of childhood, and the 'life management' requirements of young adulthood. Both *Every Child Matters* and *Youth Matters* are concerned with improving the following outcomes for children and young people:

- Staying healthy
- Being safe
- Enjoying and achieving
- Making a positive contribution
- Achieving economic wellbeing.

To this end, a dramatic reorganisation of services for children and young people at local authority level is in train. This is taking place within a wider orbit of public spending reviews, scrutiny of services for young people through inspection, and greater 'freedoms and flexibilities' for high-performing local authorities – to be gauged through local area agreements (LAAs) and comprehensive performance assessment (CPA).

As with all change, there are both risks and opportunities for youth work. There are now, more than ever, new players in the market and agendas on the table. Those commissioning services will be making choices, within the context of greater participation and consultation with young people themselves, between the claims and performance of local authority youth services, traditional voluntary youth services and a 'third sector' of entrepreneurial youth services which has expanded significantly on the back of the 'social inclusion' and 're-engagement' agendas. The public policy agenda to which youth work must connect continues to expand. The volunteering and active citizenship agenda has become more prominent, especially since the Russell Commission and the establishment of the youth volunteering initiative 'v'. Amongst particular target groups of young people, there are expectations that youth work should engage more effectively with, for example, those from Muslim communities, those with disabilities, and looked-after children. Threading through policy domains and specific target groups, and linked to the five outcomes, are cross-cutting issues such as promoting intercultural tolerance and understanding, youth participation, and community cohesion. Indeed, there is a role for youth work in attaching young people to other generations and to their local communities, particularly those young people who are most detached and most at risk of falling foul of criminal and anti-social behaviour legislation: 'Even yobs matter' (Williamson, 2005).

Few contest the aspirations of this new framework, though there are concerns about how these will play themselves out in practice. There will need to be careful thought about targets (their timescale and measurement), structures (governance, management, recording and reporting procedures) and delivery (the reach and relevance of particular interventions). The paradox of contemporary policy is that, although there is a mantra of joined-up and 'holistic' approaches to meeting individual needs, there is an equal, and sometimes conflicting, imperative to fire specific bullets to reach and hit particular targets. In the rush to produce guidelines, expectations and targets, it will be important not to lose a sense of person-centredness, a holistic philosophy that acknowledges the connectedness of needs, a time-line that can accommodate professional discretion and patience, and an assessment process that allows significantly for 'distance travelled' rather than just destination reached. Otherwise, opportunity and experience may be consolidated for the more motivated young people, but leave behind a significant minority of those with the most complex needs. That is not what the vision of *Youth Matters* is seeking to achieve. Many troubled and troublesome young people are a long way from the personal realisation of the five outcomes. Recurrent research evidence tells us that they are:

- Less healthy – in their physical, sexual and mental health, and are more likely to be involved in substance misuse.
- Less safe – not only more likely to be perpetrators of crime and anti-social behaviour, but also more likely to be a victim of crime and violence.
- Not enjoying or achieving – more vulnerable to psycho-social disorders and likely to be falling behind in learning.
- Making a negative contribution to society – uninterested in 'volunteering', occupying public space that may cause justified and unjustified anxiety in others.
- Less 'employable' – though perhaps working already in the informal and/or illegal economy; vulnerable to an unpredictable income, and health and safety risks.

Youth services, broadly conceived, should not be focusing exclusively on this latter, at-risk, group. There is also a strong case for their role in strengthening positive outcomes in the wider youth population. But it will be important to ensure disproportionate attention to the more disadvantaged. In Wales, the *Extending Entitlement* (National Assembly for Wales, 2000) youth policy agenda noted that young adults who are well-equipped for their personal, occupational and civic lives have invariably had access to a range of opportunities and experiences in their childhood and youth. Many have been provided on a private basis by their families: new technologies, music lessons, international experiences through foreign holidays, exposure to drama and culture. There are, however, young people who will *never* – for a variety of reasons – access such experience and opportunity by such private means. If such a 'package' is important for personal engagement and development, there is a moral and social responsibility on public services to extend the entitlement to those young people who will not have access to it from their family.

Finally, there is the question for accreditation – and questions about it. Judgment about youth work and youth services will rest in part on its achievement of both recorded *and* accredited outcomes with young people. A service which is concerned to promote learning has to demonstrate that it achieves it. The nature of accreditation does, however, demand careful scrutiny. One issue is the pace and ease with which accreditation can be achieved; another is the credibility of that accreditation beyond the environs of the youth work sector and those who inspect and fund it. There are now myriad pathways to different forms of accreditation: its *currency* for young people within their prospective destinations, especially in the labour market, merits sharp attention if the rush to record and certificate is not to implode upon itself.

So where do we go from here?

The 1970 birth cohort study – from which one apparently critical analysis of the impact and outcomes of some forms of youth work derives – can be interpreted in a rather different way. Indeed, the analysts of those data have themselves arrived at various conclusions. In short, though they are critical of a type of youth club provision that just allows young people to 'hang out', they acknowledge that youth work tends to attract young people from less advantaged and more troubled backgrounds – the very young people on whom a swathe of public concern and public policy continues to be focused. Building on that evidence, they suggest that youth work – if done well (and they accept that it is a sophisticated challenge) – '*can* provide precisely the form of complementary provision to formal education that is needed', and they go on to suggest that:

> Although the effects of relatively unstructured environments for young people may not be as positive as policy-makers may wish, these may be precisely the contexts in which the most challenging at-risk young people are likely to be found.

> For many such young people provision of common objectives, a range of curricula such as sport and music, and engagement in structured youth activities may provide developmental opportunities that can significantly transform their life paths at key transition points.
>
> (Feinstein et al., 2006: 324)

Thus, from perhaps this unexpected source, there is robust support for the idea of youth work but an implicit, if not explicit request for serious attention to the quality of its practice. This demands a serious debate about the duration, content and nature of youth work training at all levels, but especially at initial professional training level. Further, there is a question about the focus and style of youth work practice – should priority, for example, be given to dedicated project work on key issues with a defined group of young people, or to more open-ended and eclectic street-based work with a loose-knit constituency of young people? There is the issue of the structural location of youth work, whether in the changing context of local authority arrangements or in the voluntary sector. This raises, not for the first time, the issue of its relation and complementarity to other services for young people.

In this policy context, the agenda for the immediate future is essentially threefold:

- Youth work training and sustaining the quality of work in the field
- The focus and style of work (practice) with young people
- Institutional location and complementarity with other 'youth services'.

It is not for this chapter to address these questions in detail, except to say that clearly there are choices to be made. The overall framework and political expectations are set: under the umbrella of *Every Child Matters* and now, *Youth Matters*. Few doubt that youth work and the youth service has some part to play in the delivery of each of the five outcomes. But there are three caveats to that confidence.

1. Advanced practitioners?
It is unrealistic to expect often highly motivated but little experienced or trained practitioners, sometimes voluntary and often part-time, to bear the brunt of delivery of sophisticated practice. It is like relying on auxiliary nurses to perform complex operations. Once more a driving analogy is also useful: it is like asking Learner drivers to navigate icy mountain roads. Complex issues with sometimes challenging young people *demand* a repertoire of finely tuned skills. They need advanced skills practitioners with the sensitivity and judgment to know when to press on the accelerator and when to apply the brake.

Too often, currently, career progression requires nationally qualified youth workers to seek management and coordinator positions just as their experience offers the possibility of working effectively with more challenging individuals and 'hard-to-reach' groups of young people.

2. Hitting the target, but missing the point?

Making a difference in terms of the five outcomes and in relation to national government's expectations concerning reach, recording and accreditation is much easier with less challenging young people. Allegations of 'cherry picking' abound in the context of those youth projects that claim miraculous, speedy impact on the most disengaged: few believe them. Even amongst the hardest to reach, there are those who are more receptive to engagement and involvement and 'structured' intervention, and those who are more resistant. The latter group will need time and patience if 'targets' are to be met and aspirations for their health and well-being, contribution and achievement are to be realised. Ofsted (2005) praised detached youth work for teaching more disengaged young people but simultaneously criticised it for failing to achieve recorded and accredited outcomes. Yet 'street-based' youth work is of a very different order from centre-based or project-based work and needs different criteria for evaluating its value and effectiveness (see Crimmens et al., 2004; Harris, 2005).

3. Partnership and connected practice

There were once perceptions that youth work took place in splendid isolation from other services. Where it 'connected' – largely with and within schools – some had reservations about its appeal to (at least some groups of) young people. Such reservations – expressed as 'collaboration' in the worst sense of the word – still persist here and there but have largely dissipated in recognition that youth work can play its part in wider policy agendas without compromising its distinctive values and approach. Thus there is now a raft of evidence of successful youth work activity around, for example, formal education (school inclusion strategies, 'alternative' curriculum); health (especially sexual health, and smoking cessation); housing (street-based contact with homeless young people, floating support); and crime (within and around Youth Offending Teams, and wider prevention programmes). The issue is not, then, an absence of partnership working but a risk of dilution of professional practice, co-option into other goals and invisibility to funders. Youth work, by its very nature and definition, though not oblivious to wider public and political considerations, builds primarily from the needs, issues and concerns of young people. It gives priority to young people. It operates at the interface between the aspirations and perspectives of young people, and the expectations of public policy. If it is to retain that distinct identity – and thus a credibility with young people that is lacking with some other agencies that have more 'top-down' imperatives – it must avoid being subsumed within either children's agendas or practice specifically identified with a single thread of public policy (such as crime, or health, or schooling). Youth work is concerned with the personal and social development of young people – in the round, in response to individual concerns, through the identification of shared issues, and by means of the provision of developmental opportunities and experiences.

To that end, two points need serious attention: a sufficiency in resources to ensure young people have access to such provision, and careful consideration of the dedicated and distinctive 'space' that should be allotted to youth work so that it can work creatively within it – in the direction both of wider public priorities and the needs and wishes of young people.

Resourcing sufficient youth work

A debate on what could constitute an 'adequate' or 'sufficient' youth service has persisted since the 1944 Education Act, through the 1989–1992 Ministerial Conferences on the Youth Services (see Bell et al., 1994) and culminated in a sense of achievement with the publication of *Resourcing Excellent Youth Services* (DfES, 2002) with its clearer specification of standards for local provision. But the debate continues around both what should be resourced and at what level. The review by HM Treasury in train in 2006 may at last resolve some of these issues. Meanwhile, significant inequities remain. The National Youth Agency's annual audit of local authority expenditure on youth services highlights glaring disparities in per capita expenditure on young people between local authorities, well beyond what can be justified by local discretion. However, given the multiple funding sources through which youth work may be resourced and the practice of youth work in contexts funded by other means, an accurate assessment of 'sufficiency' remains difficult to determine. The statutory guidance promised as part of the implementation of *Youth Matters* should help to resolve at least what needs to be offered in each locality. There has, however, been a reasonable consensus over the years that a minimum level of expenditure on youth work/non-formal education should be some 2 per cent of education budgets. Alternatively, young people could be given an entitlement to 100 hours of youth work opportunity a year (two hours a week), costed at the hourly cost of formal education and this sum used as the basis for planning the scale of provision. Under new arrangements developed through *Youth Matters* (opportunity cards) and the greater freedoms and flexibilities now being accorded to local authorities, it will be important to ensure that dedicated youth work resources do not drain away – not simply to other age groups but to forms of practice which do not produce youth work's benefits. Youth work is a process of professional proactivity, not simply responsiveness to those young people who beat a path to its door for particular leisure pursuits – it is not a cinema, bowling alley or football club, pleasurable as such activities may be. It requires stable resources to build a strategic path to better outcomes within both local funding arrangements and in relation to the identified needs of young people within particular localities.

Defending a space

Fears that 'youth work' would be lost within new policy developments have been a perennial, but usually misplaced, anxiety – from the days of Intermediate Treatment in the early 1970s to the inception of Connexions in 2000. Youth work, historically, has always had a place within policy agendas of social inclusion, active citizenship, crime prevention, and health promotion. Equally, it has always had its distinctive space within the delivery of services to young people, even though that has been threatened from time to time. Too forceful a requirement that it falls uncritically in line with wider policy agendas is likely to be counter-productive. Some years ago, I tried to capture the dilemma:

> The young people who are creating social policy concern will simply draw the line at a different point. Where they previously avoided contact with the careers service or the police, they will now steer clear of such so-called youth workers…
>
> The youth service must be ready for engagement with the broad social agendas around health, training, crime and volunteering while, simultaneously, arguing forcefully for the first step requirement of open access, traditional youth work. (Williamson, 1998, quoted in Davies, 1999: 169)

Feinstein et al. (2006: 324) have also recognised the dilemma:

> Replacing what currently counts as 'hanging out' by a more structured curriculum is not necessarily going to appeal. Rather, the risk is that it may stimulate all the negative connotations of schooling that put these young people off education in the first place … The solutions to the problems of such young people therefore are not going to be simply church and sport. Rather, these contexts may offer good models of engagement with and between young people because there is a general focus on structured, joint activities towards a common goal, even where the objective is as apparently mundane as a good game of football, for example. In other words, effective

curricula – 'somewhere to go, something to do' – needs to work with the grain of young people's predispositions and interests, rather than work against them. Such an aim fits well with the key principles of effective youth work.

This is the space that needs to be defended. It is not a space for inertia, or collusion with young people, or a lack of commitment to the five outcomes. It is a space which, if occupied and used by suitably trained, alert, responsive and proactive youth work practitioners, will contribute to delivery of the five outcomes with many young people and, for more challenging, difficult and excluded young people, will help to move them on the path towards them.

References

Bell, A., Nicholls, D., Parker, B. and Williamson, H. (1994) *Towards a Sufficient Youth Service*. Birmingham: Community and Youth Workers' Union.

Chisholm, L. and Hoskins, B. with Glahn, C. (2005) *Trading Up: Potential and Performance in Non-formal Learning*. Strasbourg: Council of Europe Publishing.

Coles, B. (2001) *Joined Up Youth Research, Policy and Practice: A new agenda for change?* Leicester: National Youth Agency.

Crimmens, D., Factor, F., Jeffs, T., Pitts, J., Pugh, C., Spence, J. and Turner, P. (2004) *Reaching Socially Excluded Young People: A National Study of Street-based Youth Work*. Leicester: The National Youth Agency.

Davies, B. (1999) *From Thatcherism to New Labour: A History of the Youth Service in England Volume 2 1979–1999*. Leicester: Youth Work Press.

Department for Education and Employment (2001) *Transforming Youth Work*. London: DfEE.

Department for Education and Skills (2002) *Transforming Youth Work – Resourcing Excellent Youth Services*. London: DfES.

Department for Education and Skills (2003) *Every Child Matters*. London: The Stationery Office.

Department for Education and Skills (2005) *Youth Matters*. London: The Stationery Office.

Department of Health (2006) *Reaching Out*. London: Department of Health.

Feinstein, L., Bynner, J. and Duckworth, K. (2006) 'Young people's leisure contexts and their relation to adult outcomes', *Journal of Youth Studies*, 9(3): 305–327.

Furlong, A. and Cartmel, F. (1997) *Young People and Social Change: Individualisation and Risk in Late Modernity*. Buckingham: Open University Press.

Garcia Lopez, M. (2005) *Advanced Training for Trainers in Europe: Volume I – Curriculum description*. Strasbourg: Council of Europe Publishing.

Harden, A., Sutcliffe, K. and Lempert, T. (2002) *Young Men and Suicide Prevention*. London: Institute of Education.

Harris, P. (2005) 'Curriculum debate and detached youth work', *Youth and Policy*. 87(Spring): 57–64.

Merton, B., Payne, M. and Smith, D. (2004) *An Evaluation of the Impact of Youth Work in England*. London: Department for Education and Skills Research Report 606.

National Assembly for Wales (2000) *Extending Entitlement: Supporting Young People in Wales*. Cardiff: National Assembly for Wales.

Ofsted (2005) *Effective Youth Services*. London: Office for Standards in Education.

United Church Schools Trust (2006) *Young People's Acquisition of Attributes and Skills for Life and Work*. London: United Church Schools Trust.

Wales Youth Agency (2000) *Attitude, Attendance and Achievement*. Caerphilly: Wales Youth Agency.

Williamson, H. (2001) *Learning the Art of Patience: Dealing with the Disengaged*. British Youth Council Youth Agenda No. 17, London: British Youth Council.

Williamson (2005) 'Even yobs matter: connecting young people to community and society', in *Youth 2009: Scanning Horizons in Youth Policy*. London: Camelot Foundation.

PART 2

Practice

Given the diversity of practices which are currently available in work with young people the scope of this section is ambitious. We can't hope to illustrate, let alone analyse, even a fraction of these practices so have chosen to focus on a number of themes which have particular resonance at this time – the involvement of young people in decision making, informal education in formal settings, anti-oppressive practice, and the role of youth work in developing cohesive communities.

The section begins with Kenneth McCulloch's outline of a conceptual framework for understanding the difficult relationship between professional values on the one hand and organisational imperatives on the other. It is a framework which we hope you will find useful in thinking about each of the other chapters in this section of the book. He proposes that the actions of practitioners can be viewed as a negotiation between the culture and expectations of the employing organisation and the professional values and ethics as interpreted by individual practitioners. He concludes that the often uncomfortable dilemmas and tensions inherent in these negotiations are an essential part of professional life and when openly acknowledged and discussed become the substance of professional development and learning.

Harriet Gore draws on her long association with anti-oppressive practice in youth work to trace the different forms it has taken, and the different place it has occupied in policy. The historical trajectory described by Gore is important in helping us understand the changing face of work with young people. On the one hand it can be said to be constantly evolving as it adapts to new social and political conditions, on the other that there are certain continuities, particularly around core values. Opposition to all forms of oppression is one of these constants.

The chapter by Bill Badham and Tim Davies explores the policy and practice of participation by young people as co-creators of the services they use. They outline the policy context through which the rights of young people to participate in decision making has been established in law, before exploring some of the implications for the leadership of organisations working with young people and the forms of practice they engage with.

Tony Jeffs discusses a form of practice which has a long history but has recently come back into the policy spotlight. He describes the historical tradition of youth work in a school context, the social and political conditions which have made it once again a focus of interest and examines some of the opportunities and pitfalls it presents to informal educators.

The chapter by Paul Thomas provides a good example of the relationship between academic research, policy and practice. The idea of 'community cohesion' forms part of a policy discourse used to explain the street violence which occurred in a number of towns in the north of England in 2001. Through interviews with youth workers Thomas explores what community cohesion means to them and looks at some of the implications for youth work practice.

Ethics, accountability and the shaping of youth work practice

Kenneth McCulloch

This chapter examines the ways in which workers, managers and organisations interact to influence practice in youth work. We use hypothetical case studies to illustrate how youth workers' understanding of their own role, and the expectations others have of them, will frame the context within which problems are both set and solved. By exploring the organisational settings within which youth workers operate, we can develop a theoretical framework that illustrates the ways in which organisational size and culture can lead to differing conceptions of professionalism, accountability and ethical practice.

The term professionalism is used here in Friedson's (1986) sense, referring to a set of occupational practices, and by extension attitudes and beliefs. These practices, attitudes and beliefs form the common bond for a community of practitioners who also share a body of knowledge. Neither the particular knowledge, nor the practices that spring from that knowledge are fixed and unchanging. Recognition of the dynamic nature of the relationship between these elements is essential for an understanding of professionalism in youth work.

As Holdsworth (1994: 43) points out 'the professional has knowledge which other people do not have' and so is accountable to the rest of society for

This is a revised and updated version of a chapter previously published as McCulloch, K. and Tett, L., 'Ethics, accountability and the shaping of youth work practice', in S. Banks (ed.), *Ethical Issues in Youth Work*. London: Routledge.

the ways in which such knowledge is used. Moreover, acting as a professional requires an attitude and approach that has to incorporate critical thinking and reflective practice. We believe that the diversity of youth work practice, which includes the volunteer giving a few hours to youth work as well as those who make it a full-time vocation, is encompassed in such a definition. The idea of professionalism follows from that, as a set of attitudes and practices to which any youth worker may aspire, whatever their level of training and qualifications.

Accountability necessarily has to take account of the guiding principles of a profession and involves judgement in synthesising conflicting objectives and values. However, a key characteristic of accountability is the willingness to 'lay oneself open to criticism' (Holdsworth, 1994: 43) from both service users and the public at large. This involves accepting responsibility for providing the fullest and most open account of our activities so that others may make judgements about our actions. Accountability also involves considering to whom the worker is answerable – the profession, the organisation, the service users/young people, or their own conscience. Conflicting accountabilities often present workers with their most acute dilemmas about what constitutes ethical practice.

Ethical practice is action that leads to human well-being from a perspective that values the disposition to act truly and justly. As Smith (1994: 76) points out, ethical practice 'entails an orientation to "good" or "right" rather than "correct" action … and allows people to break a rule or convention if they judge that to follow it would not promote "the good"'. At the heart of such practice is the principle of respect for persons, which 'relates to other principles such as autonomy, non maleficence, beneficence, equity and justice' (Henry, 1994: 146).

Professionalism and accountability

The relationship between professionalism and professional values on the one hand, and organisational imperatives and accountability to an employer on the other is a central issue for youth workers. The report of the Cullen enquiry (Scottish Office, 1996) led to increasing attention being paid to who is properly entitled to the label of youth worker, and to 'means of protecting children and young people who attend clubs or other groups against abuse by leaders or others who have regular contact with them' (Scottish Office, 1996: 139). This chapter is about how professionalism is conceived, and how differing organisational contexts for youth work can both influence the ways in which professionalism is understood and constrain or direct workers' beliefs and activities.

Youth work embodies a number of different traditions, each with its distinctive value stances and notions of purpose which are manifested in varied styles of work and attitudes to such matters as training or payment for being a youth worker. Smith (1988: 57) identifies specific traditions related to histori- cal origin and differences of purpose. A key dimension of this model is the attention given to distinguishing 'professionalised' youth work both from the voluntary traditions of 'organic' small scale neighbourhood-based work and from the 'movement traditions' represented by the Scouts, Boys Brigade, religious groups and political youth groups. There are elements in all these traditions that are in some degree convergent such as an increasing emphasis on training and on what might be characterised as socially responsible or ethical practice. The fact that these trends operate right across the field tends to validate a broader notion of professionalism. For example, it is The Scout Association (an organisation that relies on volunteer commitment) that is widely recognised as operating one of the most sophisticated systems in the UK for identifying 'unsuitable' persons volunteering their services as unpaid youth workers.

A number of authors (for example, Bloxham and Heathfield, 1995; Smith, 1994) have argued that the ability of practitioners to plan, reflect, analyse, manage and develop requires them to have a critical understanding of what they are doing and where it fits into the overall aims of their work. The ways in which problems are set and solved, however, will be constrained by what is viewed as possible and the forms of activity that are engaged in. How experience is labelled and organised determines how 'sense' will be made of particular events, and in any profession this 'framing' (Goffman, 1975) will determine how situations are understood, and place limits on the ways in which practitioners can change their practice.

Youth workers traditionally had considerably greater autonomy in deter- mining their work priorities than is common in other professions such as teaching and social work (see Smith, 1988) but this also meant that the under- pinning beliefs, values and norms about what is appropriate practice might not be subject to much day-to-day challenge. In recent decades a much greater emphasis on targets, on measurable outcomes, on pre-specified learning objec- tives and on individual outcomes has emerged. External standards and regimes of inspection have increasingly shaped the ways in which workers and man- agers behave. This shift of emphasis makes it all the more important for youth workers and their managers to understand the complex relationship between ethics, professionalism and the organisational context of practice. Such under- standing is essential if the inevitable tensions between competing values, beliefs and policies are to be managed successfully.

What is judged to be 'good practice' will arise out of particular historical traditions and reflect a commitment to an elaborate, if not wholly explicit, set of beliefs. In a context where purposes (ends) are ambiguous and value conflicts exist about both ends and means then judgement is crucial and will be guided by each individual's 'theory in use' (Argyris and Schon, 1974). If youth workers are to explore their experiences and ethical accountability they need to become aware of what the prevailing norms and 'common sense' views are regarding practising what is preached in their own work settings. As Henry (1994: 145) points out:

> Professional accountability is central to the setting of standards and norms, and persons within the organisation are responsible for planning and managing the quality and delivery of the service, both individually and collectively. From a professional perspective there is personal and collective accountability for establishing and maintaining the standards of practice.

Another important consideration is the way in which workers are held accountable to their organisations for the work that they do. Different conceptions of purpose are likely to result in different emphases on what is valued, whether these are processes, outputs, or inputs. This can also lead to a tendency to prioritise what is easily measurable. For example, a small local youth club would be likely to rate its financial independence and ability to recruit voluntary leaders as key measures of success while an organisation like Barnardos or Save the Children might place emphasis on the extent to which vulnerable young people were enabled to remain in their own locality rather than requiring residential care. For many organisations externally imposed 'performance indicators' are used to assess the quality of the service that is delivered but a complex service such as that provided by youth workers can be difficult to evaluate. In local authority settings, youth workers' concerns for acting in what they regard as the interests of the young people around issues such as sexual health might conflict with a council's cautious policy. This also illustrates how concern for ethical practice can lead to conflicts that result in people breaking rules that are seen to be concerned with 'correct' rather than 'right' action.

The examples that follow illustrate some of the different organisational contexts in which youth work may take place. The case studies serve to characterise some of the different approaches and emphases that workers may experience across a range of organisational contexts in which youth work may be located and are designed to illustrate some features that may be found in settings of the general type described. They are hypothetical or 'imaginary' although based on real examples. The case studies also provide the basis for discussion of the influence of differing organisational perspectives on what is seen as ethical practice. Those questions are explored in the subsequent section.

The case studies

The local 'voluntary' youth club

The Riverside Youth Club serves a long established neighbourhood in a medium sized town. In the late 1960s a group of local parents began with the aim of providing 'worthwhile activities' for local teenagers. Over time there has been a range of volunteers helping to run the club and no one has ever been paid for being a youth worker there. The club is managed by a committee of local parents and others and their first priority has always been to maintain independence and so offers from the local authority of participation in youth forums, training events and policy consultations have been treated politely but with little enthusiasm.

The club meets for two evenings each week in the local school and the programme consists mainly of games and activities, which change according to young people's interests and those of the volunteer workers of the day. Until the mid-1990s common sense was seen as the guiding principle and cardinal virtue. However, moves towards the accreditation of youth groups and the formal vetting of adults involved in youth work have resulted in a shift towards a more 'professional' approach. Club volunteers frequently discuss what they do, how they do it and how parents and other outsiders might perceive that.

The small independent project

Woodhouse Youth Project is based in a large council estate on the periphery of a city of around 500,000 inhabitants. Initially resourced through Social Inclusion Partnership funding, it now operates as an independent organisation, but is substantially dependent on the city council since 60 per cent of costs are met by income for the local authority. The project management committee consists of local councillors, council officials and community representatives. The project runs a mixed programme of 'open' youth clubs for teenagers, a children's club and groups for young people referred to the project as 'at risk'. The latter are identified through the local social work team and local schools.

There are five full-time staff in the centre, three of whom are qualified in youth work or community education, a fourth is a qualified social worker, one has a degree but no professional qualification and was appointed on the basis of extensive experience of working with young people in a part-time worker role. There are five paid part-time sessional youth workers in the project as well as a variable number of volunteer workers.

The local city council has adopted a joint strategy in relation to young people at risk of requiring residential care. The strategy brings together education, social care and recreational services for young people, to carry out joint assessment and to develop and support projects which will help young people remain in their locality whenever possible. Alongside this the council has largely replaced grant aid with service agreements, requiring a specific range of outcomes from contracting organisations, and with explicit measures of performance applied in evaluation of the service.

The national voluntary organisation

In 1988 the Homeless Children's Society changed its name and is now known as Youth Welfare UK (YWUK). From its foundation in Liverchester in the 1890s up to the mid-1960s the society's main activity was the operation of residential care homes and centres for city children, in countryside locations. During the 1970s and 1980s the emphasis shifted away from residential care towards community-based programmes with objectives characterised as, for example, preventing 'unnecessary' referrals to residential care, diverting young people away from crime, or reducing or preventing drug use among young people.

YWUK is relatively secure in financial terms which allows the organisation to maintain a high degree of independence in its policy and practice. Typically, local projects or programmes would have three or four full-time staff and would be supervised by a regional officer; each of the five regional officers carry supervisory responsibility for up to 10 projects. The detailed arrangements for the management of individual projects vary in a number of ways. First, the different level and nature of community involvement in management committees; second, the involvement of external funders varies ranging from projects entirely funded from the organisation's own resources to service contracts under which YWUK operates a service on behalf of a local council. Of the 127 project staff now in post over half are qualified youth workers, with the remainder roughly split between those with teaching or social work qualifications. The overall gender balance is now weighted slightly towards women although among project leaders 60 per cent are male. Seventeen staff identify themselves as black or Asian; of these six are employed in two specialist projects working with black young people.

The local authority

Hillshire Council in North Central Scotland came into being in 1996 when a former regional council was disaggregated to form five new single tier authorities. The area has a strong tradition of commitment to the provision of informal education programmes for young people. The council recently merged its education service which included youth work, with the child protection and welfare arm of its Social Work (Social Services) organisation. The new department is called The Children and Families Division. The authority serves an area of some 320 square miles and a population of 137,000. There are two main towns, seven villages of various sizes and a number of smaller settlements. Management operates in a strongly hierarchical fashion, decisions and policies being 'passed down' from above.

A current debate among staff concerned with informal work with young people is that around concerns with sexuality. Most of the trained youth workers regard working with young people on issues such as sexuality, gender identity and sexual health as important. For some of their colleagues with different professional backgrounds and training this is very much unexplored territory. The (Labour controlled) council is cautious, even 'conservative' in its approach, and in developing a policy for this work is seeking to impose a restrictive and fairly inflexible framework requiring advance parental consent to participation in sessions, and restrictions on what can be said about gay sexuality which one worker characterises as 'effectively preventing us from talking about the issue at all'.

The organisational context: structure and culture

In general our focus is more on culture and processes than structural factors such as organisational systems. However, in respect of structure, Mintzberg's (1979) distinction between *machine bureaucracy* as a description of the classical hierarchical organisation, and *professional bureaucracy* is particularly helpful. The latter describes an organisational form which, while demonstrating many of the positive qualities of bureaucracy in respect of clear procedures, lines of communication and accountability, also incorporates a recognition of the legitimacy of professional autonomy. Such a setting might well be a reasonably congenial home for youth workers, and the concept of professional bureaucracy could reasonably be applied as a description of some medium and larger voluntary organisations, and perhaps to some more enlightened local authorities.

The notion of organisational culture is somewhat problematic but, for our purposes, we will use the definition offered by Bloor and Dawson (1994: 276): 'Organizational culture is defined here as a patterned system of perceptions, meanings and beliefs about the organisation which facilitates sense-making amongst a group of people sharing common experiences and guides individual behaviour at work.'

These authors offer a useful model for the interpretation of professional cultures and subcultures in their organisational context, emphasising the importance of 'patterns of signification, legitimation and domination' (Giddens, cited in Bloor and Dawson, 1994: 278). The example of medical dominance over partner professions such as physiotherapy and social work offers a useful parallel with our hypothetical local government organisation of Hillshire Council. In this context the dominance of the teaching profession within education departments may influence the ways in which issues are framed, and crucially from our point of view here, the imperatives which influence professional decision making. Similarly, youth workers practising in a context where there is a statutory social work dimension to the relationship with young people, may find their concerns and priorities subjugated to those of their social work colleagues.

Millar (1995) has argued that many youth services operate in a 'person' culture, in which the needs and desires of individuals within the organisation take precedence over the demands of the organisation itself and this orientation can lead to an oppositional stance to authority. She also points out that such services operate 'within particularly complex decision-making structures, where advisory bodies, management committees, inter-disciplinary steering groups all have a role in the process in addition to relevant local authority committees' (Millar, 1995: 51). This kind of analysis shows how, for some workers, the circumstances of their work can lead to a view of management as inherently problematic since in many of its manifestations it will be seen as antithetical to the dominant value-base that defines youth workers' professionalism. Banks (1996: 18) has summarised the principles underpinning youth work practice as 'informal education; equality of opportunity; participation; empowerment'. This can mean that activist youth workers may see managers as part of a structure of social authority that is oppressing the very people for whom they are seeking to establish equality of opportunity.

Workers experience the organisations within which they function as influencing their activities in many different ways. Organisations may impose rules or rely on workers' judgements; they may encourage or stifle innovation at the grass roots; they control resources such as time, money or equipment. The smallest and largest organisations may behave in similar ways in this latter respect even though the resource concerned might be as different as a five or six figure financial budget on the one hand, and control of the keys to the Scout Hut on the other. Such tensions between organisational imperatives and the value positions that influence youth workers' purposes and behaviour lead us on to consider the concept of 'ethical climate' in organisations.

The organisational context: four 'climates' of ethical practice

The concept of ethical climate is chosen to represent a sense of 'how it feels to work here' in terms of the range of conditions for professional practice that may be encountered by youth workers. Victor and Cullen (1988: 101) characterise work climate in the ethical sense as 'the prevailing perceptions of typical organizational practices and procedures that have ethical content'. From an organisational point of view this is the way in which individual workers perceive their activities as being prescribed, proscribed or requiring permission. One illustration is the way in which recruitment and selection decisions are conducted and understood; for example in our case studies Riverside Youth Club and YWUK may well respond differently to concerns about equal opportunity in the ways they recruit and select paid or voluntary staff.

Victor and Cullen (1988) offer a framework or typology for analysing ethical work climates and this typology is the basis for the framework represented in Figure 4.1. There are two dimensions, the first being accountability and different understandings of the 'professional'. The second dimension represents the organisational priority given to doing the right thing or conversely to such criteria as public image and reputation. This is a simple theoretical framework that can help us to understand some quite complex and subtle features of professional life.

In the framework accountability is understood in terms of control by the organisation or, by contrast, by reference to a wider professional community of practice (Wenger, 1999), and this contrast provides one dimension of our framework. The second dimension is represented as concern with organisational image and reputation versus concern to 'do the right thing'. This framework enables us to conceptualise the climates of organisations as *professional*, *regulatory*, *parental* and *bureaucratic* approaches to ethical practice. These distinctive approaches are explained as follows.

The bureaucratic climate

The classical bureaucracy (Weber, 1947) is characterised by well defined lines of communication and accountability, clearly defined job boundaries and distinct levels of authority to make decisions. Scope for autonomy is limited and professionalism becomes problematic because the organisation's imperatives acquire a higher or at least equal standing with professional codes. Consideration of the occupations characterised by Etzioni (1969) as 'semi-professions', for example

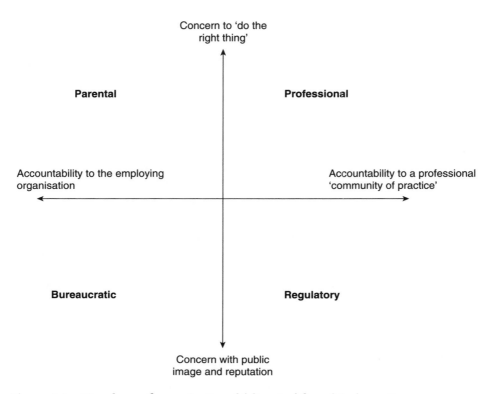

Figure 4.1   Typology of organizational 'climates' for ethical practice

social work and nursing, reveals activities which are characteristically quite highly supervised and more often than not operate within a framework of bureaucratic hierarchy such as a local government administration or a hospital.

In the Hillshire case study it would be no surprise to find that youth workers experienced it as a constraining bureaucracy, concerned primarily to achieve corporate objectives and avoid criticism, and expecting professional staff to pursue the corporate purpose and to account for their actions within that framework. It might be argued that clear organisational guidance about what is and is not desirable or permissible in practice may well help workers to clarify objectives, and to simplify some professional decision making. On the other hand an organisational context that tends to deny or stifle professional autonomy might be more likely to lead to the decline of workers' ethical sense and to a loss of the capacity to make their own professional judgements and to have confidence in their capacity to do so.

There is probably a tendency for larger, more diversified organisations to be less respectful of the professional autonomy to which youth workers might believe themselves entitled. Hillshire Council has organised its services in such a way that the work of youth workers is not necessarily supervised by professional peers (although it may be) and the autonomy of workers to follow their own judgements, or even to adopt a distinctive stance on an issue such as work with young people on sexuality issues is severely constrained. By contrast the experience of YWUK staff is much more that of being part of a peer-led community; innovation is encouraged and the taking of risks is, within limits, supported rather than criticised even when the outcomes are less than ideal.

The local authority is concerned with a wide range of issues and problems and treats youth work as part of a mosaic of services. For the worker in Hillshire Council the trade-off is some loss of autonomy in exchange for an organisational commitment to a much wider view than can be taken by YWUK. In the local authority the youth worker has a potential line of communication with colleagues such as school staff, social workers and others. It might also be argued at the policy level that a strategic approach to young people's needs and interests is something that only a local authority can develop, given also that it is uniquely legitimated through local democratic processes and structures.

The 'parental' climate

This label was chosen as an appropriate description of an organisation concerned to do the right thing but reluctant to trust the worker to make independent decisions about what courses of action to follow. The label 'parental' is drawn from a psychological theory known as Transactional Analysis (Berne, 1968) which gives us the idea of a 'controlling parent'. The emphasis on accountability through control or prescription by the organisation makes the notion of professionalism problematic. Some degree of autonomy is an important dimension of professionalism and it is difficult to see work in an organisation which functions in this way as professional, even though such a culture might be found in many of the traditional professions. For example, in many areas of medical practice highly trained doctors and nurses are required to follow particular processes and procedures rather than exercising independent judgement.

It is not hard to think of examples of settings where informal work with young people is conducted in such an atmosphere. Uniformed organisations with their quasi-military structures and symbols might be seen this way, with quite specific schemes of work and a strong hierarchy. Many organisations of the small voluntary club type operate under the control of one strong individual, or at most a very small group. The Riverside Youth Club could fit fairly neatly into this conceptual category, operating under the control of an acknowledged 'club leader'. The dominant traditions in these traditions are generally respectful and caring towards young people, and encourage a progressive involvement by club members in decisions about the programme and activities. The critical tension in such a climate is likely to be between the dominant centre and potential alternative leadership.

The regulatory climate

Here, accountability is to an ideal or professional ethic. The worker's loyalty is at least as much to a wider community of practice and to those they serve, as it is to the employer. Scope for autonomy is acknowledged and treated as an entitlement, albeit constrained by the organisation's concern with its reputation or public image. Workers cannot be permitted to exercise their discretion in ways that might appear to threaten that image. The central difficulty for the worker in this climate is to maintain commitment to the idealised notions of professional practice while avoiding challenging the organisation's expectations.

YWUK and the Woodhouse Youth Project might both be 'mapped' onto this quadrant although for slightly different reasons. The difference may be understood in terms of the source of moral authority; in YWUK the ethical boundaries are determined largely internally and are legitimated in part by the history and standing of the organisation. In the Woodhouse Project, by contrast, workers see the main source of authority lying outside the project itself, in the hands of funders. The framework of an independent project creates a protective barrier and provides the project and its workers with the standing of autonomous professionals, but at the same time the desires and priorities of funders are constantly considered by workers. Such a climate may be seen as attractive by workers, and would probably be associated with a low or moderate turnover of staff, clear commitments to ethical practice in recruitment and selection, proactive training and staff development policies and innovative practice.

The 'pure' professional climate

The combination of an organisation concerned at a corporate level to act ethically, and of individuals' independent accountability to a professional ethic might seem an ideal to strive towards. In practice there are a number of potential difficulties. The expectation of fully conscious decision making by 'autonomous professionals' creates a high level of demand on the individual worker. Constantly having to think about a professional code and principles rather than organisational rules or simply custom and practice as the source of support in ethical decision making can leave individuals experiencing isolation, doubt and uncertainty as a consequence of any dilemma with an ethical dimension.

It seems unlikely that many youth workers will find themselves working in such a climate although a lack of close scrutiny over practice, and the isolation of individual workers sometimes creates the impression of working in a professional climate when the reality is more like an ineffective bureaucracy. As a work climate it might also lack the focus for debate and the resolution of conflict. It is probably better for the nature and purpose of practice to be the focus of regular scrutiny and discussion by one's peers, in the context of practice rather than outside it. There is not a great benefit in attempting to specify an 'ideal' climate. It is important to emphasise the idealised notion of accountability to a professional ethic rather than to organisational control. That is not, however, to suggest that other climates are hostile. Professionalism is a powerful idea, able to survive and even flourish in a range of situations.

Conclusion

In this chapter we have shown how individuals, managers and organisations interact to facilitate or impede ethical practice in youth work but that individual workers have the ability to interpret their own organisational context and act to integrate professional and organisational expectations. Workers have a sense of their personal 'agency' or capacity to take purposeful action; a belief that they can act to change the world that they are in and that they can make a difference. Individual conceptions of ethical practice, that have been forged in professional training, discussions with fellow workers or through shared commitments to a particular value base will result in actions that may differ from those espoused by the organisation. For example, in terms of accountability there can be real disagreements, especially in organisations like Riverside, about how and to whom the service is responsive when disruptive young people might be construed by some workers as needing support but by others as spoiling the provision for the majority.

What this chapter has sought to demonstrate is not that such disagreements are avoidable but that placing the exploration and resolution of debate at the heart of our work is essential. Ignoring the diversity of views that arise from the interactions in and between individuals and their organisations will not avoid disputes but simply 'displace them into discontent' (Fairley and Paterson, 1995: 34). Being aware of the differing conceptions of professionalism, accountability and organisational context that we have explored is more likely to result in uncomfortable dilemmas and contradictions for individuals but, nevertheless, the struggle to resolve these will lead to growth and development and a more ethically based practice.

References

Argyris, C. and Schon, D. (1974) *Theory in Practice: Increasing Professional Effectiveness*. San Francisco: Jossey Bass.

Banks, S. (1996) 'Youth work, informal education and professionalisation', *Youth and Policy*, 54: 13–25.

Berne, E. (1968) *Games People Play: The Psychology of Human Relationships*. Harmondsworth: Penguin.

Bloor, G. and Dawson, P. (1994) 'Understanding professional culture in organisational context', *Organization Studies*, 15(2): 275–95.

Bloxham, S. and Heathfield, M. (1995) 'Reflecting the theory/practice dichotomy in youth and community work training', *Youth and Policy*, 50: 35–48.

Etzioni, A. (1969) *The Semi-professions and their Organisation*. London: Collier Macmillan.

Fairley, J. and Paterson, L. (1995) 'Scottish education and the new managerialism', *Scottish Educational Review*, 27(1): 13–36.

Friedson, E. (1986) *Professional Powers: A Study of the Institutionalisation of Formal Knowledge*. Chicago and London: University of Chicago Press.

Goffman, E. (1975) *Frame Analysis*. Harmondsworth: Penguin.

Henry, C. (1994) 'Professional behaviour and the organisation', in R. Chadwick (ed.), *Ethics and the Professions*. Aldershot: Avebury.

Holdsworth, D. (1994) 'Accountability: the obligation to lay oneself open to criticism', in R. Chadwick (ed.), *Ethics and the Professions*. Aldershot: Avebury.

Koehn, D. (1994) *The Ground of Professional Ethics*. London: Routledge.

McCulloch, K. and Tett, L. (1999) 'Professional ethics, accountability and the organisational context of youth work', in S. Banks (ed.), *Ethical Issues in Youth Work*. London: Routledge.

Millar, G. (1995) 'Beyond Managerialism', *Youth and Policy*, 50: 49–58.

Mintzberg, H. (1979) *The Structuring of Organisations*. Englewood Cliffs, NJ: Prentice-Hall.

Scottish Office (1996) *The Public Inquiry into the Shootings at Dunblane Primary School on 13th March 1996 (The Cullen Report)*. London: HMSO.

Smith, M. (1988) *Developing Youth Work*. Milton Keynes: Open University Press.

Smith, M. (1994) *Local Education*. Milton Keynes: Open University Press.

Victor, B. and Cullen, J. (1988) 'The organisational bases of ethical work climates', *Administrative Science Quarterly*. 33: 101–25.

Weber, M. (1947) *The Theory of Social and Economic Organisation*. London: Oxford University Press.

Wenger, E. (1999) *Communities of Practice: Learning, Meaning and Identity*. Cambridge: Cambridge University Press.

Wilding, P. (1982) *Professional Power and Social Welfare*. London: Routledge & Kegan Paul.

5

Leading and managing anti-oppressive youth work

Harriet Gore

Introduction and health warning

The last time I delivered a training course on anti-oppressive practice to a group of youth workers I felt a keen sense of disappointment because the group came to the session with little understanding of the subject and how it applied to their work. I found myself wondering if we had come full circle from the time in the 1980s when youth workers first struggled to get equal opportunities anti-oppressive practice on the agenda for the service as a whole and whether the achievements, learning and experiences of the 1990s had been completely lost.

I was pleased to be asked to write this chapter but as I reflected on the training programme, warning bells sounded. I didn't want readers to experience my feelings of disappointment nor to use this as an opportunity to express a growing sense that anti-oppressive practice and equality of opportunity have slipped so far down the agenda for youth work that it is hard to find examples of good practice informed by sound theoretical perspectives. I was also concerned not to use this article as a therapeutic opportunity to voice the anger and frustration I have experienced in attempting to keep anti-oppressive practice on the agenda for our work as practitioners, managers and leaders.

I am writing this introduction as a caveat; the perspectives I aim to share are sometimes of a personal nature, based very firmly in my own experience as a black person. Some of my experience has been extremely positive. I have been astounded by the bravery and tenaciousness of colleagues and young people in working to high standards and demanding the best. Some of it has been less positive; I have been saddened at how the body of learning and experience in relation to anti-oppressive practice is slipping away; that the debates surrounding the issue have become increasingly academic and unconnected with practice and that a subject that was visible at the heart of youth work has moved into the margins once again.

In this chapter I will describe the experiences and principles I bring to this area of work; I will review the legislative and societal context that has affected anti-oppressive practice; demonstrate the inter-relationship between good youth work and anti-oppressive practice and present a model designed to assist managers and leaders to provide effective support for staff and young people.

A few definitions and an assumption

Anti-oppressive practice can be a tricky term. What do we mean by it? My understanding is that it describes a methodology for our work and is about a theoretical approach that is underpinned by principles of justice and equality. This results in a belief that equality of opportunity can only be achieved if we proactively seek to address oppression in every aspect of our work with individuals and groups of young people. For me, anti-oppressive practice in youth work is about:

- Extending young people's understanding of the world in which they live and how oppression limits their opportunities and the opportunities of other groups in society.
- Identifying opportunities to engage young people in finding tools to challenge their own oppression and the oppression experienced by other groups.
- Ensuring that all young people have equality of access to resources and opportunities for personal and social development and that once they gain access that they are able to secure and achieve high quality outcomes.
- Engaging young people in building their self-esteem and pride in who they are, through celebrating their cultural, racial and religious heritages and extending their understanding and tolerance for the cultures, values and beliefs of other groups in society.

I have a firm belief that good anti-oppressive practice in youth work is a key to promoting personal development. I also work on the assumption that we all experience oppression of some kind and that if we and the young people with whom we work are able to understand and acknowledge our own oppression and how it has affected us, we are more likely to understand the oppression experienced by other groups in society and take practical action to challenge it. Unsurprisingly, as a black person much of my experience and knowledge focuses on race and racism and much of this chapter is based on the insights this has provided me. I invite you as the reader to use this as a starting point in considering how this translates into the experience of other oppressed groups.

Where it all began

I started my career as a manager and leader of youth work in the 1980s. Like many other black workers at the time I was drawn to youth work not only because of the joy and excitement I experienced when working as a volunteer but also through a sense that if only I knew as a black young person what I knew as a black adult in the 1980s things would have been much better for me. Coming to this country from Pakistan as a very young child, I had quickly learned to hide who and what I was to avoid oppression. I learned that to be safe it was important to blend in, never to speak about my life, my culture and heritage or even the food I ate, for fear of being accused of smelling of curry or being a called 'dirty Paki'. By the 1980s I had re-evaluated some of this; I felt in awe of my parents' struggle as immigrants to this country; I had grown proud of my cultural heritage and the values and principles it instilled in me (and of course, by then ethnic food was in vogue and being able to knock up a good curry was seen as a valuable skill!). All in all, I had a strong sense that I had something very important to communicate to black young people and was on a mission to do so. My message was, 'It's okay to be who you are, and in fact it is more than okay to be who you are – it's fantastic that you are who you are!'

The context in the 1980s

The 1970s saw the creation of equalities legislation in the form of the Race Relations Act 1976 and the Sex Discrimination Act 1975. This legislation made discrimination on the grounds of race or gender unlawful and raised the profile of securing equality of opportunity, particularly in public sector organisations which, in turn, led to a revision of employment practices and the provision of services.

In the field of youth work, the Thompson Report (Thompson, 1982) contained sections on work with black and minority ethnic young people, girls and young women and disabled young people, which identified the need to promote equality of access to youth service resources for these groups and mentioned separate provision as a means of meeting this aim. However, it made no mention of gay and lesbian young people and failed to identify the need to develop an anti-oppressive pedagogy. Nevertheless, the publication of the report, events such as the race riots in inner cities in 1981 and HMI reports that dealt with issues of equality, placed a greater emphasis on finding ways of working with young people that ensured that they had equality of access, developed tolerance and an understanding of oppression.

The world of youth work in the 1980s was one that was struggling to identify, understand and address issues of oppression. Many colleagues felt vulnerable and among most groups of staff there was a fear of unknowingly saying or doing the 'wrong thing'. There were debates around issues such as whether white managers could manage work with black young people or whether male managers could manage work with young women. Although these questions seemed important at the time, in retrospect they were a diversion from the real issues of ensuring that the needs of all groups of young people were considered and met and that appropriate policies, practices and methodologies were developed to provide access and address oppression.

Interventions to promote better understanding of anti-oppression seemed to add to the confusion. Training on anti-oppression tended to focus on understanding the past and less on action to be taken in the present. It was important, for example, to understand Britain's colonial history and slavery and to use this information to provide a context for the present. However, this focus on a past that dehumanised black people and stripped the colonies of wealth and natural resources often resulted in feelings of shame and powerlessness. Moreover, in its attempts to develop the debate in the 'here and now' training dwelt on premises such as all white people being racist and all men being sexist, which in turn resulted in a sense of guilt. Within youth work practice at this time, there was an emphasis on challenging oppression. In its clumsier forms this failed to promote young people's understanding of the issues and did little to foster new learning, understanding or changes in behaviour.

Many youth services established separate provision for young women, black, Asian, disabled and gay and lesbian young people during this time. This was, in many ways, a move forward as it provided a safe space within which the particular issues for these groups of young people could be explored. However, it has been pointed out that the curriculum for these groups often focused on 'cultural activities' that did not result in good educational outcomes (Chauhan, 1989).

For example, Asian girls' Groups were often located in schools; they were staffed by women who were seen as 'respected' members of the community;

and the programme focused on learning 'valuable' skills such as sewing and cooking. The activities within these groups reinforced stereotypes and there was little emphasis on developing a pedagogy that enabled the girls to explore the context in which they lived or to address issues that were important to them. Although the existence of these groups provided space for Asian young women to spend time together, they failed to deliver the personal, social and political education that was a developing feature of work in 'mainstream' provision at that time.

Over time and with training for staff the nature of these groups changed. Local and national organisations for workers in girls' groups did much to ensure that both black and white young women had access to the resources of youth services and that the curriculum was based around their needs and concerns. The voluntary and community sector also made great strides forward in meeting the needs of black and minority ethnic young people and in turn influenced local authorities. My own work with Asian staff and young women developed a sharper focus on enabling young women to define and celebrate their own British Asian identity rather than being seen as victims of a struggle between two cultures. Other aspects of this work included supporting young people in demanding recognition of black and minority ethnic cultures in schools and youth clubs through celebrations and, in turn, using this to enable young people to develop valuable practical skills that could be highlighted with families, the community and schools.

By the end of the 1980s, there was a growing recognition that youth services had to develop policies and practices that demonstrated their commitment to addressing the personal and social development needs of oppressed groups. The role and agenda for separate provision was developed to encompass programmes that addressed social and personal development. For example, in work with black and minority ethnic young people there was a greater emphasis on using experiences, interests and aspirations as a starting point for developing confidence, self-esteem, communication and organisational skills. There was recognition that separate provision could also be seen as segregated unless it was accompanied with strategies to develop the relevance, appropriateness and accessibility of 'mainstream' youth work. Finally, policies were being developed that provided a rationale for the anti-oppressive practice, identified action and allocated resources to the work.

The changing context of the 1990s

As a result of the passionate debates that took place within youth work in the 1980s, youth services were often the first council departments to develop equal opportunities policies in the 1990s. The policies that emerged tended to deal with issues of equality in recruitment and retention of staff and youth work practice grouped around the themes of equality of access, anti-oppression and the celebration of diversity. The best policies were accompanied by guidance and action plans that provided a requirement for youth workers to identify how all these themes would be addressed in their work with young people. The bolder policies included the concerns of a wider set of groups such as young people who were disadvantaged by their economic circumstances and gay and lesbian young people.

The momentum that had built up around the issues of equality of opportunity and anti-oppressive practice is illustrated by the statement of purpose for youth work that emerged from the second Ministerial Conference on the core curriculum for youth services. Bernard Davies (1999) describes how the actions of a black working group resulted in a new statement of purpose that recognised oppression:

> the new statement did not only see youth work as offering young people opportunities which were educative. It committed it, too, to promoting equality of opportunity and participative and empowering forms of practice. In applying these broad purposes, it also set the service the task of challenging oppressions such as racism and sexism and supporting young people to act on political and other issues affecting their lives.

This was a radical statement and not one which either the minister or stakeholders in voluntary and statutory youth services could embrace. Davies goes on to describe how the government distanced itself from it. Nevertheless, the events that took place at this conference demonstrate how the focus on anti-oppression in youth work had developed by this time.

Meanwhile, while local authorities and other public bodies were working to implement the requirements of equalities legislation by changing the way they recruited staff and provided services, the press and some politicians were undermining these attempts and trivialising the direction of travel by references to the 'loony Left'. In addition, legislation such as Section 28, which made it unlawful to 'promote' homosexuality in education, increased the tensions experienced by local authorities that genuinely wanted to promote equality of opportunity in employment and access to services.

Here I would like to give a practical example of how this national context affected youth work. At this time I was working with a group of young lesbians. Membership was declining as young women grew up and gained the confidence to access other social settings in which they were accepted and welcomed. The remaining members of the group wanted to advertise it and as with any other group of young people we explored ways of recruiting new members. The young women produced a leaflet explaining the aims of the group and inviting young lesbians to join. The leaflet caused immediate concern. The council's legal department would not allow it to be distributed, as in their judgement it could be seen to 'promote' homosexuality.

This situation illustrates the point made at the beginning of the chapter about how, in some situations, it is more difficult to deliver a message that says 'it's okay to be who you are'.

Where we are now

The end of the 1990s saw a change in government and the expectation that New Labour might support youth work and, in particular, anti-oppression. However, with the new government came a greater expectation that the youth service would contribute to combating a range of social issues such as youth unemployment, teenage pregnancy and drug misuse. Attention was diverted to respond to issues such as the emerging Connexions Strategy and *Transforming Youth Work* (DfES, 2001) which asserted the key elements of twenty-first century youth services. Although *Transforming Youth Work* made reference to equality of opportunity saying that, 'the youth service should be able to clearly demonstrate how the diversity of its target age range is mainstreamed through staff, provision and inclusion policies and practices', the attention of most youth services was on how they were going to resist being subsumed in Connexions partnerships while achieving the challenging standards set out for youth work (DfES, 2001). Where equality was referenced it was linked closely to social inclusion, community cohesion and meeting the requirements of legislation rather than promoting personal development through anti-oppressive practice.

Transforming Youth Work led the development of more focused youth services with greater clarity of purpose and expectations that the youth service would contribute to a wide range of issues including social inclusion and community cohesion. This might be seen as recognition of the work that many youth services were doing with young people who were excluded from society as a result of issues such as poor educational attainment, poverty, disability, sexual orientation, gender or race. However, whereas previously much of the work was based primarily on the needs and interests of young people, post-*Transforming Youth Work* it was more likely to be linked primarily to reducing social problems. Evaluation of impact focused less on what young people had learned or achieved and more on how likely they were to engage in employment, education or training, avoid unplanned pregnancies or engage in anti-social behaviour. There were merits in this new approach; youth workers were required to think about outcomes for young people for, perhaps, the first time. However, there were also losses for in the rush to develop youth work curricula, planning and recording procedures and management information systems, and to manage the implementation of these, the focus on other issues such as equality and supporting anti-oppressive practice was lost.

In reflecting on this period of time, it is clear that *Transforming Youth Work* was successful in defining a role for the youth service and placing requirements on local authorities to provide high quality youth provision. All of this was to be welcomed. However, for many youth services the pace of change that was required meant that there were also losses. A practical example, from my own experience, was that the role of my team was changed; it was refocused into working on issues of health, crime and community safety and participation. These are important issues for young people and should be addressed. It was a shame that they were addressed at the expense of other areas of the work.

The performance of youth services post-*Transforming Youth Work* was monitored by an increase in inspection activity by Ofsted. In 2004 Ofsed launched a revised framework for the inspection of local authority youth services. In July 2005 it published *Effective Youth Services* (Ofsted, 2005) a report on the performance of youth services in the 40 inspections that took place in 2004. The report commented that:

> Services had generally developed good policies on equality, inclusion and diversity and included the promotion of social inclusion among their aims. Policies on the Special Educational Needs and Disability Act (SENDA) 2001, the Race Relations (Amendment) Act 2000 and the DfES guidance Safeguarding Children in Education were in place. **Considerable differences existed, however, between services in their implementation and promotion of these policies through their curriculum. There was still much to do to ensure that good intentions expressed in policies were borne out in effective practice.**

This statement saying that there is still much to do, made over 20 years after the debate about anti-oppression in youth work first began, returns me to the question posed at the beginning of the chapter; have we come full circle in relation to anti-oppressive practice? Much was done in the 1980s and 1990s; youth work developed good practice and a greater focus on the themes of enabling young people to challenge oppression, working with groups that experience oppression and celebrating identity and diversity. Ofsted's assessment that there is still much to do to ensure that good intentions are borne out in practice indicates that a body of experience and good practice seems to have been lost or declined over the past few years.

Challenges then and now

In seeking to answer the question of whether we have come full circle since the 1980s, it is useful to compare the challenges faced then with the challenges we now face in relation to leading and managing anti-oppressive practice.

The challenges in the 1980s were:

- Getting anti-oppressive practice on the agenda.
- Understanding what anti-oppressive practice meant and identifying how it applied to youth work.
- Securing strategic support.
- Securing the support of stakeholders, staff, young people and partners.
- Formulating policies.
- Developing action plans and monitoring their implementation.
- Identifying good practice and providing good staff development and training to develop practice.
- Leading and managing anti-oppressive practice in an environment that was often unsympathetic.

The challenges now are different; anti-oppressive practice is an accepted methodology and is seen generally as integral to good youth work practice. However, it is acknowledged that leaders and managers of youth work operate in a very different context now. The *Every Child Matters* (ECM) and subsequent *Youth Matters* agendas requiring youth services to be part of integrated services for children and young people have resulted in a period of huge change for youth services. Aside from the challenge of leading and managing anti-oppressive practice, managers face a wide variety of challenges. These include:

- Ensuring that their services are seen as an essential and integral part of integrated services for children and young people by providing good quality evidence about the service's contribution to ECM outcomes and creating and maintaining a good reputation for the service.
- Facing the challenges posed by central government guidance on commissioning services, and providing evidence that the youth service is best placed to deliver social and personal education.
- Achieving Best Value Performance Indicators for the youth contribution to Local Authorities' Comprehensive Performance Assessment – a framework to measure the overall performance of a local authority council, using best value performance indicators, best value inspection reports, and audit reports. Essentially this means that what happens on

a wet Wednesday night in a youth club has a direct relationship with the assessment of the overall performance of a local authority.

- Contributing to an increasing number of corporate plans and strategies. For example, in the health field alone youth services contribute to: the teenage pregnancy strategy; the sexual health strategy; the health inequality plan; the young people's substance misuse plan; health promoting schools scheme; the 'Five a Day' campaign, and so on.
- Managing the reorganisation of services to create local integrated provision for young people.

Against this backdrop, leading and managing anti-oppressive practice could become just another priority competing with all the others. However, the key to developing and maintaining good anti-oppressive practice, and many other aspects of youth work, is performance management. Including anti-oppression in a performance management framework ensures that it is built into plans and that progress and achievements are monitored regularly. This in turn can have the effect of identifying resources and support for the work in terms of funding, equipment, staff and training.

In practice this means that, at the very least, youth services should plan to have in place:

- Policies on equality, diversity and inclusion.
- Resources allocated according to the needs of groups of young people that experience oppression.
- Service wide, area and unit plans to ensure that oppression is addressed; that groups of young people that experience oppression have access to the resources of the service and are supported to achieve good outcomes; and that provision is made for celebrating diversity.
- Training and staff development opportunities that promote and extend understanding and implementation of anti-oppressive practice.
- Systems for monitoring performance against plans, assessing quality and securing continuous improvement.

In terms of what this might look like in youth work settings, there are also some essential elements:

- Displays of information, posters and leaflets that address and promote discussion and enquiry about oppression in areas such as racism, sexism, disability, homophobia, identity and stereotyping.
- Strategies to promote access to and engagement in youth work programmes, such as targeted work and separate provision (including

meeting the requirements of the Disability Discrimination Act and the Special Educational Needs and Disabilities Act).
- Specific projects, activities and events that aim to enable young people to challenge oppression and celebrate diversity.
- Evidence of what young people have learned and achieved through exploring the effects of oppression.

The lists above can be used by leaders and managers to ensure that anti-oppressive practice finds its rightful place at the heart of youth work and that it is used to promote personal and social development, learning and the acquisition of skills.

Some conclusions and pointers about good practice

I began this chapter with a slightly pessimistic view of where the youth service is in relation to anti-oppression at the beginning of the twenty-first century. I end it more encouraged; the struggles of the 1980s have paid off. For example, there is now:

- Clear expectation from government that youth services should have strategies in place to determine the needs in their area, identifying and prioritising target groups that are vulnerable to issues such as social exclusion. This expectation helps to ensure that the needs of young people that are subject to oppression are systematically considered and met.
- A clear role and requirements for youth services to contribute to community cohesion, for example, by bringing together different groups of young people. This requirement helps to ensure that young people are supported in developing tolerance and an appreciation of the culture and heritage of other groups.
- An expectation that youth work should extend young people's understanding and aspirations and that anti-oppressive practice is a key approach in enabling young people to understand and challenge oppression and celebrate their identity.
- Public reports of youth service inspections that make judgements on local authority progress on meeting the aims outlined above.
- Good examples of work to promote social inclusion through targeted work with young people that fall into priority target groups.

However, like the Ofsted report *Effective Youth Services*, I think there is still room for improvement in developing policy and practice in this area. In the best services the following essential elements are in place:

- Needs assessment used to identify and allocate resources to priority groups thus providing access to high quality youth work. Clear communication of these strategies demonstrates commitment to equality of opportunity and ensures that stakeholders are informed of the need to target their services effectively.
- Operational plans, at service wide and unit level, to include targets and performance indicators about the type of work that is to be undertaken as well as the numbers of young people that the service seeks to contact and involve, for example, asserting that each unit will develop work that extends young people's understanding of oppression each quarter. Setting these targets helps to ensure that progress is monitored and that staff are supported in developing the work.
- A curriculum that defines the key elements of anti-oppressive practice and provides resources, training and examples of good practice to support the work.
- Effective line management, support and supervision that involves managers in monitoring progress towards targets and enables staff to reflect on their practice and develop high quality learning programmes.
- A service wide recognition that anti-oppressive practice is an integral part of good youth work.

In one service I visited recently the majority of these elements were present. The impact was evident in a youth centre where young people had developed a code of conduct that asserted that oppressive language and behaviour were unacceptable. The young people that use the centre are predominantly white and one of them proudly showed me a display and recounted how an oppressive comment had been dealt with by a youth worker. The discussion that followed resulted in a piece of work that explored culture and identity. The young woman described how this had developed her understanding of other cultures and her awareness of the effects of prejudice and discrimination. She was keen to describe activities such as using the internet to search for information, learning about religious and cultural celebrations and trying out new and different foods. The display was intended to get other young people thinking about this issue. Clearly, the young woman had enjoyed taking part in this piece of work and as a result of evaluating it was able to articulate what she had learned.

It is worth considering the role of the youth workers and their managers in developing a piece of work such as this. Staff identify a need to deal with oppressive comments and behaviour and identify strategies for raising and addressing these issues. Managers support this work by placing explicit requirements on all youth work units to develop learning programmes that explore issues of equality and oppression in the service plan. Performance against this target is explored routinely in supervision and staff are supported in achieving it through the provision of resources, training and reflection on their practice. Good practice is shared routinely so that practitioners learn from each other.

Examples such as this demonstrate that anti-oppressive practice is surviving in the twenty-first century although there is still much to do to ensure the quality and consistency of the work nationally. They also demonstrate that the core skills of leadership and management such as clarity of purpose, roles, responsibilities, clear lines of accountability, good performance management and effective use of resources, apply to implementing good anti-oppressive practice.

References

Chauhan, V. (1989) *Beyond Steel Bands and Samosas: Black Young People in the Youth Service.* Leicester: National Youth Bureau.

Davies, B. (1999) *A History of the Youth Service in England, Vol. 2: 1979–1999.* Leicester: Youth Work Press.

DfES (2001) *Transforming Youth Work – Resourcing Excellent Youth Services.* London: DfES

DfES (2003) *Every Child Matters.* London: The Stationery Office.

DfES (2005) *Youth Matters.* London: The Stationery Office.

Ofsted (2005) *Effective Youth Services: Good Practice.* HMI2445. Ofsted.

Thompson, A. (1982) *Experience and Participation – Report of the Review Group on the Youth Service in England.* London: HMSO.

6

The active involvement of young people

Bill Badham and Tim Davies

Introduction

Leading and managing work with young people is being turned on its head. The position of the service user, however young they may be, is moving from object to subject, consumer to co-creator, empty vessel to expert by experience, receiver of services to being involved by right in their design, delivery and evaluation. These are transformative times. What impact is this having and should it have on leading and managing work with young people?

This chapter explores the context of young people's participation, the pitfalls and opportunities this represents and some reflections on the changing relationships this shift in paradigm may cause.

We use the terms 'participation' and 'active involvement' interchangeably, and we refer to 'children and young people' to indicate a wider age band and a wider variety of contexts than traditional 'youth work'.

Participation: the context

This section explores the policy and practice of participation, some of the benefits and the importance of clear shared values to underpin the active involvement of children and young people. It concludes with some pointers for leaders in work with young people to help develop safe, sound and effective approaches to their participation.

Policy of participation

There are many opportunities for children and young people to take an active part in shaping where they live, the services they use and the running of local and national organisations. Creating such opportunities is not optional. It is essential. The opportunity to genuinely participate in decision making is a right, a civil right, a human right and a right of citizenship, established in law, policy and guidance. It is set out in the *Convention on the Rights of the Child* (UN, 1989). This was ratified by the UK government in December 1991 to ensure its full implementation. This right to be heard and taken seriously is further underpinned by a range of domestic legislation and guidance affecting specific groups of children and young people accessing a wide range of services, including education, health, child safety or neighbourhood renewal (Willow, 2002: 21–27). However, without full incorporation into domestic law of the *Convention on the Rights of the Child*, making breaches open to challenge in our courts, anomalies inevitably arise. Students, for example, have the vague collective right to participate in school decision making, including in governance (Department for Education and Skills, 2004a), but are still denied the individual right to attend or contribute to their own exclusion hearing.

Most recently *Every Child Matters (Department for Education and Skills, 2003)*, its underpinning legislation of the Children Act 2004, accompanying Statutory Guidance on children's trust arrangements and inspections – especially Joint Area Reviews – and *Youth Matters (Department for Education and Skills, 2005)*: these all determine that young people shall be involved in the design, delivery and evaluation of services. Their participation is essential in order to improve policy and services and ensure the best outcomes for them as set out in *Every Child Matters*: being healthy, staying safe, enjoying and achieving, making a positive contribution and economic well-being.

The stated intent of policy makers is that these requirements shall in turn promote a change in attitude and a shift in power in the management and delivery of services towards the young (Hargreaves, 2005).

> Local partners should ensure a culture of openness across their children's trust arrangements, so that listening and responding to children and young people becomes an integral part of everyday practice. They should see to it that children and young people are involved in decision-making about their lives and in designing and developing services (Department for Education and Skills, 2004b: para 32).

The services coming under such strong directive are the local authority and district council (in two-tier authorities) and services under their direction, police, probation, Youth Offending Teams, health, Connexions and Learning and Skills Councils (Department for Education and Skills, 2004b: para 17). The deliberate but extraordinary exception to those mandated in law to work together under the partnership arrangements are schools and colleges. They, along with the voluntary sector, are only encouraged to.

Statutory guidance indicates the expected range and scope of children and young people's participation in trust arrangements to include front-line staff providing integrated services, auditing, commissioning and budget processes and inter-agency governance arrangements.

Practice of participation

How children and young people get involved in decision making can be considered by using Roger Hart's Ladder of Participation (Figure 6.1). The ladder has eight rungs. The first three represent non-participation through manipulation, decoration and tokenism. Above these come increasing degrees of participation from being assigned but informed, through adults initiating but sharing decisions, to children and young people and adults initiating and sharing decisions together. The ladder highlights that participation can take various forms and happen to different degrees depending on a range of factors. It offers both a gauge to the nature of involvement and a guide to how its quality might be improved. It does not prescribe that all involvement in all contexts must operate on the top rung of the ladder, but encourages that the critical question of how young people's involvement can be developed and elevated is always asked.

What we do know is that unless involving children and young people is underpinned by a real commitment to attitudinal and organisational change and to improving services as a result, we will not get far up the ladder. Attempts will be ineffectual, frustrating and damaging. Without the active participation of children and young people in the promotion of all their rights to a good childhood, none will be achieved effectively (The National Youth Agency, 2005).

When done well, there are many benefits to involving children and young people. First, children and young people gain a voice and influence which is their right leading to opportunities for personal development and recognition as active participants within wider society. Second, organisations become more accountable, improve their decision-making structures, respond better to issues and concerns faced by children and young people and develop better quality service.

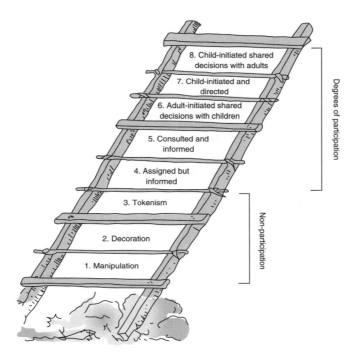

Figure 6.1   Roger Hart's Ladder of Participation (adapted from Arnstein (Hart, 1992)).

For participation to be effective it must be rooted in children and young people's rights to influence services that affect them and the right to do so safely (UN, 1989, Articles 12 and 19). It must be based on shared values. These are taken from *Hear by Right* (Badham and Wade, 2005) and are at the heart of the government's *Learning to Listen* framework (Department for Education and Skills, 2001).

- Children and young people are valued.
- The diversity and skills of children and young people are recognised.
- Adequate resources are available.
- Children and young people are involved in monitoring and evaluation.

There are, as indicated above, many opportunities and many pitfalls generated by the current climate about the active involvement of children and young people. In this context, over a number of seminars and events on participation and social inclusion between 2002 and 2004, adults and young people drew out five key aspects to help ensure participation is transformative not tokenistic (Edwards and Davis, 2004).

1. Participation involves being heard and something changing for the better as a result.
2. Participation is best promoted through opportunities for engagement in dialogue, not oppositional or confrontational processes between children and young people and decision makers.
3. Participation needs to be routed in the lived lives of children and young people on tangible issues of concern and importance to them.
4. Participation is political and is about the enfranchisement of a disenfranchised group in society to ensure effective action to make change happen.
5. Participation needs to be inclusive through opportunities for the young to take part on their own terms and on their own issues and not just through adult initiated or established models and processes.

Participation: changing organisations

Having set out the context of participation, this section looks at the implications for leadership for organisations working with children and young people. An organisation can be loosely defined as a group of individuals and resources employed towards achieving common goals. How successful it is will depend on a range of interrelated factors, including strategies, structures and staff. All of these will in turn affect its capacity to engage effectively with children and young people. Being aware of the power dynamics created by existing structures and seeing the scope for change is crucial to exploring ways of deepening and embedding a culture of participation in an organisation.

A standards framework can provide a way of seeing how different aspects of an organisation have to connect and support each other towards achieving effective change. *Hear by Right: Standards for the Active Involvement of Children and Young People* (Badham and Wade, 2005) aims to provide a robust yet flexible model and process to secure sustained and beneficial participation of children and young people and to encourage continual improvement in an organisation's activities. First published in 2001 and piloted within local authorities with its heartland in youth services, it has become established as a robust and flexible tool across voluntary and statutory sector organisations and partnerships. The standards framework encourages inclusion of a wide range of children and young people, while urging care in choosing approaches appropriate to different ages, abilities and understanding.

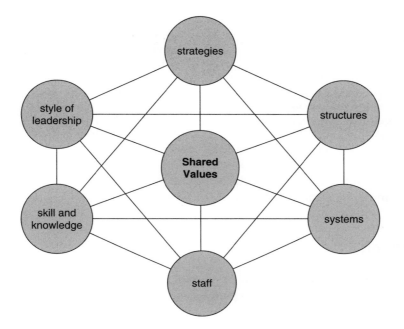

Figure 6.2   The 7S model of organisational change (Peters and Waterman, 1982)

The *Hear by Right* framework is built on the 7S model of organisational change (Figure 6.2).

There are seven standards: shared values, strategy, structures, systems, staff, skills and knowledge, style of leadership. Shared values are at the core of the framework. Each standard is broken down into seven self-assessment indicators, building one upon another across three levels: emerging, established and advanced. The central tenet of *Hear by Right* is that an organisation effectively listening and involving its 'customers' will develop better services, leading to improved outcomes for the service users.

Style leadership: the seven indicators of success

The 7S model of organisational change demonstrates the interdependence of the standards and that progress will only be made by systematic advance across each of them. The Style of leadership standard is of particular note for this book. *Hear by Right* introduces it as follows:

Leadership is always vital, especially during a time of change. Promoting the participation of children and young people means change in an organisation's culture and
requires leadership with courage and clout among staff, elected members, trustees
and children and young people themselves. While dedicated staff will be needed to
establish and develop good working practices with children and young people, support at a senior and executive level will be essential to champion the cause and build
in the structures, systems and resources for maximum impact. As active involvement
gets bedded in, leadership style will become increasingly based on partnership and
cooperation, among elected members or Trustees, staff, partners and children and
young people. (Badham and Wade, 2005: 18)

The seven indicators under Style of leadership are then set out under three
levels: emerging, established and advanced.

Emerging

7.1   Key managers and leaders act as champions for the active involvement
      of children and young people, with clearly identified responsibilities.
7.2   Managers and leaders support innovation on active involvement,
      accepting risks of mistakes and are committed to reflection and
      learning.
7.3   Managers and leaders in the organisation publicly acknowledge and
      celebrate the active involvement of children and young people and
      take an active part in key consultation and participation events.

Established

7.4   A leadership programme for managers and children and young peo-
      ple is established, based on the principles of active involvement.
7.5   Children and young people have a range of opportunities to meet
      senior staff, elected members or trustees to be included in decision
      making and promote active involvement.

Advanced

7.6   The organisation demonstrates to partner organisations an open
      style of leadership, collaboration and shared objectives on the
      active involvement of children and young people.
7.7   Leadership of specific projects and appropriate services involves
      both children and young people and adults.

In February 2006, Halton in Widnes undertook a large-scale event for adults and children and young people, using *Hear by Right* to agree priorities for their active involvement. There was significant agreement about the top three priorities under each of the seven standards, except under style of leadership. While managers and elected members saw having an effective champion as the most important indicator (7.1), the young people were less impressed by this, giving priority to celebrating achievement (7.3) and helping run different parts of the services themselves (7.5 and 7.7). Or in the wording of the young people's version of *Hear by Right*, called *Building Standards*:

> Bosses take part in our events and celebrate what we do.
> There are lots of ways that we can meet and influence the bosses and leaders.
> We help run some parts of the organisation. (Badham and Wade, 2005)

Two points arise from this. First – a champion so beloved of adults – is often for adults to promote the cause to other adults which may be of less immediate relevance to the young people themselves. The young people may find greater significance in how their achievements are recognised and valued and how power and authority are re-negotiated in managing direct services and agreeing budgets. Their participation needs to be having a tangible impact on the style of leadership and decision making as well as elsewhere in the organisation. Second, this divergence of views indicates the need for a style of leadership which encourages dialogue and mutual understanding, not the false freedom in creating a wish list or being protected from the realities of competing priorities or adult *'real politic'*.

At an event across the Nottingham children and young people's strategic partnership also in February 2006, children and young people gave significant emphasis to the training adult leaders need on the active involvement of children and young people (7.4): 'Bosses learn and get help on how we can take part.'

Adults often emphasise the need for young people to learn effective participation skills. Young people agree, but from their own experience know that adults in power have far more learning to undo to create a climate of mutual respect and develop an attitude and approach that promotes effective participation with a focus on substantial change, not smoke and mirrors. Training of senior managers and elected members needs to be at the heart, not at the periphery, of an effective participation strategy.

The participation of children and young people in organisational decision making can and needs to be transformative for the adults, including senior managers and elected leaders – be they members or trustees.

From a broadly linear structure, in which the leaders and the managers are at the top and the service user at the bottom, some organisations have

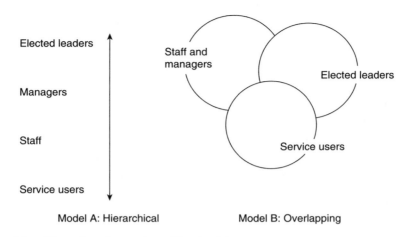

Model A: Hierarchical   Model B: Overlapping

Figure 6.3   Changing dynamics of leadership

already moved to more fluid and interacting spheres of influence. Young people as service users may be in dialogue with elected leaders. They may themselves be elected leaders. Managers may be involved in commissioning services along with young people themselves. Young people may be responsible for allocating significant funds. Young people as ex-service users may become staff members. Figure 6.3 indicates the move taking place. This may be either in the specific decision-making structures themselves, or if not that formalised, then at least in the nature of engagement, dialogue and accountability.

So what's stopping us? Attitudinal problems

Evidence from the *Hear by Right* initiative shows real progress towards strategies for setting up new structures and systems and engaging staff with new skills and knowledge to implement these changes. It seems, however, that few have grasped the implications of the cultural shift in the style of leadership that arises of necessity as participation climbs from tokenism, up the ladder towards transformative leadership. Perhaps many adults embracing the agenda have done so broadly on a utilitarian basis – 'it's useful to us' – and because 'it's good for the young people' rather than recognise the Trojan Horse effect this movement generates. Moving from hierarchical structures (Model A) to overlapping areas of governance (Model B) involving service users, staff, managers and elected members or trustees is a more challenging and perhaps unwelcome shift in leadership style that questions power relationships and underlying attitudes towards children and young people. Were this recognised at the outset, perhaps the gates would remain firmly shut!

One or more of the following concerns may surface when the participation of children and young people moves from manageable, discreet, adult controlled activity to a wider sharing and collaborative style of leadership:

1. Adult leaders have the relevant qualifications and expertise to make better decisions, especially in matters of governance.
2. They can see the strategic direction of the organisation and can best fit individual decisions into the big picture.
3. They are employed, so can be accountable to higher management and funders for the decisions made.
4. Power is not shared by adult-focused organisations with adult service users in a comparable way so why should power be shared with children and young people?
5. Young people are always moving on and getting them involved in decision making involves continuous new investment which is disruptive to effective leadership.
6. While it is possible to be a Director or Trustee under 18, it is an unfair and unreasonable legal burden to place on them.

Rather than ignore or dismiss these concerns out of hand, it is important to explore what lies behind them. They may be touching on a deeper adult's concern about the impact on attitudes, power and perceived authority. It is important to see how they can be translated into practical challenges and opportunities for the participative leader. For example, sharing power with young people is not about an abdication of responsibility. Responsibility is shared, although accountability may remain with an individual employee. A good example is in recruitment processes; whoever advises and contributes to the process (young or not so young) needs to be able to do so with transparency and clarity of role. However, even where the decision is made collectively or through aggregate scoring, the representative of the organisation is the one accountable for the appointment itself.

So what's stopping us?
Over-reliance on formal structures

When thinking about the involvement of young people in organisational decision making, the matrix in Figure 6.4 can help map particular approaches as

Ladder of Participation	A Individual complaint and feedback	B Surveys and one-off events and consultations	C Practice initiatives: time limited, focused activity	D Peer activity: training, research, evaluation	E Young representatives on advisory groups and shadow boards	F Young people involved in governance – with or without adults
8. Youth initiated – shared decisions with adults						
7. Youth initiated and directed						
6. Adult initiated and shared decisions with cyp						
5. Consulted and informed						
4. Assigned and informed						
3. Tokenism						
2. Decoration						
1. Manipulation						

Figure 6.4   Participation matrix

Note: This model was first seen by one of the authors in 2003, developed by young people in care in Gateshead. For a fuller outline see National Youth Agency (2005). Also available at *www.nya.org.uk/hearbyright*

well as how participative they are. The horizontal axis moves broadly from informal and ad-hoc methods of engagement to those which are more permanent, ongoing and structured. (The example is illustrative and further categories can be added as necessary.) The vertical axis follows the Ladder of Participation as it moves from poor participation in the shaded area, to more inclusive processes. Each approach will have its own strengths and weaknesses. Those to the left side of the matrix, such as surveys and consultations, may be targeted, of immediate relevance and cost effective. But they may also appear to be a quick fix, with lack of ownership, momentum and follow up. To the right, there may be the potential for wider and long-term organisational influence, but the risks of tokenism and lack of real say and power increase dramatically.

So what's stopping us?
Representational problems

In part arising from the challenge to established attitudes and power relationships that transformative participation provokes, a further difficulty arises from over reliance on representative models of engagement (columns E and F in the matrix). With mushrooming school councils, youth forums and youth boards working at local, regional and national levels, representative models for young people to have a voice and influence are much in fashion.

Such structured approaches run the risk of appearing to be a significant step in promoting a style of leadership open to and informed by children and young people's participation, while in reality not climbing very high up the ladder. There may be a number of reasons for this. Adults may be ignoring or underplaying the diverse and sometimes competing views of different young people. There may be the simplistic (and convenient) assumption that listening to one or a few young people equates to listening to all young people. Adult leaders may want (though they may not be aware of it) to hold onto power by listening to the representations of young people, while retaining the authority and right to interpret and judge those representations outside of dialogue and agreement with young people.

Behind these concerns lies the confusion, deliberate or not, between statistical representation (those involved mirror the wider make-up of stakeholders) and democratic representation (having a mandate to speak on behalf of others.) Where the second model is not underpinned by explicit means of accountability and feedback, those few voices remain individual opinions. In youth participation, as Liam Cairns (2006: 23) says, 'Models based on adult representational democracy have dubious democratic legitimacy'. A further worry is that making young people into 'representatives' may deprive them of their authentic voice as experts in their own lives on their own terms, providers of critical perspectives of equal validity to those introduced by adults.

This divide may be further exacerbated by investing in significant training for this small group of young people to take part in adult replica representative structures. Yet, 'Participation is not dependent upon the possession of a set of skills or attributes, although some participation practice has the effect of limiting the number of children and young people who feel able to take part' (Hill et al., 2004). The challenge for leaders is not to impose a training programme to equip a few young people to take part in a narrow band of rigid structured approaches, but to respond to a wide range of groups and agree through dialogue with them their skills development needs to take part in diverse and creative ways that they help identify.

Effective participation

Effective participation leads to young people's involvement across the work of an organisation, at different levels and in different ways. It involves seeing young people as partners in the design, development, delivery and evaluation of services, as well as being service users. Understanding this wide ranging contribution can be essential to effective leadership. This may potentially place less emphasis on formal representational structures and more on collaborative working on agreed projects, where young people contribute to a shared agenda, be that in research or evaluation, in training and staff development, as peer mentors or authors.

While partnership working and models such as peer research have strengths in being more collaborative and enabling honest conversations and decision making between young people and adults, such projects and practices are not usually tied into the overall running of an organisation. There are, however, an increasing number of organisations working with young people in a manner that also takes seriously the implications for their style of leadership and management. The *Hear by Right* website (*www.nya.org.uk/hearbyright*) has a rich archive of maps and plans indicating what this means in practice. Yet there remains a dearth of youth-led organisations, with only a small handful of projects growing into fully youth-led independent companies limited by guarantee or charities in their own right. Three current examples are UK Youth Parliament (*www.youthparliament.org.uk*), YouthBank (*www.youthbank.org.uk*) and A National Voice (*www.anationalvoice.org*). They offer insight into the cutting edge of leading and managing work with young people, where that involves empowering young people to become the leaders themselves. While UKYP,

YouthBank and ANV are pioneers, funders, policy makers and national pro-grammes are taking on the message. There is more to come, with ever increas-ing implications for the style of leadership in organisations working with young people. The Big Lottery Fund not only has young people assessing grants, but has programmes supporting young people's active involvement in governance. HM Treasury and the Department for Education and Skills Youth Opportunities and Youth Capital Fund programmes promote young people-led grant making, seeing this as a means of fostering new relationships and new organisations which are young people-led.

For this to succeed though, leading and managing youth work requires building the capacity of statutory, voluntary and community organisations to ensure the effective participation of children and young people. There are three particular challenges, the first being to increase young people's influence in the governance of smaller non-statutory organisations. The second is to provide support to emerging young people-led organisations to build their chances of survival and help them grow so that, third, they are supported in influencing policy and planning at local, regional and national level.

At the heart of this process is a transformative view of young people, not as representatives of a 'youth view' inputting into adult processes, but as autonomous actors participating in shared discussions and decision making, creating change on issues that affect them in the services they use and in wider society as a whole.

As new communication technologies lower barriers to political action, young people through informal and formal groups, are increasingly becoming creative activists and campaigners for change on the local, national and global level. Key characteristics of these new participation movements are their fluidity, their lack of need for formalised structures and procedures, their independence, their creative use of new technologies for communicating to members and coor-dinating dialogue and campaigns and crucially their emphasis on making change happen. In 2003, for example, while the Department for Education and Skills was debating the parameters of a centrally managed participation fund, young anti-war activists set up HandsUp4Peace (*www.messengers.org.uk*) with no funding at all. It blossomed into a mass movement, orchestrating highly visible and engaging demonstrations in front of Parliament and at rallies in Hyde Park.

A style of leadership that understands young people as having lives and interests reaching far beyond the bounds of a particular organisation is crucial to the full realisation of a society in which young people are equal citizens now, activists in vibrant, forward-moving communities, exercising their right to participate, including their right as citizens to dissent.

Conclusion

The active involvement of children and young people in matters affecting them is underpinned by law, statutory guidance and best practice knowledge and experience. Since the late 1990s, this has included increasingly influencing specific matters affecting the individual or group and also involvement in organisational decision making. The *Hear by Right* website indicates much progress across many of the seven standards for organisational change, including on shared values, systems such as effective protection and rewards, staff and skills and knowledge. Some concerns have come to light, including over reliance on representational models of engagement, in some cases blocking the necessary wider impact on the style of leadership this movement necessitates. The quality of participation may often be greater where there is greater emphasis on dynamic partnership or collaborative working rather than on formalised structures.

Yet, as management doors have been opened at least ajar to include youth participation in governance, one might expect more examples of a fundamental shift in the style of leadership and management of work with young people. For example, this might include a greater number of young people-led organisations, both along established organisational types and also looser, less permanent models of engagement and activism. Where such developments have occurred, they in turn have much to teach adult-led organisations working with young people. Understanding young people as autonomous agents challenges organisations to think deeply about participation. Creating 'advisory' groups is a safe option for a leader. Accepting young people as dynamic participants in the organisation – with different needs at different times – takes far more attention to creating a culture of participation and engagement.

> The truth is that children and young people are managing to survive while we base our approaches and interventions on their inability to survive. If children and young people are managing to survive, then we must conclude that they have great possibilities, potential and the strength to survive.' (ENDA, 1995: 53; translation Bill Badham)

ENDA, a Senegalese non-governmental organisation working with street children and young workers, realigned its work programmes and style of leadership to build on the evident collaborative strengths of groups of working children, supporting and nurturing their independence, rather than taking them over and subsuming them into a large adult-led organisation. This paradigm shift is no less needed in the UK, requiring bold new direction which in turn will transform the style of leadership among those leading and managing work with young people.

This journey raises a number of key issues. First, young people, building on their personal experience of participation, often have the vision, passion, skills and knowledge to take an active part in the governance of an organisation, be that adult- or youth-led. Second, an approach to promoting children and young people's participation which concentrates on structures and systems and not on staff, skills and style of leadership will not go far. Young people will be quick to spot tokenism and resistance to wider attitudinal change. This sounds a warning about offering openings to young people in affecting the style of leadership, while blocking and constraining progress. Third, where this occurs, young people will find a way, or find another route to channel their energies and action. Fourth, local leadership style in a youth project, club or programme is the essential building block to wider meaningful participation. Where this is weak, wider involvement in an organisation will risk becoming separated from its roots and irrelevant to the lived lives and priorities of children and young people. Fifth and finally, an effective style of leadership on participation must include honest dialogue, shared understanding, agreement to act and accountability for change. It must acknowledge and address issues of power and focus on the relevance of active involvement leading to improved opportunities and demonstrable change for children and young people.

References

Badham, B., Wade H. (2005) *Hear by Right: Standards for the Active Involvement of Children and Young People*. The National Youth Agency and Local Government Association: Leicester.

Cairns, L. (2006) 'Participation with purpose', in Tisdall, E., Davis, J., Hill, M., Prout A. (eds), *Children, Young People and Social Inclusion: Participation for what?* The Policy Press: Bristol.

Department for Education and Skills, Children and Young People's Unit (2001) *Learning to Listen: Core Principles for the Involvement of Children and Young People*. Department for Education and Skills: London.

Department for Education and Skills (2003) *Every Child Matters*. London: The Stationery Office.

Department for Education and Skills (2004a) *Working Together: Giving Children and Young People a Say*. Department for Education and Skills: London.

Department for Education and Skills (2004b) *Statutory Guidance on Interagency Co-operation to Improve the Wellbeing of Children: Children's Trusts*. Department for Education and Skills: London.

Department for Education and Skills (2005) *Youth Matters*. London: The Stationery Office.

Edwards, R., Davis, J. (2004) Setting the agenda: social inclusion, children and young people, *Children and Society*, 18(2): 97–105.

ENDA. (1995) *Enfants en recherche et en action*. ENDA: Dakar, Senegal.

Hargreaves, S. (2005) *Children and Young People's Trusts and Local Authority Decision-making –* Hear by Right Briefing series. The NYA: Leicester.

Hart, R. (1992) *Children's Participation: From Tokenism to Citizenship*. UNICEF: New York.

Hill, M., Davis, J. Prout, A., Tisdall, K., (2004). 'Moving the participation agenda forward,' *Children and Society*, 18(2): 77–96.

Peters, T., Waterman, R. (1982) *'In Search of Excellence'*, New York, London: Harper & Row.

The National Youth Agency (2005) *Involving Children and Young People: An Introduction*. The National Youth Agency: Leicester.

United Nations (1989) *Convention on the Rights of the Child*. UN: Geneva.

Willow, C. (1997) *Hear! Hear! Promoting Children and Young People's Democratic Participation in Local Government*. Local Government Information Unit: London.

Willow, C. (2002) *Participation in Practice – Children and Young People as Partners in Change*. The Children's Society: London.

Crossing the divide:
school-based youth work

Tony Jeffs

School-based youth work, like all youth work, is founded upon the inalienable right of young people to refuse to engage with a worker. Consequently workers must first make contact, either by attracting young people to clubs or centres, or by going to where they gather. For two centuries workers have mixed building-based work with detached work. However the balance between them constantly changes (Jeffs and Smith, 2002). Recently it has become more difficult to attract young people to clubs and centres. First because sophisticated home entertainment packages and computer games plus compulsory homework (currently 2 hours per day for 15-year-olds) have led to teenagers spending more time 'indoors'. Second, smaller families plus greater affluence mean most now have their own centrally heated room. Clubs therefore are no longer special places to meet friends, escape parents or dispel boredom. Furthermore dormitory and suburban living means many must travel further to clubs that due to under-investment are often unkempt and poorly equipped. Whereas commercial clubs can consistently attract large numbers to under-18 sessions, few youth projects can achieve this. Without investment in specialist buildings most workers will be obliged increasingly to employ detached methods to reach young people.

Essentially detached work means going to where young people gather, therefore it takes place in locales as diverse as schools, streets or Young Offender Institutions. Venue and locality are irrelevant, what counts are that those characteristics that make youth work a discrete activity remain constant. In summary these are:

- the relationship between worker and young person is voluntary allowing the latter to terminate it at will
- the focus is on the young person's needs, not those of the host institution or agency
- education, rather than indoctrination, control or behaviour modification, resides at the heart of the process (Jeffs and Smith, 2007).

Long tradition

Youth work has always used school premises and been obliged to co-exist with curriculum-led, classroom-based teaching. Much pioneering youth work was school-based. For example the Ragged Schools opened from the 1830s onwards in the poorest localities, provided an enormous range of welfare and community programmes including youth clubs, play-schemes and camps (Montague, 1904). Schools were home to many early uniformed groups invariably established by a schoolteacher who voluntarily organised after-school clubs and activities because they viewed the curriculum as too narrow to equip anyone for a life worth living and to encourage ex-pupils to continue their 'education'. However the term 'school-based youth work' signifies something different, namely the integration of youth work within the life of the school, a mélange of the formal curriculum that is the focus of school life with the informal education residing at the heart of youth work. School-based work differs from what is often called 'dual-use', where schooling and youth work are discrete since it involves both working together. For apart from sharing buildings, time and staff, it aims to fuse both in order to deepen and extend the educational experience offered to young people attending the school or living locally.

Community schools and youth work

Post-1900 progressive educators began looking beyond using school buildings as the base for delivering youth work, adult education and play work. Taking their lead from John Dewey and Robert Owen they advocated the development of schools as community centres arguing they were the only institutions within a society divided by fissures of class, race and religion, capable of crafting viable communities. Community schools, they argued, must become places where municipalities provided education from cradle to grave and a portfolio of other services. They would be hubs at the heart of every community, built around a shared responsibility for the raising of our children, incorporating theatres, sports halls and gymnasiums, libraries, attractive community rooms equipped to host meetings, classes and social events, medical surgeries and clinics and the local sub-offices of welfare agencies. In Britain the first purpose-built community school was opened in 1929. Subsequently many variants emerged, made possible by the freedom and control local authorities enjoyed over both schooling and welfare serices.

Whatever the model, the status of youth work within community schools was unresolved. Some held schools were unsuitable venues as most teachers were too authoritarian to make effective youth workers (Brew, 1943) and school buildings a poor substitute for well-designed youth centres (Edwards-Rees, 1944). However among advocates of community schooling two perspectives emerged. One maintained young people should be viewed as equally valued members of the community and that discrete youth provision discouraged this. Therefore they should be encouraged to use the community facilities, such as lounges, gymnasiums and canteens. In some cases integration entailed restruc-turing the timetable with all ages joining classes (scheduled across a day between 09.00 to 21.00 hours). The other maintained young people needed their own 'youth wings' within which noisy activities that might 'disturb' and 'disrupt' other users could be located. Many were opened but unlike traditional clubs these rarely duplicated the normal range of facilities (for example, workshops or gymnasiums) provided within the community school. Whereas some were phys-ically integrated others stood apart on the edge of a playground or playing field, even off campus. Generally wings were managed by headteachers who frequently imposed rules on the youth tutors employed to run them, such as that sus-pended or absent pupils were to be excluded. Aside from such inconveniences most tutors ran the wings like other clubs.

Early advocates of community schools and school-based youth work, such as Teddy O'Neill, Henry Morris and Stewart Mason believed success required special teachers dedicated to public service, comfortable with adults and young people, scholarly and with sufficient cultural depth to guarantee they had something worthwhile to teach. They were convinced most teachers lacked such attributes and accordingly applied harsh selection criteria which led to the appointment of a high proportion of 'unqualified' graduates, supported by volunteers and part-timers, who would provide the core workforce for youth work, community devel-opment and adult education. However bridging the gap between the formal and informal has always been problematic. For example, the difficulties compulsory schooling has in managing some pupil behaviour means teachers rely for sur-vival on punishments and distancing themselves from students. Despite these tensions schoolteachers often enjoy getting to know pupils in different contexts and educating informally beyond the classroom.

Evidence suggests this model can succeed; certainly many were remarkably successful. For instance in the 1940s over 70 per cent of ex-pupils attended clubs and classes at Impington Village College, a figure matched by Prestolee School where Teddy O'Neill was head until 1951. However this usually hinged on the presence of charismatic teachers such as Stewart Wilson at Sutton Centre (Fletcher et al., 1985), or R. F. MacKenzie at Summerhill (Murphy, 1998), or on extraordinary administrators like Stuart Mason or Henry Morris (Jeffs, 1998), committed to investing the resources essential to ensuring the schools were aesthetically attractive, well-equipped and appropriately staffed.

Changes afoot

Post-1970 changes in social structure and policy have radically restructured school-based youth work. First, encouraging young people to remain in education faded as a priority when the school-leaving age was raised to 16 and wholesale youth unemployment left few alternatives to remaining in education (Mizen, 2004). Currently 80 per cent are in some form of education until 18. Consequently educational institutions are now the prime location wherein youth workers can contact young people. Furthermore compulsory attendance means schools are the focus for government-led initiatives seeking to modify young people's behaviour. Be it concerns about political alienation, obesity, sexual promiscuity, low financial savvy or whatever these are now predominately addressed by inserting components into the national curriculum rather than via informal educational initiatives delivered by youth workers.

Second, the quasi 'market' in education introduced post-1988 views students as customers obliged to shop for the best (or cheapest) school, college or course. Therefore persuading individuals to remain in education is a priority only for unattractive institutions. High status ones can cherry-pick and discipline by threatening expulsion, consequently extra-curricular activities and support services for them become far less important. Less prestigious institutions must focus on motivating, managing and retaining students. This persuades some to employ youth workers, partly to manage reluctant attendees. These like detached street workers patrol and loiter in 'hot spots' (Reeves et al., 1993; Hand and Wright, 1997), work with troublesome and disengaged students within classrooms addressing 'issues' such as anger management and take them off-site for activity and 'training' programmes. Such interventions are not primarily youth work but examples of youth work skills being colonised to manage students who challenge the good order of the institution.

Third, growth in certification and testing means English pupils are possibly the most examined in the world – averaging 75 exams during a school career (PAT, 2002; Jeffs, 2002) – and this has transformed relationships between teacher and student. Likewise the reintroduction of the Victorian 'payment by result' system linking teacher earnings to exam performance encourages the setting aside of students' broader intellectual and social needs, mounting marginalisation of non-tested subjects and jettisoning of extra-curricular activities (Boyle and Bragg, 2006). Overall school teacher involvement in youth work and extra-curricula activities, such as running sports teams and clubs, has fallen catastrophically. Well-funded institutions employ specialist 'coaches' to deliver sporting and cultural activities and some parents pay commercial providers. Unfortunately this leaves too many with no access to the array of social, cultural and sporting activities previously offered within the curriculum or voluntarily by teachers.

Finally although community schools retain a presence elsewhere in England the determination of governments post-1988 to impose a free market model of education on LEAs has led to their virtual demise. Erosion of catchment areas, delegation of funding to schools with cash following the pupil, creation of specialist and faith schools and academies, removal of adult education and FE from LEA management, and erosion of local democratic control of schools collectively encourage parents to view themselves as consumers and schools to act as competing businesses. These changes fracture time honoured linkages between schools and their 'neighbourhood'. As fewer attend neighbourhood schools but commute to one matching their parent's faith, career aspirations or social and class affectations (Robertson, 2000), the concept of the community school dissolves. By way of compensation schools seek to construct an 'imagined' community comprising staff and students (Shircliffe et al., 2006) but such is the brevity of the attachment that few invest more than the tokenistic minimum. This is the 'community' within which contemporary school-based youth work operates.

Given that schools can opt out of LEA control and frequently cater for a minority of those living nearby it would be absurd for statutory youth services to invest in campus-based buildings or staff. Consequently even LEAs who once pioneered this approach have abandoned it. Increasingly schools and colleges have opted to hire youth workers from the statutory or voluntary sectors or employ their own. Also many schools invest in counselling, stress management programmes and various therapies of often dubious worth (Furedi, 2004) delivered by youth organisations (Hodgson and Jeffs, 2007). Where schools and colleges do employ youth workers this is not a superficial change of paymaster, for institutions want a mode of youth work that concentrates exclusively on the 'school community'. Evermore educational institutions build security fences, employ guards and install electronic surveillance equipment to keep the community and young people who are either non- or ex-students at bay (Whittaker, 2006). Within approximately a decade the fortress school has replaced the open-access community school. Even during lunchtime, as one minister explained, he now expected schools to ensure pupils:

are in school all day, no exceptions, end of story ... Students stay on the school premises, and the school provides an enriching lunchtime programme of mentoring by local business people, reading groups for support with literacy, sporting activities supervised by youth workers, as well as a wide range of language classes. ... Good for pupils. Good for the school. Good for the reputation of education in the local community. (Smithers, 2004: 6)

Within this closed environment youth work becomes viewed simply as a mechanism for eradicating problems identified by school or college managers. Rarely is it possible for young people to set the agenda, for the work takes place in an environment where they are powerless to shape the curriculum, rules or ethos and with no rights to absent themselves if under 16. Those managing the school or college may understand what youth work is and the educational role it can play if workers are gifted sufficient sovereignty to build relationships with staff and students. If so the aspiration of *Transforming Youth Work* that 'the goals for informal education through youth work complement those of more formal routes such as schools and colleges' (DfES, 2002: 11) may acquire substance. But elsewhere things are different with workers obligated to maintain order in the public areas and keep out drugs and the bothersome, provide lunchtime and after-school activities, and undertake group work with those identified as challenging. In one school the worker is on standby to go when 'buzzed' to classrooms whenever a student 'kicks off'. Elsewhere they are employed to take out of school, whenever money allows, those defined as troublesome. In another school the worker was told not to 'waste time' on academic high achievers but concentrate on the 'chavs' and disaffected. What these schools wanted was faux youth work skills to help control the difficult students classroom teachers felt ill-equipped to manage (Jeffs and Stanton, forthcoming).

Extended schools

The 'Extended Schools Initiative' hints at renewed government interest in the community school concept. It promises parents access all year round from 8.00 a.m. to 6.00 p.m. by 2010 to:

- high quality childcare either on site or through local providers
- a varied menu of activities such as homework clubs, study support, sport, music tuition, dance and drama, arts and crafts, special interest clubs
- parenting support, including family learning sessions
- wider community access to ICT, sports and arts facilities, including adult learning (DfES, 2006).

Partially based on experimental 'full-service schools' operating in the USA these only superficially resemble community schools, being time and age restricted. Rather, these are integrated school and child welfare centres offering parents, not the community, one-stop health and welfare provision for children. Services are directed towards raising school achievement and lowering dependency on state benefits by getting more mothers into full- or part-time employment within the low wage female labour market (Hutton, 2006). It is assumed a reduction in welfare costs will offset the childcare bill. The rights and wrongs of locking young people in school for 50 hours per week is an issue not yet satisfactorily aired; certainly the National Youth Agency (NYA, 2006) briefing on youth service involvement in extended schools did not raise it.

Evaluation of 'full service extended schools' first year pilots suggests they can work in more effective and sensitive ways with pupils and families (Cummings et al., 2006). Children benefit from 'wrap-around' care offering a safe pre- and after-school environment plus ready access to on-site welfare professionals. However what post-primary extended schools will resemble is unclear especially when the leaving age moves to 18. A possible pointer to the pattern of provision can be gleaned from the welcome ministers gave the policy advocated by the Institute of Policy Research (Lloyd, 2007) for:

> Young people aged 11 to 14 to participate in long-term extra curricular activity, one day a week after school, choosing from options in the Youth Matters Green Paper. This would be mandated through an extension of the school day, creating a legal requirement for parents to ensure participation. (Margo et al., 2006: xii)

Another comes from how this policy developed in the USA where agencies such as the Boys' and Girls' Clubs of America provide after-school packages located in neighbourhood centres or on site. These comprise a mix of quiet rooms and support for homework, activities, social facilities and learning packages addressing topics such as raising self-esteem, gender relationships and conflict resolution. Research showed users preferred non-school-based provision and minimal teacher involvement. Evaluators also found packaged learning materials were far less effective than informal education delivered by youth workers (Hirsch, 2005). Feinstein et al. (2006: 324) may be correct in arguing youth work can 'provide precisely the form of complementary provision to formal education that is needed'. However as Hirsch shows venue and staffing are important with schools often the least congenial place to deliver these programmes.

Working the school and college

School-based work has unique features that practitioners must take account of. These are that:

- the young people will have little control over the building
- it must function according to 'timetables' constructed to meet the needs of the formal programme
- youth work will be perceived as marginal to the focus of an organisation driven by examination results, externally measured 'academic' outcomes and the need to maximise numbers and income
- youth workers will generally be perceived as occupying a subordinate position in the hierarchy to managers and teachers or lecturers. Status and rank are distributed on the basis of office, salary, subject taught and perceived ability to control students – according to most of these measures youth workers score low (Jeffs and Stanton, forthcoming).

Besides classroom 'teaching' school-based workers carve out space to undertake youth work by exploiting gaps between lessons and public spaces. Workers allot set times to visit specific parts of the campus to 'work' the corridors and canteens. In this respect they operate like detached workers, recognising the crucial importance of 'being available' by 'being around' (see Hazler, 1998; Crimmens et al., 2004). This approach enables students to recognise workers as familiar figures and importantly allows them over time to make contact, strike up conversation, 'informally' raise issues, ask for advice or seek support. Students learn where and when they can 'bump into' the worker. These perambulations help the worker to get to know students and staff, spot isolated and rejected students and read the changing moods of the institution; to sense, for example, when tensions between groups may be developing. Often the smile from the worker may be the only one a nervous student received that day, the brief conversation in the canteen, the solitary personal exchange enjoyed all morning and the fleeting words of greeting the sole recognition of shared humanity. Working in corridors, playgrounds and canteens demands considerable skill – listening, observing, understanding, modelling behaviour, giving brief advice, offering help when required. Like detached workers or the club worker trawling their patch they must exercise care and sensitivity while retaining a faith that the innumerable brief encounters amount to more than a chimera. Certainly it is impossible to quantify the worth of the 'casual' exchanges or compute the intangible benefits emanating from the offer of friendship and possibility of help when and if needed.

Nevertheless these 'low-impact contacts', as Hazler (1998) terms them, provide the basis upon which it becomes possible to build, when necessary, deeply valued supportive relationships and perhaps more importantly, the brief contact, the hurried word may negate the subsequent need for counselling and support. Time spent out and about is critical but the worker also needs an accessible base – somewhere students can find them and where the worker can speak quietly with individuals or groups. Also they must have the resources and space to undertake group work for they are youth workers not counsellors. Consequently their focus will inevitably be on developing groups rather than addressing individual need (Luxmoore, 2000).

Finally school-based workers must be prepared to collaborate with other staff, especially classroom teachers, some of whom may be anxious about particular students and, consciously or unconsciously, perceive the worker as someone who may be helpful. At times some will be encountering problems of control and, given the ways managers judge them, may view the worker as someone with whom they can share concerns without eroding their standing or reputation. Many school teachers are unhappy with their working environment, up to a third would leave if they could find something offering equivalent pay (Smithers and Robinson, 2000). School-based workers must be aware of this. Much as detached workers seek to diffuse tensions between community wardens or the police and young people, so they must be prepared to build bridges between young people and other staff by encouraging teachers and students to co-operate and understand more and criticise less. Equally, and this may be far more difficult and professionally dangerous, they must be prepared, like all youth workers, to advocate on behalf of young people. Club or detached workers operating independently of schools or social services have greater leeway to act as advocates. Sadly schools and colleges occasionally treat students unfairly, even illegally, and when that happens the duty of the youth worker to support the victim is severely tested. In an ideal world the professional integrity and autonomy of workers in such circumstances would be safeguarded like those of chaplains working within a prison (LSC, 2006). However it is not, therefore school-based workers must appreciate they walk a tightrope and without warning may be embroiled in conflicts with management or classroom colleagues.

Conclusion

Everything points towards escalating growth in the number of school-based workers. Besides the extended schools agenda we have the remodelling of the school workforce directed by the DfES School Workforce Unit. Driven by continuing difficulties in recruiting teachers it seeks to transfer non-teaching work within schools to a growing army of quasi-professionals and assistants (Thompson, 2006). Currently there are 102,000 teaching assistants, plus a growing army of learning mentors (Cruddas, 2005) and youth workers in schools, numbers that will expand with the push towards 'personalised education' (DfES, 2006a). This envisages teachers becoming co-ordinators of learning and creators of learning units aided by an array of professionals and helpers managing the students and institution. Clearly youth workers, or youth development workers as they may become known, will figure among these.

Invited or not youth workers must actively strive to work in schools and colleges. Some FE colleges have 40,000 students, half under 20, and nationally around 250,000 under-16s attend colleges (Whittaker, 2006). With growing amalgamations some secondary schools have approaching 1,500 pupils. Given the difficulties youth workers encounter reaching so many young people they have no alternative but to find an entrée into these institutions. The composition of their student bodies also allows workers to connect with groups that neither detached nor centre-based provision currently does, however the educational focus of the institution requires school- or college-based workers to possess sufficient educational 'standing' to enjoy the respect of both students and staff. Maturity, educational experience and an enthusiasm for learning are essential prerequisites for any informal educator hoping to succeed in this setting. An absence of these will diminish their impact and make it impossible for them to engage in meaningful dialogue with those staff and students who value education as a self-evident good.

The history of youth work engagement with formal educational institutions is not a happy one (Jeffs and Smith, 1991). Youth work organisations and practitioners who wish to find a 'way into schools and colleges' must, like those who went before, tread carefully. Yet finding a way in is crucial if youth work is to avoid operating only at the margins with a tiny proportion of the potential client group. However workers must remember they have no control over funding, buildings or curriculum, that for now they are at best guests and at worst tolerated intruders.

References

Boyle, B. and Bragg, J. (2006) 'A curriculum without foundation', *British Educational Research Journal*, 32(4): 569–582.

Brew, J. Macalister (1943) *In the Service of Youth*. London: Faber.

Crimmens, D., Factor, F., Jeffs, T., Pugh, C., Spence, J. and Turner, P. (2004) *Reaching Socially Excluded Young People: A National Study of Street-based Youth Work*. York: Joseph Rowntree.

Cruddas, L. (2005) *Learning Mentors in Schools: Policy and Practice*. Stoke-on-Trent: Trentham Books.

Cummings, C., Dyson, A., Papps, I., Pearson, D., Raffo, C. and Todd, L. (2006) *Evaluation of the Full Service Extended Schools Project: End of First Year Report*. London: DfES.

DfES (2002) *Transforming Youth Work*. London: The Stationery Office.

DfES (2006) *Extended Schools: Access to Opportunities and Services For All*. London: DfES.

DfES (2006a) *2020 Vision: Report of the Teaching and Learning in 2020 Review Group*. London: DfES.

Edwards-Rees, D. (1944) *A Rural Youth Service*. London: Methodist Youth Department.

Feinstein, L., Bynner, J. and Duckworth, K. (2006) ' Young people's leisure contexts and their relation to adult outcomes', *Journal of Youth Studies*, 9(3): 305–327.

Fletcher, C., Caron, M. and Williams, W. (1985) *Schools on Trial: The Trials of Democratic Comprehensives*. Milton Keynes: Open University Press.

Furedi, F. (2004) *Therapy Culture: Cultivating Vulnerability in an Uncertain Age*. London: Routledge.

Hand, J. and Wright, W. (1997) *Youth Work in Colleges: Building on Partnership*. London: Further Education Development Agency.

Hazler, R. J. (1998) *Helping in the Hallways: Advanced Strategies for Enhancing School Relationships*, Thousand Oaks, CA: Corwin Press.

Hirsch, B. (2005) *A Place Like Home*. Washington: American Psychological Press.

Hodgson, T. and Jeffs. T. (2007) *Evaluation of the Newcastle YMCA Student Project*. Newcastle-upon-Tyne YMCA.

Hutton, J. (2006) 'Ending child poverty and transforming life chances', speech to Fabian Society 10th May.

Jeffs, T. (1998) *Henry Morris: Village Colleges, Community Education and the Ideal Order*, Nottingham: Education Now Books.

Jeffs, T. (2002) 'Schooling, education and children's rights,' in B. Franklin (ed.) *The New Handbook of Children's Rights*, London: Routledge.

Jeffs, T. and Smith, M. (1991) 'Fallacy: the school is a poor base for youth work,' in B. O'Hagen (ed.) *The Charnwood Papers: Fallacies in Community Education*. Nottingham: Education Now Books.

Jeffs, T. and Smith, M. (2002) 'Individualisation and Youth Work,' *Youth and Policy* 76: 39–65.

Jeffs, T. and Smith, M. (2007) *Youth Work*, Basingstoke: Palgrave Macmillan.

Jeffs, T. and Stanton, N. (forthcoming) 'The travails of school-based youth work,' *Youth and Policy*.

Learning and Skills Council (2006) *Towards a Whole College Approach to Chaplaincy for a Pluralist Society*. London: LSC.

Lloyd, T. (2007) 'Youth report draws early support', *Young People Now*, 17th January.

Luxmoore, N. (2000) *Listening to Young People in School, Youth Work and Counselling*. London: Jessica Kingsley.

Margo, J., Dixon, M., Pearce, N. and Reed, H. (2006) *Freedom's Orphans: Raising youth in a changing world*. London: IPPR.

Mizen, P. (2004) *The Changing State of Youth*. Basingstoke: Palgrave Macmillan.

Montague, C. J. (1904) *Sixty Years of Waifdom or the Ragged Schools in English History*. London: Chas. Murray.

Murphy, P. A. (1998) *The Life of R. F. Mackenzie: A Prophet Without Honour*. Edinburgh: John Donald.

NYA (2006) *Youth Work and Extended Services in Schools*. Leicester: National Youth Agency.

PAT (2002) *Tested to Destruction?* London: Profession Association of Teachers.

Reeves, F. et al. (1993) *Community Need and Further Education*. Nottingham: Education Now Books.

Robertson, S. L. (2000) *A Class Act: Changing Teachers' Work, the State and Globalisation*. New York: Falmer Press.

Shircliffe, B. J., Dorn, S. and Cobb-Roberts, D. (2006) 'Schools as Imagined Communities' in D. Cobb-Roberts, S. Dorn and B. J. Shircliffe (eds) *Schools as Imagined Communities: The Creation of Identity, Meaning and Conflict in US History*. New York: Palgrave.

Smithers, A. and Robinson, P. (2000) *Attracting Teachers*. Liverpool: Centre for Employment Research, University of Liverpool.

Smithers, R. (2004) 'Keep pupils in at lunch, minister tells schools,' *The Guardian*, 27th March.

Thompson, M. (2006) 'Re-modelling as De-professionalisation,' *Forum* 48(2): 189–200.

Whittaker, M. (2006) 'Now the kids are on campus,' *TES*, 17th March.

8

The impact of community cohesion on youth work

Paul Thomas

Introduction

The concept of 'community cohesion' is now central to debate about 'race relations' in Britain. Community cohesion has also become a major focus for policy designed to create improved relationships between different communities and ethnic groups. The term first appeared in reports into disturbances in a number of northern towns in 2001. This chapter explores what is meant by community cohesion, some of the context in which it has developed, and in particular what it means for youth workers and others working with communities at a local level. It is based on research carried out with youth workers in Oldham. This aimed to explore youth workers' understandings of community cohesion and ways in which it has impacted on youth work policy and practice.

The 2001 riots

The summer of 2001 saw serious street disturbances in a number of towns in the north of England. Whilst the events in Oldham, Bradford and Burnley each had specific local triggers, all involved 'race' and racism, with South Asian men clashing with the police and with white young men. The disturbances and the resulting damage were viewed as the worst in Britain since the inner-city unrest

This is a revised and updated version of an article previously published as Thomas, P., 'The impact of community cohesion on youth work', *Youth and Policy*, 93.

of the early to mid-1980s. Government's response was an inquiry and two reports (Cantle, 2001; Denham, 2001) whilst the affected local areas of Oldham (Ritchie, 2001), Burnley (Clarke, 2001) and Bradford (Ouseley, 2001) produced their own local analysis. In all of these reports the focus was *not* on the local triggers and events that led to the outbreaks of disorder. Instead, there was a shared recognition that the violence represented deeper issues and tensions below the surface of Britain's supposedly 'multi-cultural' society.

What is 'community cohesion'?

The government's main report into these riots (Cantle, 2001: 9) bluntly characterised the 'riot' towns as ethnically segregated, with an absence of community cohesion caused by a lack of shared values, respect and mutual understanding:

> The team was particularly struck by the depth of polarisation of our towns and cities. The extent to which these physical divisions were compounded by so many other aspects of our daily lives was very evident. Separate educational arrangements, community and voluntary bodies, employment, places of worship, language, social and cultural networks, means that many communities operate on the basis of a series of parallel lives. These lives often do not seem to touch at any point, let alone overlap and promote any meaningful interchanges.

Community cohesion is about people of different backgrounds actually meeting each other, and developing greater mutual respect, understanding and tolerance. The community cohesion approach suggests that individuals and communities have allowed this situation of 'parallel lives' to develop, and that we all need to do more to bridge these physical and cultural divides. From this perspective, government cannot create community cohesion on its own. The choices we all make about where we live, who we socialise with and where we send our children to school, are vital – do we deliberately avoid those that are different to us, or do we positively embrace diversity? For some critics, this analysis is a denial of the reality of structural racism in society. Such critics (Kundnani, 2001) saw the 2001 riots as being about Asian young people reacting to white racism, suggesting that ethnic minority communities have little or no 'choice' in the lives they are leading within a largely racist society.

Community cohesion is also linked with ideas of 'social capital', an understanding of the benefits of 'community' or social networks. Robert Putnam (2000), who has done most to popularise the term, warns that sometimes too much social capital or community can be a bad thing. Putnam highlights two different types of social capital: (i) bonding social capital; and (ii) bridging social capital. Bonding social capital is what gives us all a sense of place and heritage, and is found in the communities that we all feel part of – where we live, where we come from, the ethnic/religious community that we have grown up in. This is vital but too much of it can isolate us from different communities, making us fearful and suspicious of anything different. Bridging social capital is about social networks such as jobs, sports and arts groups, community organisations, that bring us into contact with people who are different to us – people who are of a different class, age or ethnic background and who may have different values and beliefs. Such contact widens our horizons and increases our tolerance, as we have met real people rather than relying on prejudice and stereotypes.

From this perspective, towns like Oldham, Burnley and Bradford have too much bonding social capital, with strong and inward looking white and Asian communities, but no bridging social capital that enables them to come together.

The policy reality of community cohesion

Since 2001, the government has moved forward with this community cohesion analysis. Advice was given to all local authorities (LGA, 2002) on how to initiate and measure the effectiveness of work around community cohesion. Experimental work was funded in different areas, and included bringing people together across generations and building links between travellers and the settled community, as well as work between different ethnic communities. Community cohesion is now a key plank of the government's race equality strategy and the promotion of community cohesion has become a duty for all public bodies (Home Office, 2005). This policy shift has had a direct impact on youth work, with the National Youth Agency offering good practice guidance (NYA, 2002; 2004) and Ofsted Inspection of Local Authority Youth Services and Joint Area Reviews of Councils now including a focus on performance in this area (Ofsted, 2004).

This government focus on the need for community cohesion activity has been heightened by the July 7 bombings carried out in London in 2005. These suicide attacks by four Muslim young men brought up and educated in the north of England, one of whom worked as an (unqualified) voluntary youth worker, raised further concerns around apparent separation within British society. Proposals originally made in the wake of the 2001 riots – such as citizenship and English tests for new immigrants, more focus on the use of English within ethnic minority communities, and an end to funding for projects and organisations that only benefit one ethnic group – have since been implemented with more urgency. This makes it all the more urgent for youth workers to better understand what community cohesion means, and what implications it has for youth work practice.

The research: community cohesion and youth work

To investigate what community cohesion actually means for youth work, I interviewed over 30 youth workers in Oldham. Oldham was chosen as the research focus not only because it was one of the 2001 'riot towns', but also because it is close to my workplace, the university of Huddersfield. The university has strong links with youth work organisations in Oldham, both voluntary youth work agencies and the local authority youth service, and these links were useful in getting agreement from those interviewed. Youth workers from all levels of responsibility, from Principal Youth Officer/Chief Executive to part-time workers, were interviewed on a one-to-one basis.

Interviews were used because the ability to develop a meaningful conversation is seen as the most crucial skill of youth workers (Smith, 1982), and this interview approach seemed to play to the strengths of youth workers. Interviews were 'semi-structured', meaning that the same issues were discussed with all youth workers, however the way and the order in which they were asked varied from interview to interview. All the youth workers interviewed had an alias, a different name that they wished to be known by, so they couldn't be identified, and neither could areas of the town.

The interview approach was also important because the focus of the research was not on the 'facts' of community cohesion. It was concerned with the meanings and understandings held by youth workers, and with their personal opinions on the subject. Indeed, such social research cannot 'prove' anything about a topic such as community cohesion; what it can do is provide evidence drawn on real experiences and make arguments as to how policy and practice should be altered. Here, my own interest was important. My youth and community work experience has focused heavily on issues of prejudice and racism, and the research topic represented a chance for me to reflect on some of the work approaches in which I had been involved.

The research findings discussed below are my own conclusions but I hope that they reflect the experiences and opinions of the youth workers that I interviewed. What they show is that community cohesion has had a significant impact on youth work practice in Oldham, and on the thinking of many of the workers involved in that practice. Indeed, community cohesion seems to have led to youth work agencies developing a different type of youth work practice. One of the key features of youth work's history is that what government or funders want is often interpreted differently and subtly changed by youth workers on the ground. Therefore, this research is not claiming that the changes I highlight have happened because of what government has said or done. Instead, it is about how youth workers individually and together within agencies have reflected on past work and interpreted the new ideas and concerns of community cohesion. Within this, leadership from managers has been crucial in developing new thinking.

Youth worker's support for community cohesion

Many critics have questioned the claims of community cohesion that ethnic segregation in Britain is significant and getting worse, but all the youth workers interviewed agreed that Oldham is highly segregated, with little positive contact between different ethnic groups. Further, the workers agreed that individuals and communities themselves had to take a lot of the blame for this state of affairs. Rather than blaming 'other' communities for this, the youth workers interviewed blamed their 'own' ethnic community. They also accepted that in the past, youth work had reinforced this segregation by making little effort to bring young people together across ethnic or geographical lines – virtually all local youth clubs and projects were used by one ethnic group only, and little had been done to counter this. Indeed, this can partially be seen as a downside of the policy change of the 1980s (Davies, 1999) that led to separate youth work projects and provision for particular ethnic minority groups. Such separate provision was probably needed, because of clear evidence that ethnic minority young people felt marginalised by racism within supposedly 'open access' youth clubs (often dominated by white boys), and the need to provide support in the face of racism in wider society. However, this policy change seems to have suggested to many youth workers that there was no need to bring young people together, or even that it was inappropriate. Alex, the dual-heritage background Principal Youth Officer of Oldham Youth Service (OYS), took over just after the 2001 riots, and found that previously:

> They (youth workers) never even met each other, let alone worked with each other – some of them had never seen each other's areas or buildings.

Understandings of community cohesion: 'meaningful direct contact'

This shared analysis of the problem led to a clear shared understanding amongst youth workers of what community cohesion therefore means. For those interviewed, community cohesion is all about direct contact between young people of different backgrounds, with the emphasis being on actually meeting and getting to know and understand each other better. Stacey, an African-Caribbean origin part-time OYS worker studying for her professional qualification, believed that:

> You've got to mix to learn – if you don't mix, you aren't learning anything.

There was a clear acknowledgement that such direct contact between young people will not automatically be positive (see below), so it must be well planned and 'meaningful'.

There were clear differences of opinion, though, over who should be included in such community cohesion direct contact work. For some youth workers, community cohesion is all about tensions between different ethnic groups, and work in Oldham needs to be squarely focused on building contact and mutual respect between Asian and white young people. Other workers, however, felt that community cohesion should also include work to bridge divides over class, geographical location and other forms of difference. Many of these workers highlighted the fact that the worst examples of youth violence and tension in Oldham are *not* between white and Asian housing areas, but between different white working class areas and housing estates. Underpinning this wider 'social cohesion' perspective was a concern that by focusing community cohesion on ethnic difference, we are assuming that 'race' or ethnicity is the biggest factor in young people's lives, whereas many of them saw class, poverty and location as equally important.

Putting community cohesion into practice

The research clearly established that youth work agencies are now thinking and acting differently in response to the community cohesion agenda. In particular, they have altered their priorities to ensure that all their youth work programmes promote 'meaningful direct contact'. The discussions below can only give a flavour of the range of work being done, but these new approaches are being carried out by a range of voluntary youth work organisations, as well as by OYS. They include:

- Linking arrangements between youth centres and projects.
- Events and projects designed to promote direct contact.
- Strategic use of youth work staff across ethnic lines.

Youth centre linking

Oldham Youth Service has created linking arrangements between different youth centres, with the expectation that joint events and activities are held together regularly throughout the year. This means that community cohesion underpins *all* youth work activity and it allows young people's relationships to develop over a longer period. Rather than a 'twinning' approach that simply links a mainly ethnic minority youth centre and a mainly white centre, this arrangement involves links between three or four centres. Here, differences between urban and rural areas, and between different geographical areas of the same ethnic background, are seen as just as crucial as differences in ethnicity. Johnson is a white-origin Area Manager for 'Newton', a mainly Asian area. This role involves managing the staff and youth centres in a geographical area, as well as direct work with young people. Johnson commented that:

> We have a 'triangulation' with myself, 'Thorndale' (club based on an urban white estate) and 'High Moor' (affluent rural white area), so we're getting the young people out, and I think that works because that breaks down the barriers.

The joint activities within such arrangements are deliberately designed to be experiential and fun, involving outdoor activities, trips and residential weekends. Nevertheless, the challenge involved for the young people taking part in this contact across ethnic and geographical boundaries should not be underestimated, as Johnson showed when discussing a recent residential weekend involving young people from all three youth centres:

> We went for an Indian meal on the first night; we took them to Whitby ... and one of the white lads said, 'God, if people on 'Thorndale' knew what we're doing now, we'd get leathered', and that was just going to a restaurant!

Events and projects designed to promote direct contact

Both OYS and a range of voluntary youth work organisations have planned and delivered events and projects deliberately designed to promote meaningful direct contact between young people of different backgrounds. One example is an 'Eid Party' organised by OYS to celebrate the Muslim New Year. This involved young people from all OYS youth centres and projects coming together for a party involving music, food and dancing. Mark, an African-Caribbean part-time worker, took an all-white group to the Eid party, and commented that:

> Yes, it was hard getting them out of there. We had to come back for a certain time and they didn't want to leave!

Another example is the annual 'Fusion' residential. 'Fusion' involves young people from every high school in Oldham, including young people with physical and learning disabilities, taking part in a residential experience facilitated by workers from OYS. The residential consists of experiential, fun activities carried out in teams and requires young people to get to know others very quickly. Jane, the white/Irish Assistant Head of OYS in charge of planning 'Fusion' highlighted how careful planning enables 'spontaneous' dialogue between young people:

> We sort of set the scene, grow the seeds during the day and through the week, but once those young people start establishing relationships with each other, that's when a lot of the discussions were happening, and people were asking questions. For instance, one of the (Muslim) young women was praying at night, so the other girls watched her pray and asked her really interesting questions about it. The fact was that it was done at one o'clock in the morning, and they should really have been in bed, but I didn't stop it because it was a really interesting piece of dialogue that was going on.

Peacemaker is a voluntary youth work organisation established long before the 2001 riots to promote direct contact across the ethnic divide in Oldham. Their projects include bringing diverse groups of young people together to train as peer mentors, and the Bangladeshi-origin Director and founder Rafiq clearly highlighted that such direct contact youth work is possible in most areas of Britain:

> In towns like this and in inner city areas … that positive interaction is possible as soon as you step out of the community that you live in.

Youth workers crossing ethnic lines

The 'meaningful direct contact' youth work being promoted in Oldham in the name of community cohesion has been underpinned by the strategic use of youth work staff, a deliberate decision by OYS, and by voluntary organisations, to create ethnically mixed staff teams. This policy provides young people with adult role models of different ethnic backgrounds. Qummar, a Pakistani-origin Area Manager was asked by OYS to take over a 'notorious' white estate targeted by the British National Party:

> It was a big challenge coming to a predominantly white community as a black worker, but the experience from youth work training ... enabled me to settle down quickly here. I've never had a problem here working as a black worker ... yes, people have taken me very well.

Qummar went onto describe how he has expanded junior youth work provision through his community development work with a group of (white) young mothers. A number of the workers interviewed were working across 'race' divides, and pinpointed the opportunity this gave young people to ask questions and test assumptions with a real person of a different ethnic background. This approach can be seen as challenging the previous assumption of 'anti-racist' youth work practice that young people are always best served by workers from the same ethnic/religious background. Instead, this new policy enables individual youth workers to promote community cohesion through their day-to-day conversation with young people. Sometimes, this involved workers having to deal with racist comments and prejudices from young people, but they saw this as an important and legitimate part of their educational role.

A return to 'traditional' youth work?

The 'meaningful direct contact' being promoted in Oldham through community cohesion youth work can be seen as a return to 'traditional' youth work priorities and approaches. The centre 'linking', and the events and projects have been built around experiential and informal activities, using sport, art, drama and outdoor activities that bring young people together in ways that allow dialogue and relationships to develop naturally. In particular, what is being promoted is 'association', the opportunity for young people to be part of a group experience that involves young people of different backgrounds. The stress on experiential activities, learning by doing, can be seen as a contrast to the type of youth work activities previously carried out in the name of 'anti-racism'. Previous research by the University of Huddersfield (Thomas, 2002) found youth workers nervous and confused about anti-racist work. Youth workers interviewed thought that anti-racism meant that they had to 'teach' young people to not be racist and to condemn and ban young people who continued to make racist comments. This belief that they should deliver formal 'lessons' on anti-racism was partially why youth workers were so unconfident of their ability to put anti-racism into practice.

Those previous findings were echoed by youth workers in Oldham. Michael, a white-origin full-time worker for a voluntary-sector youth work agency commented:

> I think that anti-racism … automatically has quite a negative spin-off, because its anti-something, you're immediately challenging people's views.

In contrast, there was clear understanding of, and enthusiasm for, community cohesion. This is because the youth work being carried out in the name of community cohesion plays to the strengths of youth workers in asking them to organise and facilitate fun group activities that provide young people with new experiences and informal learning without making the educational content 'heavy' or formal.

The report into the Oldham riots (Ritchie, 2001) criticised OYS not only for the low level of funding given to it by the Local Authority, but also for what it did with those resources. In the years before the riots the importance of open access youth centres had been downgraded, with more emphasis on project work involving smaller groups of young people and a more 'formal' curriculum and educational content. Ritchie (2001) criticised this approach as it had meant more bored young people on the streets, and less contact with young people who were likely to get involved in violence, but who had no interest in the youth work 'projects' on offer. The experiential and fun work in the name of community cohesion is responding to that criticism alongside an expansion of detached and outreach work (partially through new 'mobile' buses), and an increase in centre opening hours.

Planning for the spontaneous

The focus on association and informal activities within community cohesion youth work does not assume that 'meaningful direct contact' will automatically be successful. Indeed, a number of youth workers interviewed offered examples of when bringing different groups of young people together in the past had gone badly wrong. This means that careful planning and preparation is vital to ensure that informal activities are actually an enjoyable and educational experience for young people. Alex highlighted this in relation to the large-scale 'Fusion' residential:

> Certainly, within the planning it's not up for grabs whether it's successful. It is planned with incredible detail to be successful, to make a difference with every single

person in terms of their perceptions of young people from different cultural backgrounds, different genders and different geographical areas within the borough.

Mary explained how such preparation translates into the reality of the young peoples' residential experience:

> It's how the staff managed the group, how the staff got young people interacting, how they bring issues in that young people would then look at then or discuss. So, it's not so much the activity, it's the workers, the staff are the key for me.

The role of leadership in community cohesion

The enthusiasm and support for community cohesion youth work approaches discussed above have not come simply through a formal change of policy, or by orders of managers. Indeed, the history of youth work (Davies, 1999) shows that youth workers have always used the relative freedom of their role (compared with teachers and social workers) to alter official policies that they don't agree with. 'Anti-racism' may have been the official policy approach in youth work and education for the past 15 or 20 years, but there is clear evidence (CRE, 1999) that many youth workers avoided the role it expected of them.

Therefore, the support for community cohesion in Oldham has come as much from 'leadership' and example by senior managers as it has by the traditional 'management' route of passing a policy and instructing staff what to do differently. Youth workers interviewed clearly described how senior managers had convinced and 'sold' workers the need to operate differently after the 2001 riots. This leadership role also involved demonstrating and 'modelling' good practice by actually being involving in planning and delivering pieces of community cohesion youth work. Alongside that has been a determination to emphasise the positive results of youth work and to actively seek funding and recognition for youth work on the basis that it can offer positive ways forward for community cohesion.

Such leadership and positive attitudes led to early community cohesion events and programmes being successful, which in turn convinced many workers to be enthusiastic and confident about future work. June, an African-Caribbean origin OYS Officer saw the leadership of the Principal Youth Officer as crucial:

> It's probably Alex herself as an individual who's really pushed for this. I think she's got so much drive and energy, and so much positivity, she won't turn up an opportunity, she never misses anything.

Part of this leadership approach within community cohesion work has been to trust the professionalism and judgement of youth workers rather than simply tell them what to do and constantly check up on them. Alex explained that:

> What I try to do here is create a culture that actually requires people to be creative and innovative by not providing them with the step-by-step 'how to do it' guidelines – and that is quite deliberate.

Having made community cohesion, and the importance of fun and experiential activities, central to the purpose of OYS, senior managers have then left workers to take this forward creatively. Louise, a white-origin Area Manager, highlighted how having community cohesion as an organisational principle underpinning all youth work activity helped:

> If you've got it (community cohesion) there, then you're thinking about doing joint activities, you're getting people together ... we use the word loads now, and I think that it does help.

Problems and limitations

Despite the positive developments outlined above, youth workers also identified problems and limitations with community cohesion. In particular, these centred on:

- The apparently superficial and 'one-off' nature of some 'direct contact' work
- The possible downplaying of 'anti-racism'.

Tokenistic one-offs?

A number of youth workers felt that direct contact across ethnic lines is now happening, but that the impact is questionable. This viewpoint was summed up by Habib, a Pakistani-origin, full-time OYS worker:

> In the paper work it could look like it's community cohesion, but in reality it is that they are just doing the normal thing of getting a few Asian kids in a room with white kids and vice versa and saying, 'this is community cohesion'. It doesn't mean that they talk to each other.

A number of youth workers felt that funders and managers had wanted a 'quick fix' in the wake of the 2001 riots, so that something was seen to have been done. Some criticised this approach as being about 'one-offs', but the example of the 'Fusion' residential discussed above shows that even one-off events, if planned and facilitated properly, can have a real impact on young people.

The real danger of superficial, or even negative, community cohesion work comes from the more general youth work problem of poor planning and preparation. The successful examples of community cohesion work in Oldham saw full-time workers and senior managers actively involved in the planning and delivery of the work, so leading by example and demonstrating good practice to less qualified and experienced colleagues.

A down-playing of anti-racism?

Possibly the most serious question mark against community cohesion is the concern that by moving away from the language and methods of previous anti-racist work, community cohesion is retreating from a focus on combating racism. Workers such as Salma, a Pakistani-origin part-time OYS worker, felt that racism must be talked about openly and honestly, and that community cohesion may be avoiding doing that:

> I would say that work doesn't tend to touch on anti-racism because there might be a taboo on that. 'Don't talk about that word because it brings trouble'... I would say that cohesion is an easy option because you can get negatives and positives out of it, but when you talk about racism, you do get a lot of hatred and a lot of negativity out of it, but it needs to be talked about.

Such concerns can partly be seen as a frustration with the continued existence of racism in young people's lives, but it may also represent a lack of confidence in the wider, informal and experiential approach of community cohesion. From this perspective, more formal sessions, conferences and programmes of 'anti-racism' clearly demonstrated that 'racism' was being addressed, but there is growing evidence that not only have such anti-racism programmes not worked with many of the white young people that they were usually aimed at, but that they have actually been counterproductive and created resentment (Thomas, 2002).

Conclusion

My research in Oldham showed that the new term 'community cohesion' is both understood and supported by youth workers from a variety of agencies.

Their shared understanding of community cohesion as 'meaningful direct contact' between young people of different ethnic backgrounds has allowed youth work agencies to develop new approaches to practice. These new approaches are built around fun and experiential activities that bring young people together and which enable them to get to know each other better, so challenging stereotypes and misconceptions. In many ways, this community cohesion activity is 'traditional' youth work, focused on association and informal, rather than formal, education. This explains why youth workers are so positive about community cohesion, in contrast to their feelings on 'anti-racism', which they understood as being about 'closing down' discussions, and the delivery of formal 'lessons' on racism.

The success of voluntary youth organisations and the local authority Youth Service in Oldham in developing such community cohesion activity potentially points to a 'unique selling point' for youth work agencies nationally. The promotion of community cohesion is a clear priority for local and national government, and youth work organisations have the skills and experience to develop programmes that allow young people to come together and build relationships in safe but challenging situations. Clear and positive leadership from managers is needed here, but the challenge above all is to ensure that racism and other forms of oppression are still addressed within the community cohesion programmes of fun and experiential activity.

References

Cantle, T. (2001) *Community Cohesion – A Report of the Independent Review Team*. London: Home Office.

Clarke, T. (2001) *Burnley Task Force Report on the Disturbances in June 2001*. Burnley Borough Council: Burnley.

CRE (1999) *Open Talk, Open Minds*, London: CRE.

Davies, B. (1999) *A History of the Youth Service in England and Wales*. Leicester: Youth Work Press.

Denham, J. (2001) *Building Cohesive Communities – A Report of the Inter-departmental Ministerial Group on Public Order and Community Cohesion*. London: Home Office.

Home Office, (2005) *Improving Opportunity, Strengthening Society: The Government's Strategy to Increase Race Equality and Community Cohesion*. London: Home Office.

Kundnani, A. (2001) 'From Oldham to Bradford: the violence of the violated' in *The Three Faces of British Racism*. London: Institute of Race Relations.

Local Government Association, (2002) *Guidance on Community Cohesion*. London: Local Government Association.

National Youth Agency (2002) *Spotlight: Promoting Community Cohesion*. Leicester: National Youth Agency.

National Youth Agency (2004) *Justice, Equality, Our World*. Leicester: National Youth Agency.

Ofsted, (2004) *Report of Inspection of Oldham Youth Service*. London: Ofsted.

Ouseley, H. (2001) *Community Pride, Not Prejudice – Making Diversity Work in Bradford*. Bradford; Bradford Vision.

Putnam, R. (2000) *Bowling Alone – The Collapse and Revival of American Community*. London: Touchstone.

Ritchie, D. (2001) *Oldham Independent Review – One Oldham, One Future.* Government Office for the Northwest: Manchester.

Smith, M. (1982) *Creators not Consumers: Rediscovering Social Education*. London: NAYC.

Thomas, P. (2002) 'Youth work, racist behaviour and young people – education or blame?', *Scottish Journal of Youth Issues*, 4: 49–66.

People

Leading work with young people requires an ability to work effectively with a range of individuals and teams, both in your own organisational context and, increasingly, outside it. This section explores different aspects of this important area of professional practice. Common themes include the importance of making time to reflect on your practice, including ways in which you manage and lead.

Mike Hudson's chapter 'Managing People' examines key elements of successful people management, including the importance of managing your own managers. If staff are an organisation's most important resource, then the way they are supported, challenged and led is crucial. Hudson demonstrates how successful leaders learn how to handle and deal with relationships, including their inevitable frustrations. He emphasises the importance of building strong teams based on a shared understanding of what they are aiming to achieve. He also highlights the importance of learning, both for organisations and individuals, and the need for all of us to take responsibility for our own learning and development.

The theme of learning organisations is developed by Peter Hawkins and Robin Shohet in their chapter, 'Towards a Learning Culture'. They look at aspects of organisational culture and ways that they impact on the work of teams and individuals. They emphasise the importance of understanding the culture where you work and explore how aspects of policy and practice, including supervision, are influenced by organisational culture. They present the view that practitioners work best in situations where they have opportunities to keep learning and developing themselves, including the importance of having opportunities to reflect and discuss work with others.

The final two chapters in this section continue to develop this focus on supervision as a key aspect of good professional practice. Neil Thompson's chapter 'Using Supervision' begins by acknowledging that the tasks involved in people work can be messy, complex and demanding. Given these difficulties and challenges, the ability to provide and receive effective supervision is an essential part of the role of leaders and managers. Supervision is a complex and skilful process, but these skills can be learnt and developed. He looks at the different functions that supervision can take on in an organisation, and explores ways in which a good supervisor balances managerial functions with supporting and developing staff and their learning.

In 'Structuring Support and Supervision for Different Contexts' Hazel Reid explores supervision in the particular context of professional practice with young people. She considers how supervision can help practitioners to establish and maintain boundaries and good, ethical practice in their work with young people. She suggests some frameworks for establishing and supporting a supervision relationship, particularly in the context of developing integrated support services for young people. Like Thompson, she sees supervision as an essential form of support that provides valuable 'space' for reflective professional practice. She also looks at a number of different models of supervision, including the potential to develop group and peer supervision.

9

Managing people

Mike Hudson

Developing people is an art

The ability of third-sector organisations to achieve their objectives depends almost entirely on the skills of their people. The capacity of their staff and volunteers is determined by the quality of the people who are recruited and by the organizations' investment in developing their expertise.

Investing time and effort in developing the capabilities of managers at all levels of the organization brings great benefits both to the individuals and to the organization. It presents people with new challenges to the way they work and consequently makes work more interesting and stimulating. The new skills and abilities they gain make them more rounded and capable individuals. Organizations that strive to develop the capabilities of their staff attract more talented people, who grow personally and perform to higher standards.

The potential for increasing the effectiveness of third-sector organizations by developing people's skills is huge. Many managers could improve their delegation skills and give their staff greater responsibility within clearer boundaries. They could also learn more from the people to whom they delegate.

This chapter sets out how to increase the capacity of organizations to be really effective. It describes how to:

- manage your boss
- get better performance from teams
- delegate work and empower people
- supervise, develop and coach people.

This is an edited version of material first published as Chapter 12 in Hudson, M., *Managing without Profit: The Art of Managing Third Sector Organizations*. London: Directory of Social Change.

Managing your boss

Managing your boss (an idea propounded by John Gabarro and John Kotter in *Harvard Business Review*) is a foundation-stone of being a good manager.

Managers and staff can do their jobs more effectively if they have a strong and constructive relationship with their boss. Each is dependent on the other: bosses need help, guidance and advice from their managers in order to do their jobs. They need to feel confident that they can depend on their managers. Similarly, managers and staff depend on their bosses for guidance and support. Managers and staff need to understand how their work fits in to the wider context; they need information from their boss and, most of all, they need their boss to help procure the resources required to achieve their objectives.

Poor relationships are often put down to personality conflicts. 'I don't get on with the boss,' is a common sentiment. However, this description sometimes conceals simple misunderstandings about the mutual dependencies in the relationship. Managing a boss is not about political manoeuvring to seek advantage. It is a process of working with him or her to obtain the best results for the organization and using every opportunity to learn from each other.

The first step in managing bosses is to understand their context. This means having a sense of their priorities, their aspirations and the issues that are being addressed at a higher level. It means tapping into their information systems, networking with other managers and asking questions when the broader context is not clear.

The second step is to understand her or his strengths and weaknesses. Successful people avoid making the assumption that their boss is omniscient. They recognize that all bosses are different: some are full of creative ideas but need guidance to come to decisions; some are decisive but need to have all the options developed for consideration. Some are good at networking outside the organization but need to be briefed on developments within the organization. People who understand their bosses actively exploit their strengths and support them in their weaker areas.

The third step is to understand his or her preferred working methods. This requires watching their behaviour and gaining insights into the way they work. Some people prefer to learn about things on paper; others prefer an oral report. Some like solitary time to think; others prefer to work things out together. Some are lateral thinkers, others are better at making quick judgements.

Managers and staff can conceive of their boss as a resource which needs to be used effectively. A boss's time is always limited, so it needs to be used judiciously. Wasting time involving the boss in detailed issues which people ought to resolve on their own is a common mistake; briefing the boss on the issue and the action taken is far more helpful. Similarly, judging when an issue needs the boss's attention, preparing thoughts about the problem and knowing what to ask helps make effective use of the boss's time.

All relationships have frustrations. Successful people learn how to handle them. Those who rebel against their boss and who undermine him or her are not creating the conditions for succeeding in their own job. Similarly, people who bottle up all their frustrations and do not share their concerns with their boss are storing up problems for the future.

They also seek opportunities to learn from their relationship with their boss. There is a potentially rich resource to mine here, provided both parties are willing to strive to learn.

In summary, people who wish to learn should:

- understand the broader context in which their boss is working
- discover their boss's preferred working style
- use their boss to help with tasks they are good at
- expect their boss to provide them with support and one-to-ones
- see the relationship as an opportunity for each to learn from the other
- look elsewhere for the support their boss is unable to provide.

Getting performance from teams

In addition to creating relationships upwards, managers also have to create relationships with the people who work for them. More than anything, managers need to create and lead a team of people who are dedicated to achieving agreed objectives. Their job is to build strong teams, release the potential that is within team members and ensure that the achievements of the team as a whole are much greater than the sum of its parts. Teams are important not only in the line-management structure, but also as an essential integrating mechanism across the departmental structure.

Characteristics of effective teams

Organizations have different types of team including:

- **Management teams** – consisting of managers and their boss (e.g. the Senior Management Team)
- **Staff teams** – consisting of staff and their manager (e.g. the Help-line Team)
- **Project teams** – consisting of a cross-section of managers and their staff (e.g. the Lottery Project Team).

When teaching about teams, Ashridge Management College, a research and management school, summarizes the characteristics of highly effective teams as groups that are:

- persistent in pursuit of their goals
- inventive in overcoming obstacles
- committed to quality in all aspects of teamwork
- inspired by a vision
- action-orientated
- committed to the success of the organization as a whole
- able to distinguish the important from the urgent
- willing to take risks and be innovative and creative
- always looking for ways to do things better.

This, no doubt, reflects many team leaders' intentions. However, two special characteristics of third-sector organizations have to be overcome in order to attain this ideal. First, there is the fact that the sector attracts an extraordinarily wide range of characters to its organizations, many of whom are intelligent, charismatic, opinionated, but sometimes obstinate when it comes to being a team player.

Secondly, managers have to understand that their role is different from that of other members of the team. The democratic values of some organizations and the deeply held desire to represent users' views can spill over into team behaviour. Sometimes managers start from an assumption that their primary duty is to represent the views of their staff or service users. They put their loyalty to their staff or service users ahead of their role as a member of a more senior team in which they have to make trade-offs between the interests of different parts of the organization. They feel more accountable to the people they represent than to the senior team. They find it hard to accept collective responsibility for management decisions and to support those decisions when they have to report back to their own team.

Creating the team

The first issue to consider is the **size of the team**. Teams that are too small may not contain all the skills required or generate enough variety of thought. Teams that are too large are cumbersome and frustrating for members.

Larger teams are appropriate when:

- some of the posts are similar (for example, managers of similar centres or regions) because they will have common problems
- members are experienced team players who require less support, one-to-ones or coaching

- a wide range of skills is essential to the team's effectiveness (for example, resolving very complex problems).

Smaller teams are appropriate when:

- there is high interdependence between members (for example, an assessment and rehabilitation centre where tight co-ordination is required); they need time to work closely together
- the team works in a rapidly changing environment (for example, a campaign team); people will need lots of short meetings.

Any rule has exceptions, but for many situations a team of between four and seven people is a common compromise.

The next issue to consider is the **characteristics of team members**. For teams to perform to the highest standard, people have to work closely together, support each other and balance team needs with their own. A balance has to be found between having people with similar backgrounds and experience who work together well but who see issues only from one perspective, and having a more heterogeneous team drawing on people with different skills. The need for homogeneous teams increases as the tasks they have to undertake become more complex. Heterogeneous teams are more productive when dealing with more straightforward tasks, but they can expect to experience more conflict.

Then there is the issue of **sensitivity and trust**. Groups of people who get along well, who trust each other and are sensitive to each other's needs, are more productive than those where members are suspicious of one another. Sensitivity and trust should grow as the team works together and as members gain deeper insights into their colleagues' strengths and weaknesses.

The fourth aspect of creating an effective team is allowing **time for people to get to know each other** both professionally and personally. Teams are more effective when people understand each other's personal backgrounds and personalities. They work more efficiently when members have a deep understanding of each other's strengths and weaknesses.

Changing team membership

Sometimes managers need to change the size, structure or membership of a team in order to improve its performance. Another option for changing team membership is to make judicious use of opportunities created by people leaving or retiring. A departure gives managers the space to reconsider everyone's responsibilities and either reduce or enlarge the team.

Another, more subtle option is to **change the definition of the team**. Team membership can be adjusted by redefining the scope and purpose of the team and incorporating or excluding people to increase its effectiveness. For example, if a team is too small and the organization has talented people who are not on the team, it can be expanded for certain types of meeting. A quarterly review of strategy, for example, or a series of planning meetings provide an ideal opportunity to enlarge the team. If the team is too large, it may be necessary to reduce the frequency of meetings and create a smaller group to co-ordinate activities between meetings.

Creating a team with an appropriate size and composition is an essential prerequisite for getting performance from a team. However, there is a trap to avoid. Some managers mistakenly assume that getting the right group of people is their single most important task. They continually adjust the structure and the membership of the team – not recognizing that **each adjustment is a disruption** to team dynamics. Developing appropriate team behaviour and coaching members so as to help them become better team players can have more effect than adjusting its membership. In short, oversize or undersize teams with good team behaviour can be more productive than a team with appropriate size and composition and no accepted ways of working.

Developing the team

Teams need objectives. Everyone on the team needs to be totally clear about what the team is trying to achieve. The team needs both to have words that define the objectives and to be clear about the context in which they have to be achieved. The objectives need to be understood from many different perspectives and from the different viewpoints that each team member brings.

Ideally, all team members need to be directly involved in agreeing the objectives. Everyone also needs to believe in them. It is easy to support the words, but the high-performance team needs people who are motivated to achieve the objectives and demonstrate by their behaviour in and outside the team that they believe in the objectives. This can be achieved only by working on the objectives, taking time away from the office to explore the options and develop the thinking. Objectives can then be tested on other groups (up, down, across and outside the organization) to make them more robust.

Teams plan together. Successful teams spend time planning their work. Sometimes individual members of sub-groups will prepare plans for achieving a particular objective and bring them to team meetings. In other situations, planning the work will be done in team meetings. Whatever the circumstances, effective teams are clear about how the objectives will be achieved.

MANAGING PEOPLE

Teams need coaching. Managers are responsible for setting the standards for team behaviour. As well as guiding the team in its work, managers encourage members to contribute constructively. They praise good team behaviour, they criticize loose or poor contributions and they help people to improve their work.

Teams need good administration. Preparation for meetings and communication outside meetings are essential elements of effective teams. The major topics for meetings need to be planned so that papers can be commissioned, reviewed by the manager and distributed in advance. Timing of meetings, appropriate venues and circulation of action notes may all be details, but they are crucial elements of an effective team.

Leading teams

Finally, the most effective teams are those that have strong leadership which is sensitive to team members' needs and not dominant or authoritarian. The critical elements of effective team leadership can be summarized as follows:

Start modestly. Managers should set realistic objectives at the beginning, build the team's confidence in itself and then increase expectations. If leaders are too ambitious, they risk losing credibility when the objectives are not achieved.

Promote the mission. Teams are motivated by missions. They need to feel that their work is vitally important and be able to set it in the broader context of the organization's overall objectives.

Encourage openness. Teams under-perform when individuals have private agendas or when one group is making different assumptions from those of another.

Support each other. Members of high-performance teams take particular care to support each other. They build on each other's arguments in meetings, show concern for each other's welfare and assist each other in their work.

Face up to differences. Managers with strong teams encourage differences of opinion. They expect members to make their differences clear, but to be willing to compromise when decisions are required.

Review performance regularly. Managers set aside time for the team to review its own performance. They identify behaviour that worked well and review situations where improvements could be made. They encourage critical discussion of the team's performance and expect the team to agree actions to improve team performance.

Encourage systematic decision-taking. Teams make better decisions if they are systematic about gathering information, diagnosing problems, seeking opinions and evaluating options before taking decisions.

Make the team visible. Managers promote their teams both inside and outside the organization. They communicate up, down and across the organization, ensuring that their team's work engages with the rest of the organization.

Encourage action. Managers encourage action. They clarify what needs to be done and ensure that agreed actions are followed through.

Celebrate success. Managers make sure that successes are celebrated. They mark achievements with praise, publicity and parties.

Different styles for different tasks

Leading an effective team also requires the selection of an appropriate style of working for the task at hand. When the team needs to crack through the routine work of communicating with each other, co-ordinating activities and making regular decisions that do not raise wider issues, it is appropriate that there should be tight chairing, short interventions and timetabled agendas. Where there are disagreements on minor matters, the team leader can impose a decision on the group.

However, where there is a great deal of uncertainty around the issues being addressed and the decisions will have widespread repercussions, an entirely different mode is required. All the skills and all the experience of team members are required to consider the issue. Chairing needs to be more flexible, ownership of the way the discussion is going may move around the team, and timetables need to be less fixed. Table 9.1 shows the stages of the development of a team.

Delegating work and empowering people

Delegation is the art of sharing work among the team, giving people the freedom to make decisions, but retaining responsibility for achievement of the task. Empowerment is a broader concept; it is concerned with giving people more latitude around how tasks are completed and holding them accountable only for the results. It implies less detailed monitoring and an expectation that the delegatee will request assistance when required.

There are many forces that work against delegation in third-sector organizations. Managers are often highly motivated by the nature of the work they are doing; they believe in the cause they are working for, put in long hours and enjoy the detail. It is very tempting not to delegate enough in these circumstances.

Then there is the fact that staff feel overloaded. They too are committed to the cause and often believe that they could not work harder. So, before work

Table 9.1   Stages of the development of a team

Characteristic	Undeveloped team	Experimenting team	Consolidating team	Mature team
Atmosphere, feelings and conflict	Tense, individual self-interest; feelings not dealt with; conflicts seen as inappropriate	Dynamic; expressions of mutual interest; feelings begin to be opened up; group's inward-looking	Confident, open approach; resolves interpersonal issues	High commitment to the task and each other; individuals' needs for recognition low; confrontation handled easily
Talking and listening	Very little listening; points of view queuing up	More listening and thinking, less talking in unconnected ways	Listening very good, constructive use of ideas, good balance of agreeing, disagreeing and behaviours	Easy but careful listening; lots of building and extracting benefits of ideas; summaries stated regularly
Working method	Stick to the established method; scared of changes; little time spent considering how to operate	Increasing dissatisfaction with procedures initially established; increased concern with internal processes	Further examination of methods; willingness to change; better understanding of method through discussion	Conscious observation of group process; discussion of its effectiveness; flexible use of procedures and time-keeping; readiness to change
Time management	Ignored; 'speaking clock' tends to operate	Realization of need to plan and manage time; tentative steps	More realistic time-allocation to the various stages of working	More flexible use of time-allocation and readiness to change to facilitate the task
Understanding the task	Leader's view is often different from the rest; others tend to be confused	Understanding increases through discussion and questioning, but little willingness to vary it	Better understood through questioning, leading to a group version of the task	Continual monitoring of the task; modification depending on progress and feedback
Decisions	Mostly taken by the leader	Decisions still taken mostly by the leader or by voting	Shared responsibility for decisions; group tries for consensus	Taken by the group by consensus, but leader's role in reasoned arbitration is recognized

(Continued)

Table 9.1 (Continued)

Characteristic	Undeveloped team	Experimenting team	Consolidating team	Mature team
Using each other's abilities	Individuals keep to narrow roles; low recognition resources available	Increased readiness to deal with quiet members	Clear understanding of strengths and weaknesses; moves to use resources outside the group	As for consolidating team, but stronger
Personal weaknesses	Covered up; mistakes used to judge people, not to identify learning opportunities	Increased readiness to look at people's preferences and at tasks they feel unhappy with	Now well understood and taken account of in a positive and acceptable way	As for consolidating team, but stronger
Resilience to the outside	Defensive to outside 'threats'; proposals increase bureaucracy	Increasingly insular and competitive	External demands and conflict handled constructively	Team copes constructively with problems

can be delegated, managers have to find ways to help their staff review priorities and stop doing some things that they believed were important in order to create the time to do the new work managers wish to delegate to them. The issue is usually not lack of willingness but the ability to set priorities that are consistent with the manager's view of their relative importance.

A frequent obstacle to delegation is the pressure of time. The work needs to be done quickly, so the easiest solution is for managers to do it themselves. It takes time to brief someone, explain what is required and help them to adjust their priorities, so it often appears easier just to do the task. This, however, is a recipe for overload. Effective delegators anticipate the need for the work and decide how it can be done before they become trapped into doing it themselves.

Another obstacle to delegating is the fear that the individual will not be able to do the task. Sometimes this may be entirely justified and the task should not be delegated to that person. But sometimes managers have to take small risks in order to give the person who is delegated the task an opportunity for learning. They can assist in these circumstances by being particularly clear about the objective of the task, its scope and its time-frame, and explicitly checking that the person concerned understands the task.

Successful managers delegate as much as they possibly can. They delegate in stages as people's skill and experience grow; they monitor the individual's performance; and they maintain the level of control needed to ensure a successful outcome. They start by delegating low-risk tasks and, as the person's experience grows, higher-risk tasks are delegated.

However, delegation is not simply a matter of handing over tasks to another person. It is the skill of giving someone additional responsibilities that are within his or her abilities and providing appropriate advice and support as that person takes greater responsibility for the task. The amount and nature of work that can be delegated depends on the person's experience, the confidence of the manager and the risk attached to the task.

Learning the art of delegating

Becoming an effective delegator requires a new attitude of mind. Good managers instinctively think ahead and ask themselves how to achieve each task for which they are responsible. Anticipation is the critical ingredient. Managers have to allow time to brief people to whom tasks are delegated and for those people to fit the work into their already busy schedules. They have to allocate time to review progress, to give advice and to support the delegatee.

Managers also need to clarify why they are delegating tasks. They can delegate:

- **To make better use of time**. Managers are paid to manage, not to do the work. They have to create time to discharge their many managerial responsibilities, and this invariably means delegating as much work as their staff can handle.
- **To give staff development opportunities**. All staff need to develop their skills and abilities. Giving staff responsibility for additional tasks is an ideal method of enabling and encouraging professional development. It provides new challenges within carefully selected boundaries.
- **To use people's skills**. Staff have strengths in areas where the managers may have weaknesses. Managers delegate to maximize the use of staff members' skills.

Some activities cannot be delegated. **People-management responsibilities**, such as one-to-ones, performance reviews, chairing team meetings, discipline, praise and resolution of disputes, are responsibilities that managers should retain in all but the most unusual circumstances. **Policy-making** cannot be delegated. The work of preparing papers, doing research and making proposals can be delegated, but decisions on matters that have widespread repercussions cannot be delegated. **Crisis management** usually requires judgements to be made from a broader perspective; these situations can seldom be delegated. Matters involving **confidential information**, such as sensitive personnel information, cannot be delegated. Finally, the **rituals** of celebrating successes, rewarding long service and representing the organization or department at major occasions should not be delegated. Position and status both add significantly to the value of rituals.

Improving delegation skills

Good practice in delegation involves:

- Creating a well-informed team of people who understand the broader context into which their work fits. When tasks are delegated, people will understand why the work needs to be done.
- Giving people appropriate information about the task. Hard information about what needs to be achieved is as important as soft data about the people and problems that might be encountered.
- Being clear about the objective but allowing the individual to take the initiative in how it is achieved.
- Being clear about available resources, the milestones that will mark progress, the timescale for achieving the result and the arrangements for reporting on progress.

- Being honest about the task and what it will involve.
- Leaving no confusion about accountability for the work.
- Giving credit for a job well done, and taking responsibility if it does not go well.
- Using mistakes as learning opportunities and not as reasons for allocating blame.

Delegating is a skill that is learned with practice. It is an essential ability that managers need to grasp. Too often managers fail to delegate and so overload themselves, or they delegate without providing the support and guidance that are needed to produce the required outcomes. Managers need to practise delegation so that it becomes an instinctive way of working.

Empowering people

Empowering people is a process of giving **greater ownership** of a task or a set of responsibilities to an individual or a group. It is about going one step further than delegation, being very clear about the 'ends' that people are expected to achieve, but allowing them greater freedom in managing the 'means' of achieving the desired end. In an empowered organization, people are held accountable for their achievements and not for the methods used to accomplish them. Empowering people allows them to take charge of their situation within clearly agreed boundaries and to take more decisions. Empowering people requires that the fundamentals of good management are securely in place. It is appropriate in organizations that already have very clear objectives, strong teams, well-established management processes and good personal relationships.

Initiatives to increase empowerment also require managers to have reached a comparatively experienced stage of their personal development. They should be sufficiently mature to be able to share their anxieties with other people, willing to learn from failures, and able to challenge people confidently, to stand back from detail and to command people's respect.

In its most developed form, the manager is not a 'member' of the empowered group. He or she builds the environment in which the group can do its job, coaches people when support is required and monitors the results.

The most critical judgement that managers have to make is the **extent of empowerment** that is appropriate. On the one hand, managers who hold on to too much power frustrate their staff and do not allow them to perform at the highest level. Staff end up wasting time, working out how to 'get round' the system. On the other hand, managers who expect people to work to very wide briefs when they are not ready to have so much scope run into great difficulties. Activities start to feel less well controlled and people begin to express anxieties about the abilities of their managers. This is a particular problem when it is inherently difficult to set clear and limited objectives for work, such as in campaigning. At its worst, this leads to an element of organizational anarchy in which everyone is running his or her own initiatives with insufficient co-ordination to allow a coherent strategy for the department or the organization as a whole to be constructed.

Similarly, attempting to give people power over huge issues with long timescales is just as inappropriate as giving people power over trivial matters. A useful catchphrase is to think about giving people '**freedom within a framework**', in which the manager is responsible for defining and agreeing realistic conditions within which the empowered person can work.

Empowerment is likely to be appropriate in organizations that are well established and which, over the years, have developed controls and procedures that are now an obstacle to effective entrepreneurial working. However, care needs to be taken to avoid raising inexperienced managers' expectations that they will suddenly have more power over the organization and will be participating in all the major decisions. They need to be aware that increased empowerment also means increased responsibility, both for their own work and for their interventions into broader management issues.

Increasing empowerment is a long-term process, requiring changes in trustees', managers' and employees' behaviour. A **two-year time-frame** might be appropriate in many circumstances. Empowerment should therefore be treated as a change management project, with stages including a diagnosis of the problem, building commitment to the need for new ways of working and the preparation of plans and actions to bring about the required changes.

Empowerment generally requires greater change from managers than from the people they manage. Managers have to put more effort into clarifying objectives and boundaries, coaching staff, giving them links to other people and resources, and encouraging two-way feedback.

Actions to empower people

Managers can take many actions to empower people. Choices will depend on circumstances and on people's views on what will have the greatest impact. The stages of increasing empowerment might include:

- **Involving people in planning** so that they share the ownership of objectives in addition to the means of achieving them. A deep understanding of the purpose and boundaries around the work of an individual or a group is a prerequisite for devolving power.

- **Communicating extensively with staff** to keep them well informed about the changing context in which they are working and how their work affects the organization's overall effectiveness. Such communication should be a two-way dialogue that also encourages people to submit new ideas. The best of these can then be fed back in subsequent communications to maintain the dialogue.
- **Removing institutional barriers** that prevent people making changes in their own area of responsibility. Managers should have freedom to make changes that they know are necessary and feasible. Where such changes cross departmental boundaries, set up a 'bureaucracy-busting' task force to find imaginative ways of overcoming obstacles. Examples include forms that gather data that has been collected elsewhere, statistics that hardly anyone uses, onerous authorization procedures and requirements to consult committees on matters of tiny detail.
- **Asking staff to keep you appraised** to ensure that you get feedback on your performance.
- **Increasing people's spending limits** to indicate confidence in their ability to make good decisions.
- **Reducing the formal reporting requirements placed on staff** to an absolute minimum and requiring reports on results not activities.
- **Encouraging people to come with solutions** rather than presenting problems.

Empowering people to take greater responsibility significantly increases an organization's capability. It releases senior people to put more effort into their critical role of integrating changes in the external environment with the current work of the organization. However, it cannot be done in short timescales. It is achieved over months and years, and results from incremental behaviour changes that become embedded in the organization's culture.

10

Towards a learning culture

Peter Hawkins and Robert Shohet

Introduction

In this chapter we focus on the wider context in which supervision happens. One of the core contexts is the culture of the organization in which the supervision is happening. The culture of the organization can not only influence and frame the supervision, but even block effective supervision from happening. In this chapter we will illustrate different types of culture that are prevalent in helping organizations and how these affect supervision.

What is culture?

Following Herskowitz (1948), we define culture as the different explicit and implicit assumptions and values that influence the behaviour and social artefacts of different groups.

   The understanding of culture derived from anthropology has been more recently used to understand the deeper context of organizations. McLean and Marshall, in their book *Working with Cultures: A Workbook for People in Local Government* (1988), quote the definitions of various writers, including themselves, who have studied organizational cultures. Organizational culture is:

   ... how things are done around here.

(Ouchi and Johnson, 1978)

This is an edited version of material first published as Chapter 12 in Hawkins, P. and Shohet, R., *Supervision in the Helping Professions: An Individual, Group and Organisational Approach*. Maidenhead: Open University Press.

... values and expectations which organization members come to share.

(Van Maanen and Schein, 1979)

... the collection of traditions, values, policies, beliefs and attitudes that constitute a pervasive context for everything we do and think in an organization.

(McLean and Marshall, 1988)

McLean and Marshall (1988) go on to explore how culture is carried not only in the high-profile symbols of an organization such as logos, prestige events and training programmes, but also in the low-profile symbols: 'Essentially everything in an organization is symbolic; patterns of meaning in the culture mirrored in multiple forms of expression – in language, relationships, paperwork (or its lack), physical settings ... how meetings are called and conducted, who sits next to whom, who interrupts, what time different topics are given, what lines of reasoning prevail and so on'.

Thus the organization's culture of supervision can be seen in the high-profile symbol of its policy about supervision, but can be more accurately seen in its low-profile symbols; where supervision takes place, who supervises, how regular the sessions are, what importance is given to them and what priority they have when time pressures necessitate something being cancelled. Some social services departments have a policy with grand phrases about the key importance of supervision and ongoing development and support of staff; yet supervision is the first thing to be cancelled when there are staff shortages.

Other writers have referred to the organizational culture as representing the unconscious of the organization, as it is embedded in the ways of experiencing what happens; thus they see culture as less to do with what is done and more to do with how it is viewed, heard and experienced.

Levels of culture

Hawkins (1994) has built on this work as well as the writings of Geertz (1973) and Schein (1985) to develop a model of five levels of organizational culture, each level being fundamentally influenced by the levels beneath it:

- *Artefacts*: the rituals, symbols, art, buildings, mission statements, policies etc.
- *Behaviours*: the patterns of relating and behaving; the cultural norms.
- *Mind sets*: the ways of seeing the world and framing experience.
- *Emotional ground*: the patterns of feeling that shape the making of meaning.
- *Motivational roots*: the fundamental aspirations that drive choices.

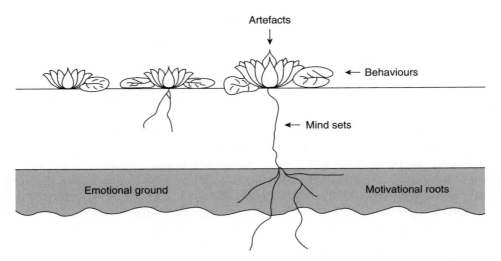

Figure 10.1   The five levels of organizational culture (after Schein, 1985)

Like Schein (1985) we have utilized the water lily to illustrate this model (see Figure 10.1). The water lily illustrates that what is most noticeable about culture is the artifacts: the building, logo, mission statement, annual report, etc., which equate with the flower of the lily. Just above the surface of the water the leaves of the water lily represent the typical behaviours of the culture. If the artefacts demonstrate the espoused values of the organization, the behaviours show the values in action. Many organizations have run into difficulties when there has been a rift between their rhetoric (what they say) and the reality of what they do. Beneath the surface are the mind sets, which hold in place the belief systems of a culture. These in turn grow out of the emotional ground or climate of the organization. The motivational roots are about the alignment of individual purposes and motivations with those of the collective organization.

Cultural dynamics and supervision

In working as organizational consultants to a number of health services, social work departments, probation teams, counselling and psychotherapy organizations, and voluntary organizations, we have come to recognize certain distinct and typical cultural patterns that exist across all the helping professions. We have called these 'cultural dynamics':

- Hunt the personal pathology
- Strive for bureaucratic efficiency

- Watch your back
- Driven by crisis
- The addictive organization.

We do not want to create another typology or classification of organizational cultures, as there are already many in existence (Handy, 1976). Rather we would see these patterns as recognizable system dynamics within the dominant organizational culture. Indeed, an organization may contain a number of these dynamics at the same time. Each of these cultural dynamics will create different motivations, emotional feelings, attitudes, behaviours and policy around supervision. Each, in time, will lead to degenerate and even perverse forms of supervision.

Hunt the personal pathology

This culture is based on seeing all problems as located in the personal pathology of individuals. It is highly influenced by psychodynamic case-work theories, but has little understanding of either group dynamics or how systems function.

If there is a problem of one department not functioning, the first thing that managers with this cultural mind set do is to look for the problem *person*. This is often the head of the department. The belief is that, if we can cure the sick individual, the department will be healthy. If the sick individual does not seem to respond to treatment, then you look for a way of removing him or her.

This approach can happen at all levels of the organization and can degenerate very quickly into scapegoating. The residential home for children will report that all their troubles would be solved if only they could find a way of moving young Tommy somewhere else. However, when and if they do move Tommy to another home, then Sally becomes the problem child, and so on.

We have also worked with teams where the team has located all its problems in one member. 'If only Jack would take early retirement', they all sigh. This attitude ensures that they are impotent in addressing the collective team problems, as you cannot solve a problem that you do not first own as, in part, yours.

In one large voluntary organization, individual homes were elected one at a time to be 'the problem child' of the organization. The unspoken belief was that if *this* home could be sorted out then the whole organization would be problem free!

In this culture supervision can become problem centred and aimed at treating pathology. This can create a subtle form of paranoia in the supervisees who fear that, if they do not keep the focus on the pathology of their clients, they themselves may become 'a suitable case for treatment'. In this culture we also find that staff will sometimes say: 'I do not need supervision this week as I do not have any problems'. Team leaders will tell us that they give supervision on an ad hoc basis 'when problems arise'. This culture creates the belief that, if you go for supervision, you must have a problem or, more perniciously, there must be something wrong with you.

This attitude is intensified by the policy of giving students the most regular supervision, the new staff the next largest amount, and senior staff no supervision at all. The message in this low-profile symbol is very clear: 'if you want to get on in this culture, demonstrate that you do not need supervision'; and 'Supervision is only for the untrained, inexperienced or needy'.

Strive for bureaucratic efficiency

This form of organizational culture has been extensively written about by Isobel Menzies (1970) in her classic work on nursing cultures in hospitals. This form of culture is high on task orientation and low on personal relatedness. There are policies and memos to cover all eventualities and all meetings have tight agendas.

In this culture supervision is mostly concerned with checking that all the tasks have been done correctly. We have worked with team leaders who have arrived at supervision with their staff with an agenda which is like a mechanic's checklist. When they have ticked off all the items, the supervision is finished. They may say as they walk out of the door, 'Oh by the way, how are you?' but they may not stay to hear the answer.

For the supervisee the supervision is one of reporting back what they have and have not achieved. Again the culture is problem centred but this time the ethos is that of mechanics rather than sickness and treatment. There is little space for understanding in the rush for tidy answers.

Watch your back

This form of organizational culture becomes prevalent where the climate is either very politicized or highly competitive. Some departments are riven with internal power battles between subgroups. Sometimes this is on political or racial grounds, but sometimes it is more to do with cliques and who is on whose side. In this atmosphere much energy goes in ensuring that the other sides do not have all the information for fear of the possibility that they will use what they know against you. Meanwhile you make sure that you use everything you can to expose the other group.

Charles Handy (1976) in his book *Understanding Organizations* points out: 'In all organizations there are individuals and groups competing for influence or resources, there are differences of opinion and of values, conflicts of priorities and of goals. There are pressure groups and lobbies, cliques and cabals, rivalries and contests, clashes of personality and bonds of alliance'. Often in the helping professions power and rivalry are denied and then become even more powerful as shadow forces that are not recognized.

This form of culture can also develop in a very hierarchical organization where the climate is set so that those who 'keep their noses clean' will get promotion. This leads staff to ensure that they cover up any difficulties, inadequacies or problems they are having, as it would be detrimental to share these: 'I have regular meetings with my supervisor, but always steer clear of my problems in coping with my report work. Can I trust her? I need her backing for my career progress, but will she use this sort of thing as evidence against me? There are some painful areas that are never discussed but need discussing so much. It is an awful dilemma for me' (Fineman, 1985: 52).

What happens to supervision in this culture depends on who your supervisor is. If you are supervised by one of your own power subgroup, it becomes conspiratorial and falls into discussing 'how awful the other sides are'. If you are supervised by someone who is 'one of them' or a manager you do not trust, then it is centred on covering up, putting a good gloss on the work you have done and making sure you are seen in a good light.

Driven by crisis

We have visited homes and departments where the staff never have uninterrupted time to meet, as one of them is always responding to the latest crisis. In this type of organizational culture there is never time to reflect properly on the work or the plan ahead – the focus is always on the intensity of the moment. Clients pick up this culture and realize that, if you want to get attention around here, produce a crisis.

When we first worked in a halfway house for the adult mentally ill, cutting one's wrists seemed to be contagious. Even those who had no previous record of wrist-cutting seemed to be starting. The staff were always rushing to the local casualty department, holding hastily bandaged arms. Eventually we managed to stem the flood of crises long enough to hold a staff meeting to reflect on this. We realized that those who cut their wrists were getting far more attention than the other residents. We, as a staff group, were perpetuating this particular crisis culture. The staff made it clear to the community that in future they would not visit clients in the hospital who had overdosed or cut their wrists and would instead give more attention to the clients who avoided such behaviour. Immediately the number of crises dropped dramatically.

In other organizations staff have told us that the only way to get time with the director is to have a crisis in your section – then the director, who is always too busy to see you, sends out an urgent summons for you to see them. In this culture supervision is rarely a high priority and will get cancelled regularly, always for very important reasons. When it does happen, it often creates the atmosphere of being in a tremendous rush and having to solve problems in a hurry before the next wave or onslaught bears down upon us.

The addictive organization

In 1991 we wrote a review (Hawkins and Shohet, 1993) of the book by Ann Wilson Schaef and Diane Fassel, entitled *The Addictive Organization* (1990), in which we described the four major forms of addiction in an organization as:

- Where the key person in an organization is an addict. We have known directors and chief executives who have been alcohol dependent or workaholics, who's whole life was absorbed in their professional life.
- Where there are a number of people in the organization replicating their addictive or co-dependent patterns. In another book, Schaef (1992) quotes the shocking statistic that in one study of nurses in the USA 83 per cent were found to be the eldest children of an alcoholic parent.
- Where the organization itself is an addictive substance, eliciting high degrees of dependency and workaholism from its members. This can be fuelled by the covert messages that say if you want to get on here, you do not take lunch breaks or leave until late in the evening.
- Where the organization itself is the addict. Here, the organizational system functions in a parallel way to an addictive personality. The organization becomes unable to face its own truth and confront its own difficulties, and starts to rationalize and defend dishonest and abusive behaviour.

One of the key notions in the field of addiction that is used by Schaef and Fassel (1990) is that of co-dependence. These are the partners, family or work colleagues who service, accommodate and protect the addict and their addiction. In the case of the addictive organization the entire workforce can be either acting addictively or colluding as a co-dependent.

If the organization has a culture of addiction, then it is important to interrupt the denial and dishonesty before attempting any other mode of development. Schaef and Fassel (1990) are sharply critical of many of the approaches to organization development that facilitate the client organization in being more skillful in staying addicted. They criticize:

- stress management programmes that provide individual managers with techniques to keep their workaholism even longer and more intensively
- programmes in worker participation which become subtle ways of staying in control
- mission statements that become a 'fix' – 'It reassures us that we are important and do important work'.

Shifting the cultural dynamic

The first step in shifting the cultural dynamic is to become aware of the culture. This is not as easy as it sounds, for in the words of the Chinese proverb, 'The last one to know about the sea is the fish'. Our current favourite definition of organizational culture is: 'what you stop noticing when you have worked somewhere for over three months'. Newcomers and visitors can often offer insightful feedback on your culture. There are also a number of exercises devised by the Bath Consultancy Group for accessing your own culture (Hawkins, 1994):

- looking at typical patterns of behaviour
- collecting stories of organizational heroes, villains and fools
- common metaphors
- staging the unofficial induction programme
- listing the unwritten rules, etc.

Using such exercises a group can produce a detailed description of your own organizational culture, at all the five levels previously mentioned.

Just bringing the organizational culture to the surface can lead to some degree of change. Individuals and organizations may suddenly realize that they do not have to carry on with the same beliefs and ways of working that have become institutionalized. Their new awareness leads to greater choice.

Having *surfaced an awareness* of their culture, an organization can move on to exploring how they wish this culture to shift. One way of starting this process is known as 'three-way sorting' (Hawkins, 1994). The team or organization may have generated a great amount of data about their culture from carrying out the above exercises – they are then asked to create three new lists:

- What lies at the heart of the organization? What are the core values, the root metaphors, etc.? What needs to be safeguarded and nurtured as the organization moves on?
- What can be discarded, is no longer appropriate and has outlived its usefulness? What is the excess baggage that is slowing down change?
- What needs to be incorporated, acquired, done differently – how does the change represent a time of possibility and opportunity?

This exercise represents the first step towards creating a cultural shift. To really change the culture in a sustainable way is a much longer and more difficult process which is beyond the focus of this particular chapter.

Creating a learning developmental culture

Supervision best flourishes in a learning developmental culture. Such a culture is built on a belief system that a great deal of the work in all helping professions is about creating the environment and relationships in which clients learn about themselves and their environment, in a way that leaves them with more options than they arrived with. Further, it believes that helping professionals are best able to facilitate others to learn if they are supported in constantly learning and developing themselves. An organization that is learning and developing right from the top of the organization to the bottom is far more likely to be meeting the needs of its clients, because it is also meeting the needs of its staff. We will summarize here the key attributes of such a culture and how they affect supervision.

- Learning and development are seen as continuous lifelong processes. Thus in a learning culture the most experienced and the most senior staff ensure that they have ongoing supervision or consultancy and do not see supervision as just for the untrained and inexperienced. The actions of the senior managers speak louder than their policy statements and it is important that they conspicuously exemplify the learning culture by, among other things, having supervision themselves.
- A learning culture emphasizes the potential that all the different work situations have for learning, both individually and collectively. Learning is not just something that happens in the classroom or on a training programme, but is built into the very fabric of work.
- Problems and crises are seen as important opportunities for learning and development, both individually and organizationally. Major crises are seen as growth points and the culture is one where it is safe

to take risks, as failures are seen as events to be learned from, not as evidence for the prosecution of individuals.

- Good practice emerges neither from an action culture that is always dealing with the latest problems and crises, nor from a theorizing culture that is withdrawing from the real issues to draw up theoretical policy papers. Good practice comes from staff, teams and departments that are well balanced in all parts of the learning cycle, which goes from *action,* to *reflection,* to *new thinking,* to *planning* and then back to *action* (see Kolb et al., 1971).

- This means that supervision needs to avoid rushing for quick solutions, but also needs to avoid getting lost in abstract theorizing. Rather, it must start with reflecting on the concrete experience and try to make sense of this in a way that allows the experience to challenge one's own way of seeing and thinking about the world. But supervision must not stay at the point of new insight, but rather use this new insight to generate new options, evaluate these options and choose what new strategy to put into operation. This new action then needs to be reviewed in the following supervision so that the learning cycle does not become a one-circuit process.

- Learning becomes an important value in its own right. Supervisors carry the attitude 'How can I help these supervisees to maximize their learning in this situation so that they can help the client learn too?', rather than the attitude 'How can I ensure that the supervisees make no mistakes and do it the way I think is right?'

- Individuals and teams take time out to reflect on their effectiveness, learning and development. In a learning culture there are team development sessions or 'away days' (see Brown, 1984). There are also 360-degree staff appraisals that go well beyond the senior grading the staff member on performance. They should involve a cooperative process of the staff members' appraising their own development, their own strengths and weaknesses and then receiving feedback on and refinement of their own appraisal from both their peers and their senior.

- A good appraisal system will focus, not just on performance, but also on what the staff member has learned, how they have developed and how their learning and development can best proceed and be nurtured in the forthcoming period.

- There should be a high level of ongoing feedback, both from peers and between levels within the organization. Also, feedback would be encouraged from those with whom the work team or organization relate: customers, other helping organizations, professional networks, politicians, etc.

- Time and attention will be given to the transition of individuals: how new staff are welcomed and inducted into the team and organization; how they are helped to go through leaving and changes in status within the organization. Time would be given to this in both team, and individual supervision.
- Roles will be regularly reviewed and negotiated. They will be allocated not just on the basis of efficiency, but also on the potential that each role provides as a learning opportunity for its incumbent. This would include the role of supervisor which would not just be allocated to the automatic person in the hierarchy.
- In such a culture the learning does not reside just in individuals, who may up and leave. Rather, it is ensured that the learning happens at the team and organizational levels and is both recorded and lived in the developing culture.

Supervision, the learning organization and the learning profession

Where organizations have confronted the cultural dynamic that leads to degenerate supervision and have developed a healthier learning and developmental culture, there is likely to be effective individual learning and development. However, this is not enough, for there is still a danger that despite the learning of all the individuals, the organization itself will have stopped learning and developing.

Supervision can also be the place where a living profession breathes and learns. For too long we have reduced the concept of supervision to a cultural socialization process where the elders of the professional community shape the practice, behaviours, understanding, perceptions, feelings and motivations of the apprentices and noviciates.

All the approaches discussed in the cultural patterns above have learning flowing from the supervisor to the supervisee. The learning is about conforming to the pre-formed professional norms and precepts – the culture's written and unwritten rules. Certainly, both quality control and inducting newcomers into the professional collective wisdom are important aspects of supervision, but if supervision is reduced to just these two aspects, as is often the case, we create a self-reinforcing profession which ceases to learn and develop. Eventually the profession becomes ossified, operating more and more within well-worn grooves of practice.

Supervision has a key challenge to move beyond the three central roles as defined by Kadushin (1976):

- Managerial (quality control)
- Educative (development of the supervisee)
- Supportive (ensuring the supervisee is able to process their experience, rather than be overwhelmed by it).

If we are to create learning professions that constantly renew their cultures, then supervision needs to become the learning lungs that assist the professional body in its learning, development and cultural evolution. Supervision needs to be practised in a way that allows learning to emerge in the interaction between the three unique areas of experience that are brought into relationship with one another:

- The client situation and context
- The supervisee's experience and understanding
- The supervisor's experience and understanding.

Too often we have seen supervision reduced to the exchange of pre-existent 'thoughts' and knowledge. The supervisee tells their supervisor what they have already thought and know about their client, and the supervisor shares their pre-existent knowledge about similar clients or processes.

One useful test to review whether a supervision session has provided new generative learning is to ask four questions at the end of the session:

- What have we learned that neither of us knew before we came into supervision?
- What have we learned that neither of us could have arrived at alone?
- What new capability have we generated in this session?
- What new resolve have we each created?

The answers to these four questions will show the possible outputs of the dia-logical learning that is generated in the space of our thinking and feeling together, rather than what has transpired from the exchange of pre-existent 'thoughts' and 'felts'.

For a learning profession it is not enough to shift supervision from an exchange of thoughts to dialogical and generative thinking. We also have to consider how the learning that emerges from these supervisory dialogues can flow into the learning and cultural evolution of the wider profession. How do the learning lungs provide the necessary oxygen to the lifeblood of the organization?

We believe that any organization or profession working in the helping professions needs to create learning pathways, which can be used for harvesting emergent learning from supervision sessions, and for taking this learning into new collective practice and standards. Such learning pathways can include:

- supervision case reviews and action learning sets
- supervisor seminars for the exchange of learning
- conferences on new practice
- new papers, articles and guidelines on professional practice using case material, appropriately disguised, from supervision.

Conclusion

In this chapter we have tried to show how supervision is not just an event, but an ongoing process which should permeate the culture of any effective helping organization. Nearly all organizational cultures have a mix of several of the organizational dysfunctions that we have illustrated and caricatured. We have yet to meet an organization that fully lives up to the ideals of the learning developmental culture. This said, some organizations do go a long way along the road to creating such an environment.

Developing supervision policy and practice should include attending to the organizational culture and helping it to evolve away from some of the patterns illustrated in this chapter, towards being a learning developmental culture. In such a culture, learning and development are an intrinsic part of every aspect of the workplace. Ultimately we believe that clients of all helping professions learn, develop and heal best in places where the staff are continuously learning.

References

Brown, A. (1984) *Consultation: An Aid to Effective Social Work.* London: Heinemann.
Fineman, S. (1985) *Social Work Stress and Intervention.* Aldershot: Gower.
Geertz, C. (1973) *The Interpretation of Cultures.* New York: Basic Books.
Handy, C. (1976) *Understanding Organizations.* London: Penguin.
Hawkins, P. (1994) *Organizational Culture: Evolution and Revolution.* Bath: Bath Consultancy Group.
Hawkins, P. and Shohet, R. (1993) A review of the *Addictive Organization* by Schaef and Fassel. *Management Education and Development,* 24(2): 293–6.
Herskowitz, M. J. (1948) *Man and His Works,* New York: Knopf.
Kadushin, A. (1976) *Supervision in Social Work.* New York: Columbia University Press.
Kolb, D. A., Rubin, I. M. and McIntyre. J. M. (1971) *Organizational Psychology: An Experiential Approach.* New York: Prentice Hall.

McLean, A. and Marshall, J. (1988) *Working with Cultures: A Workbook for People in Local Government*. Luton: Local Government Training Board.

Menzies, I. (1970) *The Functioning of Social Systems as a Defence Against Anxiety*. London: Tavistock Institute of Human Relations.

Ouchi, W. E. and Johnson, J. B. (1978) 'Types of organisational control and their relationship to emotional well being', *Administrative Science Quarterly*, 23(2).

Schaef, A. W. (1992) *When Society Becomes an Addict*. Wellingborough: Thorsons.

Schaef, A. W. and Fassel, D. (1990) *The Addictive Organization*. San Francisco: Harper.

Schein, E. H. (1985) *Organizational Culture and Leadership*. San Francisco: Jossey Bass.

Van Maanen, J. and Schein, E. H. (1979) 'Towards a theory of organizational socialization', in M. B. Straw and L. L. Cummings (eds) *Research in Organisational Behaviour, Vol 1*. Greenwich, CT: JAI Press.

11

Using supervision

Neil Thompson

Introduction

The tasks involved in people work can be extremely demanding at times. They are often complex and 'messy' with no simple or straightforward solution (Schön, 1983). They often need to be thought through very carefully, and there is much to be gained from discussing issues with a senior colleague who is not directly involved in the situation. This is a key aspect of supervision and underlines the benefits that can be drawn from effective line management. This chapter therefore explores the important role of supervision in developing and maintaining personal effectiveness.

What is supervision?

Supervision is, in principle at least, a process through which an organization seeks to meet its objectives through empowering its staff. This involves a range of tasks:

- Monitoring work tasks and workload
- Supporting staff through difficulties
- Promoting staff development
- Acting as a mediator between workers and higher management, where necessary
- Problem-solving
- Ensuring legal and organizational requirements and policies are adhered to
- Promoting teamwork and collaboration.

This is an edited version of material first published as Chapter 7 in Thompson, N., *People Skills*, New York, Palgrave Macmillan.

These are achieved partly through day-to-day contact, and partly through more formal meetings or 'supervision sessions'.

For people workers there is considerable variation in the use of supervision. For example, social work and youth work have long traditions of supervision, while its use is far less well established in other professions such as nursing, although mentoring, a process closely akin to supervision, is being increasingly emphasized. The significance of supervision is none the less of major proportions, regardless of the extent to which it is commonly practised, as it can play a vital role in the success or otherwise of people work. It is therefore worth considering the benefits of supervision, and it is to these that we now turn.

The benefits of supervision

Effective supervision can often be the difference between: success and failure; stress and job satisfaction; worry and reassurance; good practice and excellent practice. Its significant role should therefore not be underestimated. In particular, we should appreciate the positive benefits that can be derived from supervision. These include:

- An opportunity to share concerns
- A forum for reviewing actions and checking plans
- A more objective perspective on work currently being undertaken
- Constructive feedback, both positive and negative
- A source of confidence and reassurance
- Opportunities for personal and professional development.

This is by no means an exhaustive list but should suffice to paint a clear picture of the potential benefits of supervision. Furthermore, we should also consider what may occur as a result of adequate supervisory support not being available. That is, a lack of effective supervision may not only rob workers of the support they need, but may actually act as a source of pressure in its own right (Thompson et al., 1994).

Morrison (1993/2001) also emphasizes the importance of supervision and outlines a set of beliefs on which his view of supervision rests. These are:

- Supervision is the worker's most essential professional relationship.
- What goes on *under* the 'supervisory table' is often as significant as that which goes on *over* the 'supervisory table'.
- Supervision is a complex and skilful process which can be learnt – you are not born with or without those skills.
- Supervision is improved by analysing what we feel, think and do and by trying new things out with support for ourselves as supervisors.

- Supervision is one of the most important managerial activities in an organization.
- Supervision is a major organizational strategy for the protection and empowerment of minority or vulnerable groups whether they are clients or our own staff.
- Supervision can be one of the most rewarding tasks in social care work.

These are principles that are also endorsed here and inform many of the points made in this chapter. They reinforce both the value of supervision and its complexity.

The elements of supervision

Kadushin (1976) describes supervision in terms of three elements which relate to: managerial accountability, staff development and support for staff. Richards and Payne (1991) add a fourth dimension of mediation. I shall outline each of these four elements in turn.

Accountability

Line managers have some degree of responsibility for the work of the staff they supervise. They will therefore need to have some oversight of the work being undertaken. This will allow a process of standard-setting which plays an important part in contributing to the overall process of quality assurance.

In this way, the supervisor can ensure that legal requirements are met and that organizational policies and procedures are followed. However, this is not simply a 'checking up' procedure. It can give workers a sense of confidence and reassurance that any mistakes that are made (and, of course, mistakes inevitably will be made) are likely to be picked up at an early stage so that any damage done can be kept to a minimum.

If this role is fulfilled sensitively and skilfully by the supervisor, it can create a strong sense of security and a feeling that there is a reliable safety net if things should start to go wrong. However, if undue emphasis is given to this element of supervision at the expense of the others, supervision can become very 'heavy-handed' and can be resented and resisted by staff – a positive tool becomes a problem.

Staff development

The staff of an organization are its most important resource, in the sense that the success or failure of the organization depends to a great extent on the actions and attitudes of staff. Staff are a 'human resource' and so, to be of maximum benefit to the organization and to the people who use its services, it is important that steps are taken to promote staff development.

This is often achieved through courses and other forms of training. However, the line manager also has a significant role to play through supervision. The supervisor can help to identify opportunities for learning and help to capitalize upon them. He or she can also play a crucial role in identifying barriers to learning and helping to break them down. This does not mean that the supervisor is expected to be an 'expert'. However, it does mean that he or she should have the skills of facilitating and promoting learning and the confidence to put these into practice.

Staff care

People work is fraught with a number of pressures that can easily lead to stress. The role of the supervisor in helping to insulate staff from these pressures is therefore a very important one in terms of staff care.

There are many dangers in undertaking people work unsupported, not least because of the emotional demands of this type of work. Morrison (1993/2001: 22) includes the following in a list of important aspects of the supportive function:

- To create a safe climate for the worker to look at her/his practice and its impact on them as a person
- Debrief the worker and give them permission to talk about feelings, especially fear, anger, sadness, repulsion or helplessness
- Helping the worker to explore emotional blocks to their work.

Mediation

The line manager is in an intermediate position between the staff he or she supervises and the senior management hierarchy. The supervisor is therefore well placed to act as a mediator between the two sets of people, and indeed has a responsibility to do so.

A key part of this is the process of negotiation. It may involve representing staff's interests to higher management or guiding staff through organizational changes imposed from above. In this respect, the mediation role reflects elements of accountability, staff development and staff care.

The four elements are not mutually exclusive and do overlap to a certain extent. Unfortunately, a weakness that is relatively common is that of supervisors

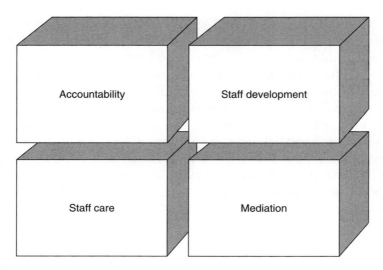

Figure 11.1   The four elements of supervision

sticking too closely to their 'favourite' element, the one with which they feel most comfortable. For example, a supervisor who enjoys the role of standard-setting may engage in 'snoopervision' by being too zealous and defensive in checking staff's work. Such an approach is likely to cause resentment and mistrust. Similarly, a supervisor who enjoys the staff development element may focus almost exclusively on promoting learning, and thereby neglect other significant aspects of the role. A good supervisor is therefore one who is able to balance all four elements of the role.

Problems and barriers in supervision

Supervision is a skilled activity, and some of these skills relate to being able to negotiate barriers and resolve problems that stand in the way of effective supervisory practice. These problematic areas include:

- *Destructive processes*   Avoidance behaviour is one such very common destructive process, and creating a dependency relationship is another. If we are not careful, supervision can become a non-productive forum for game-playing (Morrison's notion of what goes on *under* the table, as discussed earlier). It is sometimes necessary to 'name' the process, for one party to bring the process out into the open by commenting explicitly upon it.

- *Unfinished business*   This relates to previous experiences of supervision. If there have been previous problems in a supervisory relationship, these may be 'carried forward' to the current situation. There may, therefore, be a need to exercize the ghosts of previously problematic supervision.
- *Personality clashes*   These do occur from time to time, but the term can also be applied inappropriately on occasion. For example, the clash may have more to do with a conflict of values than personality *per se*. Similarly, there may be conflicts arising from differences of ethnic group, gender, class or age. For example, a worker may resent being supervised by a younger person.
- *Imbalance of elements*   As mentioned above, an overemphasis on one of the elements at the expense of the others can be very problematic. This applies not only to the supervisor but also to the worker. For example, a worker may seek to guide supervision in a particular direction and thereby make it difficult for the supervisor to maintain the necessary balance.
- *Burnout*   Where staff have reached a point of emotional exhaustion, their commitment to supervision is likely to be very low, as they have probably given up hope of making progress in their work. Indeed, it is a characteristic of burnout that work is undertaken in a routine, emotionally sanitized way, and so supervision is likely to be a difficult process.

These are just some of the ways in which supervision can be blocked or rendered ineffective. It is primarily the supervisor's responsibility to remedy the problems encountered. However, there are steps that the supervisee can take to contribute to a successful process of supervision – making supervision work is, after all, a joint responsibility.

The worker's responsibility

The skills of personal effectiveness can be seen to include those of making the best use of the supervision opportunities available. These skills can be developed, in part at least, by following certain guidelines. Chief amongst these are the following:

- *Avoid 'macho' attitudes*   To take advantage of the benefits supervision can offer, we have to be open to accepting help and support. A 'be tough' attitude (Pottage and Evans, 1992) is a significant barrier to effective use of supervision. All staff, even the most highly competent, can benefit from supervision. Being open to receiving help and support should not be seen as a sign of weakness.

- *Do not collude* If you have a supervisor who indulges in game-playing or destructive processes, it is important that you should not collude with this. It may be very difficult to challenge your 'boss', but playing along with games can lead to even worse problems in the long run.
- *Ensure you receive supervision* You can play a proactive part in receiving supervision, if necessary. If a supervision session is cancelled, make sure you book an alternative time. If no one receives supervision, raise the subject at a staff meeting and try to get a system of supervision organized. If your line manager is unwilling to provide supervision, try to organize supervision from a senior colleague or develop group supervision (see Morrison, 1993/2001).
- *Identify your own needs* Be clear about what you need and expect from supervision. Once you have identified what you need, make sure your supervisor becomes aware of what these needs are.
- *Be assertive* An assertive approach towards supervision can pay dividends. In particular, it can promote an open supervisory relationship in which constructive feedback works both ways. This can make a significant difference in terms of realizing the positive potential of supervision.
- *Use time management* Some people comment that they are 'too busy for supervision'. This is a misguided approach to the subject as it fails to recognize the need to invest time in order to save time. Effective supervision can prevent mistakes being made, increase motivation and encourage creative solutions. In this way, supervision can actually help to save a great deal of time and make the best use of the limited time resources available. It is therefore important that we are able to make time available for supervision.
- *Prepare for supervision* The time that can be allocated to supervision is inevitably limited. It is therefore helpful to prepare for supervision so that the time can be used to maximum effect. For example, it is a good idea to set priorities, to plan in advance what are the most important issues to be addressed. This helps to set an agenda at the beginning of the supervision session so that discussions do not become unfocused and unproductive.

A positive, proactive approach to supervision can be seen to be a very important part of personal effectiveness. Workers who neglect the significance of supervision or adopt a passive approach to it are seriously undermining their own potential for effectiveness.

Conclusion

Supervision can be seen to play a critical role in promoting good practice. If it is positive and constructive, it can be a tremendous source of confidence, learning and support. However, where it is handled badly or does not take place at all, workers can be left feeling unsupported, unappreciated and lacking guidance. The role of the supervisor is therefore a very important one.

The responsibility for providing supervision lies clearly and firmly with the line manager. However, the central point to be emphasized is that the worker too has some degree of responsibility for ensuring high-quality supervision by not colluding with the absence of supervision and by taking whatever reasonable steps he or she can to make supervision a success.

References

Kadushin, A. (1976) *Supervision in Social Work*, New York, Columbia University Press.

Morrison, T. (1993/2001) *Staff Supervision in Social Care*, 2nd edn, Brighton: Pavilion.

Pottage, D. and Evans, M. (1992) *Workbased Stress: Prescription is Not the Cure*, London: NISW.

Richards, M. and Payne, C. (1991) *Staff Supervision in Child Protection Work*, London: National Institute for Social Work.

Schön, D. A. (1983) *The Reflective Practitioner*. New York: Basic Books.

Thompson, N., Murphy, M. and Stradling, S. (1994) *Dealing with Stress*, London: Macmillan Press – now Palgrave Macmillan.

Structuring support and supervision for different contexts

Hazel L. Reid

Introduction

> Perhaps our job is more difficult because it has fewer boundaries and some people are getting into difficulties because they don't know how far they should be going, and to what extent they should be doing certain things. (Reid, 2005)

The above is a quote from a practitioner working as a personal adviser with young people. It is taken from a study that explored the different meanings attached to the practice of supervision within a service aimed at cross-agency help for young people. For many of these practitioners the holistic nature of the role often involved them working in ways which were not covered by their initial training in career guidance. Whilst they sometimes worried that they were 'not doing enough' for their clients, they did feel that their previous training gave them a sense of where boundaries should be drawn, as they were able to identify the limits of their expertise. The advisers in this study expressed concern about those 'new youth support workers' who did not have previous training within a helping profession. They felt there was a real danger of 'doing too much', as their genuine desire to help was not framed by the ethical boundaries provided by an established professional identity.

This chapter argues that a structured approach to support and supervision can help to establish and maintain those boundaries when leading work with young people. Support and supervision can provide the framework for the development of the practitioner, including the necessary 'ethical watchfulness' (Reid, 2004), alongside offering the required support that can avoid a difficulty turning into a disaster. 'Disaster' is a strong word, but lack of support and supervision could be instrumental in turning practice that is challenging into practice that is disturbing and even dangerous. Both the young person *and* the practitioner have a right to expect that helping organisations will take an ethical approach to their support needs.

The chapter will discuss what is meant by holistic services to young people in order to examine the diverse context for the work, before exploring the purposes of support and supervision. These meanings, across organisational contexts, affect the understanding of what it is for; who gets it and who gives it. Having considered purpose, the chapter will move on to describe existing models and suggest a framework for structuring a support and supervision relationship. Methods will then be outlined, with inclusion of ideas that can be adopted for less 'traditional' contexts.

The context for youth support work: together and apart

Within the context for youth support work, and in other health and social services, there has been a trend in policy development within the UK for 'joined-up' services. For example, the establishment of the Connexions Service in England provided an opportunity to establish a collaborative service to support young people, paying particular attention to those who required additional support (SEU, 1999). With the publication of *Every Child Matters* (DfES, 2004) the sector for providing support to children and young people has grown in significance. The policy agenda resulting from *Every Child Matters*, and the subsequent *Youth Matters* Green Paper (DfES, 2005), is likely to turn a spotlight onto how integrated services for young people are managed and evaluated. However, words like 'integrated', 'holistic' and 'partnership' give a positive spin to practice that is often experienced as 'separate', 'isolated' and 'frustrating'. In other words, partnerships are easier to talk about than make happen in practice: they can be experienced as working within the rhetoric of togetherness whilst feeling apart – why?

Many youth support workers will be full time, within an established agency or institution (albeit the frameworks may be changing for some), working from a central office, a school or within community settings. They may have access to registered networks of other helping agencies alongside the personal contacts they have created in the work. Conversely, many other youth support workers will be part time, or voluntary workers who may work in the evening or weekends in non-office surroundings, outside of established institutions and in several different locations. In addition, they may not be members of a professional association and their knowledge may be based on their experience of working with young people, rather than acquired through formal training. Within both groups there will be those who are new to working with young people; but whether a novice or a veteran, support and supervision is at the very least useful and perhaps essential.

The purpose of support and supervision

So far in this chapter support and supervision has been written as if one word: 'support and supervision'. This reflects the view that both aspects of the process are important. Before moving on to look at structuring a support and supervision relationship, it will be useful to consider definitions given to its function from a number of viewpoints.

There is no clear-cut view of the purpose of support and supervision, even where it is an established practice. Approaches vary between and within professions as a response to practitioner need and the context in which support and supervision takes place. Not surprisingly, this often determines the methods used. There is a growing body of literature that can be referred to, for example, within counselling. Bradley and Kottler (2001: 3) discuss purpose via the 'principles, process and practice' of supervision. They state that the term supervision can be divided into two words 'super' and 'vision'. The implication is that an experienced person looks over, from above (super) the work of a less experienced person and has a view (vision) of the work of the other.

According to the British Association of Counselling (1988: 2) the primary purpose of supervision 'is to address the needs of the client'. Within counselling, Inskipp and Proctor (1993) have described support and supervision as having *formative*, *normative* and also *restorative* qualities. Kadushin (1976) writing from a social work perspective offers a similar definition, employing the terms *managerial*, *educative* and *supportive*. The time spent on each of these functions may not be equal and the focus may be dependent on the context, be that professional or situational. It will also depend on the experience of both the supervisor and supervisee. Woods (2001), writing from a youth work perspective, views support and supervision as offering practitioners a 'space' in busy practice to reflect on their work in order to understand it more clearly. Cottrell and Smith (2003) write that in the field of nursing supervision, greater emphasis is placed on the function of support and less emphasis is placed on the control or surveillance function of supervision. Supervision is a broad enough concept to attract a diversity of purposes which it can be said to address; including care of the client, support for the worker or a management tool for improving performance.

The focus on the support function was highlighted in the study referred to earlier (Reid, 2005) where the importance of 'care of self' was placed above other, at times more powerful discourses related to caring for the client (Reid, 2006). So, despite the many similarities with regard to defining purpose, it is evident that there is a difference in emphasis across sectors as to the central or prime purpose of support and supervision.

Other issues related to a difference in emphasis can be linked to who needs support and supervision and who gives supervision. For some professionals, for example, counsellors registered with the British Association of Counselling and Psychotherapy, supervision is not optional but a requirement to practice. This has the advantage of removing any stigma that may be attached to negative connotations related to 'being in need of supervision', as it is universal. Making it a requirement is not the same however as saying that all practitioners value it or receive adequate or 'good' supervision (Feltham, 2002). Feltham takes this critical perspective further, suggesting that supervision is not always a 'good thing' for the practitioners who receive it, and that it can encourage dependency and a reluctance to accept responsibility.

Youth support work can include dealing with 'issues' ranging from helping young people to make choices about a college course, to coping with bereavement, to dealing with self-harm or substance abuse. Often the issue as first presented may appear relatively straightforward, but other 'problems' emerge once a young person works with a practitioner prepared to listen to their story. For others the issues are multilayered and complex, requiring the help of a number of services and a significant investment of time and resources. Where it is not obligatory, who gets support and supervision should be determined by the context; by the work, by the experience and the stated need of the practitioner. All too often the provision available will be determined by resources. In voluntary organisations in particular, funding for any activity that takes resources away from direct delivery of the service is an ever-present issue.

Who gives support and supervision can also impact on the purpose and effectiveness of the practice. Whilst it may be desirable to keep support and supervision away from the line management of the practitioner, many services combine the role. However, the insertion of management agendas in supervision can lead to subterfuge in the supervisee, as the supervisee hides difficult cases so as not to appear incompetent (Dryden et al., 1995). Distortions of the supervisory relationship can also occur where effective use of resources and meeting 'targets' becomes the focus of supervision. In some cases practitioners have taken a pragmatic view, accepting that scarce resources make it desirable to combine the roles of line manager and supervisor (Turner, 2000).

Structuring a support and supervision relationship

In many ways the supervisory relationship needs to mirror the helper–young person relationship. In other words, a contract is negotiated which works towards a shared agenda. Confidentiality, and its limits, needs to be discussed as the supervisor has a duty to the profession, the supervisee and the young person. A sense of working towards shared goals should be present, with a discussion of strategies and actions for achieving those goals. In short, a structure is required within which the supervisor will use communication skills to facilitate the process. Within counselling and psychotherapy the process for structuring supervision will often resonate with the theoretical perspective of the counselling approach. There are explanatory models, grounded in such theory, from the field of counselling and psychotherapy which can be applied to support and supervision for work with young people. These include the model derived from developmental theory described by Stoltenberg and Delworth (1987) and the Seven Eyed Model of Hawkins and Shohet (1989).

Stoltenberg and Delworth's model takes into consideration the developmental stage of the practitioner and helps the supervisor and supervisee to understand the dynamics at work within the supervisory relationship. The discussion of this should be open to aid self-awareness and progress. The model presents a four-level process of professional development, as follows:

Level one: self-centred

At this level the youth support worker will have a high level of dependence on their supervisor. They may be feeling anxious about their work and be relatively inexperienced, unable to engage in informed reflection. Their view of self-competence can be negative.

Level two: people centred

At this professional development stage, the supervisee oscillates between feeling secure in their work and feeling unsure and, at times, overwhelmed by its complexities. They can be very enthusiastic and/or defensive.

Level three: process centred

The development is such that the youth support worker has increased their level of professional security and is less dependent on the supervisor. The supervisory relationship becomes more equal and greater time is spent on the process of the work, in a more holistic manner.

Level four: process in context

At level four the professional development of the supervisee could be described as autonomous. The level of skills is high and self-awareness, insight, and reflection are evident through the observations made on a wide range of aspects within the work.

The role of the supervisor in using the developmental model is to consider which level their supervisee is working at and to support them to move on – develop – to the next stage.

The Seven-eyed Model of Hawkins and Shohet (1989) identifies aspects of supervision which the authors argue should be present in the supervisory relationship. For the context of youth support work, the seven key areas of focus are:

1. The young person
2. The intervention
3. The relationship
4. The supervisee
5. The parallel process
6. The supervisor
7. The socio-cultural context.

Within the model, a balance needs to be struck in terms of the time spent exploring each of these aspects. So, for example, it would be appropriate to 'set the scene' by describing the (1) young person's history, circumstances and the assessment of the 'case', but supervision needs to focus on the practitioner too:

their practice. The work should move on to consider (2) the intervention. What work has been completed so far? Together, supervisor and supervisee can examine the actual practice and evaluate its effectiveness. This can lead to discovering new techniques and to discussions on how to implement these. It will also be important to explore (3) the relationship with the young person. How does it feel, working with this young person? Are there difficulties that need to be explored? Time spent on this aspect will allow the supervisee to reflect on the quality of the relationship with the young person and to think about where this could be changed, as appropriate.

Moving on, the support function of supervision can be enhanced by time spent on discussing how the supervisee feels about themselves in this work (4). How do they feel and think about their role as a youth support worker – how does this relate to 'their story', both personally and professionally? How do they feel about the supervisory relationship? This focus can provide 'space' to offload some of the difficulties of the work and to celebrate success. The parallel process (5) is described in more detail below, but attention paid to what is happening in the supervisory relationship can provide insight into what might be happening in the work with a young person. And, reflection is two way: the supervisor (6) will be thinking about their supervisory practice as a result of the discussion. How does the supervisor feel about the supervisory work? Are they able to put to one side their own work, other roles they may have within the organisation, are they able to focus on the needs of the supervisee? The final aspect to consider is the socio-cultural context (7). The work, whether we are talking about the work with the young person or the supervisory work, takes place within wider organisational, social and cultural contexts. It is vital that this wider context is considered. At times the impact will be obvious: for example, if the young person has broken the law or if helping services or resources have changed. At other times the impact may be less obvious and may relate to the cultural background of those involved. For example, it may be appropriate to explore the power issues present in a relationship between a white, male worker and a black, female young person, or a black, young worker and white, older supervisor. The aim in considering such issues would be to work towards anti-oppressive practice, both for work with young people and work within the supervisory relationship (Bimrose, 2006).

The above models can be used to inform an integrative approach to support and supervision. An integrative approach will be developmental, but provides a structure which combines both skills and process, placing the supervisee at the centre of the work. Other models, like those described above, can be selected and 'integrated' into the approach according to their suitability for the work 'in-hand'. This allows for flexibility and recognises that a 'one-size-fits-all' approach may not be helpful. In other words, there is a difficulty in applying any singular or fixed model where youth support workers are operating in the circumstances described earlier. That is, part time – often not available in the day time – in diffuse locations and working with and across different helping agencies. The resources available in terms of time, funding and expertise are likely to be limited. Whilst, in themselves, these are not reasons to avoid introducing a system of support and supervision, they are the realities of practice. In addition, many youth support workers will not have received training in a model for structuring helping relationships with 'clients' (e.g. Egan, 2002; Reid and Fielding, 2007). For managers of services in these circumstances, it can be a challenge to develop a system of support and supervision which is 'fit for purpose'. In the next section a range of methods will be considered that can be used for the different contexts described, but first it will be useful to consider two further approaches that are flexible and can be adapted for such work.

Egan's (2002) three-stage model is a useful starting point as the model is relatively simple and reflects, or 'parallels', an approach that many professional helpers use. Egan's model mirrors a natural process of problem resolution from identifying the issue, considering options and planning for change. The simplicity is beguiling and can be overstated: effective use of any approach is dependent on the careful use of counselling skills and the core attitudes of the helper. The latter are summarised by Rogers (1951) as empathy, congruence and unconditional positive regard.

There is a danger here that the proposed integrative model is treated superficially and readers not familiar with a three-stage model of helping are recommended to research this further (Egan, 2002; Reid and Fielding, 2007). The three stages can be summarised as:

1. Helping the client/supervisee to tell the story of 'where they are' at the current time with their 'problem'/or a particular case
2. Helping the client/supervisee explore the options available to resolve the problem/move forward with the case
3. Helping the client/supervisee suggest, evaluate and plan action for the future.

Those familiar with a three-stage model of helping will know that the process is rarely as linear as the three stages above suggest. There is movement back and forward between stages, work can get stuck in a particular stage and it is often the case that several meetings are required before resolution is achieved. Work may not always start in the first stage, and in some cases a successful outcome may never be reached. All that said the model provides a useful framework for work with young people and by extension a scaffold for supervision to support that working relationship. The particular advantage of a three-stage model is that it is rooted in practice as it follows a recognisable pattern of problem solving. Or put in simple terms for the work of the client, practitioner or supervisor, the structure has a beginning, middle and end.

As indicated earlier counselling or if preferred, communication skills, must accompany the structure. Perhaps, as Rogers (1961) concluded, the key skill is active listening. To be able to express feelings, thought and actions in a relationship of trust, enables the supervisee (or young person) to 'hear' the problem and to reflect, often helping them to find their own answers. This then becomes a learning process where the supervisor, by active listening, facilitates that process.

So, the supervisory 'space' can help the youth support worker to evolve new approaches, alongside 'checking' the boundaries of the work and expressing their frustrations and anxieties. The aim, as in work with young people, is for the supervisee to see the problem with greater clarity and, using the insights gained in supervision, to work towards their own conclusions of what might be the 'best' solution. This facilitative approach avoids the danger that the supervisor will view themselves, or be seen by the supervisee, as the expert; there to solve problems and give advice. The type of learning described above is not about teaching the 'right way of doing things', but about engaging in a dialogue. It fulfils the educative function of supervision in a collaborative manner, allowing the supervisee to engage in professional development that becomes genuinely self-motivated. The dialogue however, is more than a cosy chat: it does need a structure, but the structure needs to be flexible.

To achieve this, in addition to active listening, the supervisor needs to ask appropriately phrased and challenging questions. In discussing learning and understanding from a youth work context, Bamber (1998: 42) suggests that supervisors, after the initial contract is agreed, should begin with a number of open questions designed to get the practitioner to consider their internal perceptions within the social context of their practice. For example:

- What did you 'see'?
- What did you feel?
- What did you think?
- What did you do?

The replies will encourage a conversation which can proceed within a framework that enables the practitioner to explore their particular frame of reference (FOR): in other words the ways in which they view the situation from their own knowledge and experience. Through this collaborative process the supervisor and supervisee can then develop the practitioner's understanding, by acknowledging the 'world views' or FOR in use; expose what is hidden or ignored; combine internal and external influences within the context of the work; focus on areas where there are gaps, where new learning will promote professional development, good practice and relate the issues to theoretical knowledge, as appropriate (Bamber, 1998).

This process helps to make visible and clear that which may be hidden and confused. The approach moves beyond internalised notions of what is often referred to as 'professional common sense' and helps to avoid ignoring or underestimating the emotional impact of the work. It assumes learning is part of the process and can help to achieve a balance between the normative, formative and restorative functions of supervision (Inskipp and Proctor, 1993). This later point is important as it is often the case that both supervisor and supervisee will avoid the areas of supervision they may feel less 'at ease' with. For example, a supervisee may avoid discussing an aspect of practice if they feel their work is going to be judged negatively, and a supervisor may (subconsciously) avoid discussing the emotional impact of the work if they feel ill equipped to work at an appropriate psychological depth with their supervisee. Again the concept of boundaries is important here, as in client work; after all supervision is not counselling albeit there are similarities. In addition a collaborative approach ensures engagement in the process is shared and avoids taking a 'deficit' view of the practitioner.

Having outlined an integrative process for structuring a supervisory relationship, and the importance of using active listening and appropriate questioning skills, the next section of the chapter will move on and consider methods for implementing support and supervision. But first, a cautionary word on the recommendation for integrative practice. The aim is not to replace existing theories, models and methods with a 'new' singular approach. Clearly this would work against the desire for integration which celebrates the benefits derived from diverse approaches. Perhaps, rather than think of integration as a blend which becomes a singular approach, it is more fruitful to think about the mix as ideas that can exist together: a confluence rather than a merger.

Methods: traditional and alternative

Support and supervision is a complex practice and opinions about the 'best' method of implementing it are not straightforward. What follows is therefore partial, but offered as an overview of a range of methods from those that are well established, to those that can be viewed as alternative.

One-to-one supervision is common in many helping services. As part of the supervisory contract, time, frequency, venue, privacy and confidentiality (and its limits) will be discussed. The method has the potential to ensure that the supervisee's agenda is addressed. However, as touched on earlier, the lone supervisee may be reluctant to expose weaknesses if these are viewed as failures or where competence is an issue. In addition, unless an external supervisor is used, the supervisor cannot remain 'outside' the needs of the organisation or the service targets that constrain the work of both supervisor and practitioner. This aspect is not limited to line managers who are also supervisors, although it is perhaps more apparent. By design, one-to-one supervision gives a greater degree of confidentiality than group supervision, but where youth support workers are working in public services, absolute confidentiality cannot be guaranteed.

The other established approach is group supervision, facilitated by a supervisor, who may be a peer or someone with particular expertise, or by the group sharing the task of co-ordinator. Group supervision that is led by a specialist has the advantage of economies of scale, in that a group of practitioners can be 'supervised'. This may result in a limited opportunity to discuss issues or cases of immediate or particular interest to the individual, which may reduce the perceived value of the method. Despite this, group supervision provides an opportunity to learn from the experience of a number of practitioners, although it may be the more talkative or extrovert practitioner that monopolises the time. Using an experienced supervisor to facilitate group supervision can help to avoid this occurring. Then again, peer group supervision without a specialist supervisor or 'manager' can be viewed as less threatening for it can lead to possibilities for the individual to engage more comfortably in restorative supervision.

Within one-to-one and group support and supervision it is possible to vary the approach by incorporating creative methods for exploring issues brought to the process. More creative approaches require an element of risk-taking and are dependent on trust within the relationship, but are worth exploring. For example, role play and the use of a dramatic space (i.e. not being fixed to a 'seated' discussion); using diagrams, drawings or graffiti, incorporating the use of colour for expressing aspects of the problem, or perhaps using artefacts to represent the 'players' in a situation, for example, through differently shaped pebbles or plastic building blocks.

Where access to supervision is difficult, developing a system 'at a distance' can be a viable option, through using the telephone or, where available, video-conferencing. Other electronic means are also a possibility via email, and other 'on-line' access. Some practitioners find a reflective journal is helpful for focusing on aspects of their practice in supervision and this method can be applied 'at a distance'. These alternative solutions should not of course be viewed as 'quick fix' and 'cheap' solutions and require the same careful planning and consultation that any process should involve. There are times when support and supervision is required instantaneously, but for many the option of walking down the corridor and consulting a colleague is not available. In these circumstances a 'phone call or email may suffice, but for structured support and supervision to take place 'at a distance' a range of methods should be considered.

Another alternative would be to adopt meaningful forms of self-supervision (Morrissette, 2002). Self-supervision does recognise that the experienced practitioner can engage in creative reflection on their work, although for those who already work in 'isolated' circumstances this may accentuate their isolation. Where the opportunities to engage in support and supervision are infrequent, for whatever reason, it is helpful to consider a mix of methods and to negotiate with individuals what will best fit their needs, alongside the needs and resources of the organisation. At times supervision may not be the best way of supporting the practitioner: a short course or consultation with an expert in a particular area of knowledge, for example, on eating disorders or substance abuse, may be more effective.

Conclusion

This chapter has suggested a structure for support and supervision for work with young people and has outlined a range of methods. The aim is of course for support and supervision to be beneficial – 'good' – for all involved: the organisation, the supervisor, the youth support worker and the client. As services for young people develop and change in response to government policy, it will be important to negotiate with those on the 'front line', which model and what methods are best suited to their needs and circumstances. Any model put into place needs to navigate the difficult path between structure on the one side and flexibility on the other: both aspects are important for effective support and supervision to take place.

References

Bamber, J. (1998) 'Learning, understanding and the development of critical practice', *Youth and Policy*, 60: 30–45.

Bimrose, J. (2006) 'Multicultural issues in support and supervision', in Reid, H.L. and Westergaard, J. (eds) *Providing Support and Supervision: An Introduction for Professionals Working with Young People*. Oxon: Routledge.

Bradley, L.J. and Kottler, J.A. (2001) 'Overview of counselling supervision', in Bradley, L.J. and Ladany, N. (eds) *Counselor Supervision: Principles, Process and Practice*. Philadelphia: Brunner-Routledge.

British Association of Counselling (1988) *Code of Ethics And Practice For The Supervision Of Counsellors*. Rugby: BAC.

Cottrell, S. and Smith, G. (2003) *The Development of Models of Nursing Supervision in the UK*, *http://www.clinical-supervision.com/developmentofclinicalsupervision* (accessed 10 April 2003).

Department for Education and Skills (2004) *Every Child Matters: Next Steps*. Nottingham: DfES.

Department for Education and Skills (2005) *Youth Matters*. Norwich, UK: Her Majesty's Stationery Office.

Dryden, W., Horton, I. and Mearns, D. (1995) *Issues in Professional Counsellor Training*. London: Cassell.

Egan, G. (2002) *The Skilled Helper: A Problem-management and Opportunity-development Approach to Helping*, 7th edn. Pacific Grove: Brooks/Cole.

Feltham, C. (2002) 'Supervision: A Surveillance Culture?,' *Counselling and Psychotherapy Journal*. February: 26–27.

Hawkins, P. and Shohet, R. (1989) *Supervision in the Helping Professions*, Milton Keynes, Bucks: OU Press.

Inskipp, F. and Proctor, B. (1993) *The Art, Craft And Tasks Of Counselling Supervision, Part 1. Making The Most Of Supervisors*. Twickenham: Cascade Publications.

Kadushin, A. (1976) *Supervision in Social Work*. New York: Columbia University Press.

Morrissette, P. J. (2002) *Self-Supervision: A Primer for Counselors and Helping Professionals*. New York: Brunner-Routledge.

Reid, H.L. (2004) 'Jiminy Cricket on my shoulder: professional common sense and formal supervision as routes to ethical watchfulness for personal advisers', in Reid, H.L. and Bimrose, J. (eds) *Constructing the Future: Reflection on Practice*. Stourbridge: Institute of Career Guidance.

Reid, H.L. (2005) 'What advisers want from support and supervision: "pit-head time to wash off the dust of their labours"', *Career Guidance Today*, 13(1), Stourbridge, UK: Institute of Career Guidance.

Reid, H.L. (2006) 'A cautionary note on support and supervision', in Reid, H.L. and Westergaard, J. (eds) *Providing Support and Supervision: An Introduction for Professionals Working with Young People*. Oxon: Routledge.

Reid, H.L. and Fielding, A.J. (2007) *Proving Support to Young People: A Guide to Interviewing in Helping Relationships*. Oxon: Routledge (in press).

Rogers, C. R. (1951) *Client Centred Therapy*. Boston: Houghton Mifflin.

Rogers, C.R. (1961) *On Becoming a Person*. Boston: Houghton Mifflin.

Social Exclusion Unit (1999) *Bridging The Gap: New Opportunities for 16–18-Year-Olds Not in Education, Employment or Training*. London: Stationery Office.

Stoltenberg, C.D. and Delworth, U. (1987) *Supervising Counsellors and Therapists*. San Francisco: Jossey Bass.

Turner, B. (2000) 'Supervision and mentoring in child and family social work: the role of the first-line manager in the implementation of the post-qualifying framework', *Social Work Education*, 19(3): 231–240.

Woods, J. (2001) 'Supervision from an informal education/youth work perspective', in A. Edwards (ed.), *Supporting Personal Advisers in Connexions: Perspectives on Supervision and Mentoring from Allied Professions*. Occasional Papers Canterbury: Canterbury Christ Church University College.

PART 4

Change

Work with young people is taking place in the context of a rapidly changing policy environment. This presents all of us working with young people, including leaders and managers, with a series of challenges. Potentially, it offers the opportunity to respond to young people's needs and interests in new and exciting ways. Less positively, it can feel as if there is a constant pressure to respond to agendas and demands outside of our control, with little time to reflect on the implications and outcomes of one set of change before the next begins. In this section we explore some of the issues that working with and seeking to manage change present for practitioners and leaders of work with young people. We have selected three chapters that we hope offer ideas and perspectives that will help you to retain some ability to shape and influence change, rather than feeling totally overwhelmed and disempowered by the process.

In Chapter 13 entitled 'Managing Change', Mike Hudson analyses change from the perspective of third-sector organisations, though the approach he takes is equally useful for practitioners leading work with young people in other organisational contexts. He looks at the range of factors that create pressures for 'more frequent, more rapid and better managed change' and explores some of the principles and practices of effective change management. He also considers the key role of 'change leaders' in driving and supporting organisational change and the importance of combining leading with listening.

You might not be working in a context where you have a formal position as a 'leader' in an organisational hierarchy. Nevertheless, as Neil Thompson's chapter 'Influencing Skills' demonstrates, there are other ways in which you can influence change and the ideas of those around you. The chapter explores some of the skills involved in trying to influence others, and highlights a number of strategies for maximising the effectiveness of how we engage with other people in our work. He draws a clear distinction between influencing and manipulating, which he views as unethical. Instead he encourages us to make positive connections with others, to be prepared to listen and empathise with perspectives different to our own, and to work wherever possible to create 'win–win 'situations and solutions.

The chapter by Bryan Merton, Rob Hunter and Harriet Gore, 'Getting Better All the Time', provides a case study of how one local authority youth service planned, led and managed change in order to respond more effectively to the increasing demands placed upon it. Issues highlighted in the case study include the importance of good communication across different levels of the organisation, the importance of building a 'guiding coalition' of others who will support change; the need to establish clear expectations and support staff, including through training; and perhaps most important of all from their perspective, the importance of effective leadership in guiding and supporting the process of change.

Managing change

Mike Hudson

Managing change is an essential skill

Third-sector organizations have had to respond to an increasingly turbulent and competitive external environment in recent years. Rising expectations of users, funders, staff and the public have all contributed to the need for more frequent, more rapid and better managed change:

- Users expect to be more closely involved in organizations providing services than they were in the past.
- Staff and volunteers expect to get learning opportunities as part of their compensation for working with the organization.
- Funders expect to give fewer handouts for loosely defined purposes and more contracts with tightly specified performance requirements.
- The public expects good governance, low overhead costs and high standards of probity.
- Developments in technology are having an increasingly significant impact.
- Partnerships and coalitions with other organizations are presenting new ways of working.

Taken together, these mean that organizations face a significant 'change management' agenda, and all the evidence suggests that these pressures are all likely to grow in coming years.

This is an edited version of material first published as Chapter 10 in Hudson, M., *Managing without Profit: The Art of Managing Third Sector Organizations*. London: Directory of Social Change.

The principles of change management can be used to underpin the successful implementation of a wider range of tools and techniques for making an organization more effective. Examples include people development programmes (such as Investors in People or the introduction of management competencies), quality standards initiatives (such as the Excellence Model), customer care projects, cost-reduction programmes or process redesign projects.

Change management has to be led by a 'change leader'; this is the person responsible for managing the change initiative. Change leaders have to drive change with enthusiasm and commitment in order to maximize the probability of success.

This chapter sets out the principles and practices of effective change management. It starts with a short section on the theory of organization culture, because understanding organization culture is an essential prerequisite to a successful change programme. Insights into culture help managers to identify which levers of change will have the greatest impact, to understand which communication methods will be most effective and to ensure that changes are fully embedded into culture.

The chapter then describes:

- The fundamental concepts of change management
- Some characteristics of change processes
- The eight critical stages of a major change initiative
- The essential skills of successful change leaders.

Introduction to organization culture

Culture has been described in many ways, including:

- The way we do things around here
- The way we think about things around here
- The commonly held and relatively stable beliefs, attitudes and values that exist within an organization.

Three levels of organization culture

Culture is best understood by considering the three different levels at which it is expressed. At the most superficial level, there are the **visible representations** of an organization's culture – its buildings, the routine procedures of meetings, the management structure and the language that people use. Visit a well established housing association with its offices in the business park, and one cannot help but notice the smart photographs of its properties on the wall, the tidy reception area and the sense of calm organization. Contrast this with a campaigning organization with its offices in a dilapidated property in a run-down area of town, newspapers piled high waiting to be clipped, desks cramped close together, walls piled to the ceiling with T-shirts, pamphlets and posters, and the sense of pressure and urgency. Two extreme cases, perhaps, but they illustrate the different physical manifestations of culture.

At the second level of culture, there are common patterns of **group behaviour**. This level is about how people act and react in various circumstances. Organizations work in subtly different ways: decision-making processes are different, respect for different groups varies, and the processes that are important and those that are disregarded are different. Examples of group behaviour include:

- How the organization treats users
- How trustees behave towards staff
- How the senior management team behave towards staff
- How staff treat each other.

Once behaviour patterns have been established, they strongly influence people who join the organization. New managers and trustees watch how people conduct themselves and adjust their own behaviour accordingly. As a result, the way the organization works becomes embedded in their unconscious behaviour patterns.

At the third and most fundamental level, there are the **underlying beliefs** held by the staff, trustees and members of the organization. These are assumptions that are taken for granted. They are the unconscious values that inform people's behaviour. For example:

- Social welfare providers may have underlying beliefs about respecting service users
- Managers may have underlying beliefs about the costs and effectiveness of services provided
- Campaigners may have underlying beliefs about social policy.

The underlying beliefs of the different groups of people and different departments will vary within an organization, but there are also common values that exist across the whole organization. These values are virtually invisible, which is why it is so difficult to change them. Their power in determining how an organization works should not, however, be underestimated.

Embedding changes into an organization's culture requires action at all three levels. The easiest level is the visible representational one – but this also has the least long-term effect. The most difficult level to change is that containing the underlying beliefs. When these are altered, change becomes part of the unconsciously accepted culture of the organization.

Characteristics of culture

The concept of culture can be understood more thoroughly by considering some of its characteristics:

1. **It is learned**. It results both from people's experiences before they joined the organization and from the influences of the organization itself.
2. **It is determined by the organization's history**. It is defined by decisions people have taken in the past, particularly those taken by significant individuals such as the founder.
3. **It is partly subconscious**. Over time, assumptions develop and become implicit influences on people's behaviour. These beliefs and assumptions affect the way people think about things.
4. **It is heterogeneous**. Different parts of an organization have different cultures. A commonly observed difference is that between staff in the headquarters of an organization, who may be concerned with public profile, fund-raising, lobbying and the inevitable politics of large organizations, and people in the local, branches, who may be more concerned with service delivery and valuing volunteers.

Change management concepts

This section:

- Defines change management
- Describes different types of change
- Explains the art of combining leading and listening.

The nature of change management

The ideas that underpin change management are vitally important to managers who wish to introduce significant change into their organization.

Organizations are littered with examples of changes that did not produce the desired results. Indeed, much of the cynicism that managers encounter when they wish to make changes results from the failure of previous initiatives to have a significant impact. Introducing change is a subtle and sensitive process and a misjudgement in any of the stages of change can easily result in good proposals being consigned to the pile of failed management initiatives.

Change management is **the skill of catalyzing significant improvements in the performance of organizations**. It is a set of skills that managers need to apply in order to achieve the greatest results for their efforts.

Change management **involves people from many parts** of the organization. The actions usually cut across departments and may involve users, branches and board members.

Change management is a **combination of substance and process**. It is about developing a clear view of the improvements that are needed and integrating this with a sequence of activities for achieving the change. It combines the head (the vision and the analysis) with the heart (the people and their emotions).

At a more fundamental level, change management is about **'re-framing' a situation** so that people see their circumstances in a different way. It is about creating a new mental model or 'paradigm' that enables people to think and act in ways that will help the organization achieve its objectives more effectively.

There is **no one approach** that can be applied to all change situations. While this chapter aims to help managers to plan and implement major changes by setting down some principles and a general approach, there is no avoiding the harsh reality that good judgements at each stage of a change process are critical to success. It is impossible to predict how the change process will evolve – something will always go awry in a complex set of changes.

Flexibility is therefore critical. Plans have to be prepared, communication methods agreed and timetables established. But, particularly in large-scale change, effective managers are always ready to make adjustments and sometimes to take a different approach in order to achieve the desired objective.

Types of organizational change

Three types of organizational change have been defined (by L. Ackerman, 1984):

- **Developmental change** – concerned with the improvement of current activities or ways of working (for example, by doing more or doing it better).

- **Transitional change** – concerned with replacing current activities or ways of working with new ones (for example, introducing new services or systems).
- **Transformational change** – concerned with changing beliefs and awareness about what is possible, requiring a leap of faith (for example, redefining the mission or adapting an entirely new strategy).

Transitional change may also involve an element of developmental change, and transformational change may involve both the other types.

Two particular types of transitional change that are common in the third sector are project management and programme management. The term 'project management' is often used to describe the planning and implementation of specific pieces of work with well-defined boundaries. Programme management is concerned with the management of a number of projects simultaneously. The principles of change management can be applied to both project and programme management. However, the stages of change are likely to be much more compressed, and some will be done more informally. Nevertheless, the ideas that underpin transitional and transformational change provide a rigorous basis for managing projects and programmes.

The key point for aspiring change leaders is to determine the type of change they are embarking upon, since the complexity and resource requirements grow exponentially from developmental to transformational change. This chapter focuses on transitional and transformational change.

Combining leading and listening

Change management has two historical roots. One root was a 'top down' approach to change, inspired by a vision, pushed by senior management and driven energetically through the organization with plans, briefings and an element of razzmatazz. This approach tended to be strong on analysis and aimed to achieve a predetermined objective. The other root was a 'bottom up' approach in which leaders facilitated change, managers helped their staff to use skills and experience that were already embedded in the organization, and the development of people was seen as the key to successful change. In this approach, sometimes called 'organization development', change happened in incremental steps.

Modern views of change management stress the need to adopt both approaches simultaneously. The most effective change happens when there is a combination of:

Leading	Listening
• a clear view of the future	• a desire to build on the best of the past
• strong leadership	• strong commitment to listen to the concerns of people at all levels of the organization
• a focus on action	• time for reflection
• investment in training	• commitment to learning
• a plan with targets and timetables	• freedom to act within broad guidelines

This combination is particularly important because trustees, managers and volunteers place a very high value on the meaning of their work to them personally. People are closely attached to their work because one of their fundamental motivations is to improve an aspect of the world in which they live. Since change management is about altering an aspect of people's work, it can threaten to take away some of the value of that work to those people. It may therefore be perceived as the organization placing less value on that person, department, region or branch.

These concerns are expressed in many different ways. Sometimes they are expressed in terms of the implications for service users of the proposed changes. Sometimes the objections are practical and sometimes they are philosophical. They are seldom expressed in terms of people's anxieties about how the organization is perceived to be placing a lower value on some people's work. In these circumstances it is difficult to untangle people's concerns about the value of their work from legitimate views that they are expressing about the proposed changes.

If these concerns are not listened to, or if their underlying meaning is not understood, there is a danger that change will be opposed. Such opposition may be voiced through the organization's formal decision-making processes, but it may also arise through the powerful networks of informal communications that determine how any change initiative is viewed in the organization. Successful change managers go out of their way to meet concerns head-on and to understand what people have to gain and to lose from the proposals.

Broadly speaking, people affected by a change initiative can be divided into those who are committed to change, those who are uncommitted and see it neither as an opportunity nor as a threat, and those who are likely to oppose change. The key group to win over is that of the uncommitted, who may well be the silent majority. They need to be motivated by the proposed changes, and their concerns about the consequences need to be given particular attention.

The stages of a change management initiative

The success of transitional and transformational change is highly dependent on following a series of stages, and not falling into the trap of beginning a new stage prematurely. This section sets out eight essential stages that need to be followed in order to implement change successfully. It draws on the experience of third-sector organizations and the thinking of a number of people who have written about change, including Professor John Kotter of Harvard Business School.

Reduced to the core, these stages are:

1. To **clarify the scope and scale** of the proposed change initiative.
2. To **establish a change team** with the power and expertise needed to ensure the change will succeed.
3. To **prepare a diagnosis of the problem** so people can understand why change is needed.
4. To **build strong commitment** to the need for the change and listen to people's concerns.
5. To **develop a motivating vision** for what the change will achieve.
6. To **plan and communicate** extensively about the proposed change.
7. To **implement by empowering** people to take the required actions.
8. To **incorporate change** into the culture of the organization.

The key to successfully managing change is to start the stages in order and not be tempted to jump on to a new stage before the preceding stage is substantially completed. The change leader and members of the change team need to be thinking ahead about subsequent stages, and indeed these thoughts may influence their approach to a current stage. However, ensuing stages should not be rolled out more widely into the organization until people have understood and internalized previous stages.

Stage 1. Clarify the scope and scale of the proposed initiative

Before deciding to proceed with a change initiative, critical judgements need to be made about its scope (what its boundaries will be) and its scale (how significant it will be).

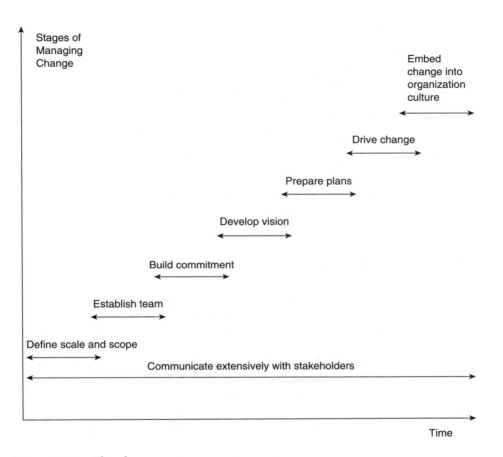

Stages of
Managing
Change

Embed
change into
organization
culture
←——————→

Drive change
←————————→

Prepare plans
←—————→

Develop vision
←—————→

Build commitment
←———→

Establish team
←———→

Define scale and scope
←————→

Communicate extensively with stakeholders
←——————————————————————————→

Time

Figure 13.1   The change management process

Scope: It is all too easy for a change initiative to stray into many different areas that seem to be connected to the issue, leading to loss of the sharp focus required for success. Clear boundaries need to be established around levels of the organization to which the initiative applies, the departments or divisions covered and the issues that should and should not be considered. Connections with other change initiatives should also be identified at this point and different change initiatives should be dovetailed to ensure that they are properly integrated by management before they are presented to the organization. A common mistake is to present a number of change initiatives to the organization in ways that appear to other people to be unconnected.

Scale: Change initiatives need two resources, staff time and budget; staff time is usually the hardest to obtain in the required quantities. Although it is difficult to make accurate estimates before plans for the initiative have been agreed in detail, the scale can be clarified by considering:

- Who will be involved?
- How much of each person's time is required to ensure that the initiative will be a great success?
- What will the key individuals *not* do to free up the required time?

In the third sector, one of the most common problems is that workloads of the key people can spiral out of control so that change initiatives lose all their momentum. For change to succeed, it is critical to keep significant amounts of time free to cope with the unexpected.

Stage 2. Establish the change team

All change management initiatives require a team to ensure that many perspectives can be considered, to give the initiative champions in different parts of the organization, to improve the quality of decision-making and to take effective action.

The team needs a leader who cares about the issue and has the skills and authority to deliver a successful result.

Four types of team can be considered:

- A **line management team** – consisting of the managers responsible for the areas where the change is happening.
- A **cross-cutting team** – consisting of managers from the different parts of the organization that will be affected by the initiative.
- A **representative team** – consisting of carefully selected representatives from those levels and parts of the organization that have a stake in the initiative (including trustees, front-line staff, regions, branches and volunteers). This is sometimes called a 'diagonal' or 'slice' team.
- A **mixed team** – consisting of a combination of the above.

The critical tests are whether the team has sufficient:

- **Expertise to do the job**. The specialist and managerial skills required to review the problems and implement solutions should all be represented.
- **Power to drive through the changes**. People with the power to make the change happen and those with the power to block it should all be

represented. This may include board members, staff association officials, branch members, user representatives and individuals who are significant opinion-formers who may not hold any formal positions of power.

- **Connections to listen to the views of everyone affected**. The tentacles of the team should reach out to all parts of the organization that will be affected by the changes.

When change is transitional, the chief executive should create the team. This confers immediate authority on the initiative – though, as time passes, the team will have to earn their authority from their work and their actions. When it is transformational, the chief executive will almost certainly be the team leader.

The team leader should estimate the time that will be required from each team member from the start so that everyone realizes the level of commitment that is likely to be required. The team leader will then need to agree people's availability with their managers. Being explicit about the time required and reducing team members' other commitments ensures that they can allocate sufficient time to make a success of the initiative.

The team is the core of people who champion the initiative. Their influence will need to spread out across the organization as the initiative gains momentum. In particular, they will need to listen to, involve and influence the key stakeholders as the change process gets underway. These key stakeholders will in turn have to do the same with an ever-widening group of people.

Stage 3. Prepare a diagnosis of the problem

The first task of the change team is to develop a diagnosis of the situation. This may involve an analysis of the issues that led to the creation of the team and the development of a shared understanding of the underlying causes of the problem.

Start by thinking through how the diagnosis should be prepared. Topics to consider include:

- The issues to be investigated
- The division of the issues into manageable chunks of work
- Responsibilities of individuals and teams preparing parts of the diagnosis
- The method of bringing elements of the diagnosis into an overview
- The timescale for the work
- The process for agreeing the diagnosis.

For a comparatively minor change initiative, members of the change team may do all the work. In larger initiatives, sub-groups may be needed to do specific jobs and feed their work into the change team. Involving people across the organization in gathering data helps to build commitment to the change process. Setting up task groups to gather information on specific issues, each of which could be led by a member of the change team, is one way of gaining support. External and internal sources of information will be needed to review the current situation, identify the key issues and summarize the reasons why change is required.

External information ensures that the case for change is based on the perceptions of people who see the organization from outside. These external views and comparisons are valuable, even when the change initiative is mainly about internal matters, because they bring new perspectives which can catalyse change.

User information is particularly valuable because it helps to challenge any complacency that may have developed about the quality of the services provided. With appropriate support, and guarantees about confidentiality, information can be gathered from virtually everyone who receives services from third-sector organizations. People with learning difficulties contributed to Mencap's strategic review; people attending counselling with RELATE provided feedback at specified times after the counselling was completed; and drug misusers gave feedback on the use of illegal substances.

Other sources of information include funders, members, visitors, other organizations in the same field, suppliers, prominent people who know the organization, past employees, trustees, patrons and people from the media, and others (such as elected representatives who know the organization).

Internal information is equally important in building the case for change. Gathering people's views – as well as facts and figures – has the added advantage of involving people in the initiative and listening to their opinions. People need to be given time to raise their concerns about the issue and to explain previous decisions that led to the current situation. This ensures that people feel fully involved in the change process.

When pulling new information together, task groups and the change leader should go to great lengths to **be respectful of the past**. Acknowledging the commitment people have given to improving the organization in the past ensures that their previous work is appreciated and is not unintentionally devalued.

The diagnosis stage usually involves the preparation of a summary document that clarifies the many issues raised. It is the first point at which people should be clear about why change is needed and how the process will proceed. The stage can end by confirming the original thoughts on the nature and extent of the problem. Alternatively, it can end by redefining the problem. In either case, the diagnosis will clarify the issues and provide the evidence needed to convince people of the need for change. The stage can also end by concluding that no change is necessary or that the costs and upheaval of change outweigh the anticipated benefits.

Whichever way it ends decisions will be required from the sponsor of the change about how to proceed.

Stage 4. Build commitment to change

Change initiatives are most successful when a critical mass of the people involved has a deep understanding of the need for the changes and the benefits that will be gained. The best way to achieve this understanding is to build a **robust case for change**.

Change is easiest when there really is external pressure for change: a financial crisis, loss of public confidence, demonstrably poor performance or a succession of missed opportunities. However, well managed organizations anticipate change. They see new opportunities or issues on the horizon and introduce change in anticipation of their arrival. Such changes require stronger and even more robust cases to be made.

The case for change needs to **take account of both the facts and the emotions** of the situation. Change therefore requires hard information on the situation which can be analysed and summarized for presentation to key stakeholders. It should diagnose the problem and pinpoint what needs to change, without making proposals for the actual changes required. The case for change also requires a deep understanding of people's concerns about the current state of affairs and their future aspirations, both for the organization and for themselves. By taking these on board, the change team will earn the support and respect of the people who may be most affected by the change process.

One way of ensuring that all the appropriate groups are considered is to list key stakeholder groups and, for each, to identify:

- Their major concerns
- The key contribution they need to make
- The obstacles they might present
- The actions required to win their support.

The summary case for change should be limited to the arguments for change. Although proposals may be beginning to emerge, do not be tempted to put them forward at this stage; that would be premature and would risk generating opposition about proposals before the reasons for change had been accepted.

Stage 5. Develop and communicate the change vision

Change initiatives need a vision that describes the desired improvements. The change vision should state as succinctly as possible the ultimate objectives of the initiative. It should describe **desired objectives and outcomes** and, where possible, these should be quantified.

The vision should be **motivating**. It should inspire people to support the project by connecting its aim with the overall mission of the organization. People should be able to see how the initiative will help the organization to achieve its overall objectives more effectively.

A clear and powerful vision provides a solid foundation for a change initiative. It should help to identify both appropriate and inappropriate actions of the people who will be involved in the initiative. This also enables task groups and other people to work with a degree of autonomy, and it should result in easier decision-making. It is therefore worth taking time to get the vision right.

The acid test of clarity is whether team members can describe the purpose and vision of the change initiative to people inside and outside the organization in a few sentences.

When it is reasonably well developed, the change team can sound out key stakeholders both to get them to 'buy in' to the vision and the change process and further to improve the vision itself.

The case for change and the vision should be communicated to stakeholders in the change initiative and more widely through the organization. A wide variety of means should be used to ensure that people get the messages by different methods and at different times. Workshops and briefing sessions are likely to be more powerful than written communications, which tend to get swamped in the morass of internal communications circulating in any organization. Events also have the advantage of allowing two-way communication, so people can raise their concerns and alert the change team to potential obstacles to change.

Effective change leaders do not expect to get things right first time, so both the case for change and the vision should go out as drafts to enable people to improve and buy into them before they are finalized.

Stage 6. Plan the changes

It is tempting to start a change initiative by thinking about solutions and preparing detailed proposals for change. This is a mistake. Unless the preceding stages have been completed, proposals are likely to land on unfertile ground. However, once the preparatory steps have been concluded, a plan is an essential element of any change initiative.

The plan needs to address both the substance of the change and the process for implementing it. The substance may include:

- **Models** – of different ways of working in the future.
- **Options** – setting out alternative solutions to the issues.
- **Proposals** – describing what the changes will be.

The process part of the plan needs to address:

- **Practical issues**: what will happen, in what order.
- **People and group issues**: who will do things, who needs to be consulted, and how activities will be co-ordinated.
- **Timetable issues**: deadlines, milestones and fitting in with existing decision-making processes.

A critical judgement at this point is the **division of the work into manageable pieces** that can be completed within available resources and the available time. This provides another opportunity to involve people through task groups. The change team should identify each of the tasks that need to be undertaken and estimate the number of days required to complete the task and the time it will take to complete the change. When this has been done, tough decisions may have to be made either to cut out some activities or to increase the resources available to the team.

This is the stage when pilots of possible ways forward may be appropriate. This allows managers to discover whether proposals will really work. Practical experience helps to improve the proposed solutions and, most critically, it helps to build commitment to the proposals. Pilots may delay organization-wide implementation, but they ensure that when change is rolled out it is rooted in practical experience and has champions who have real credibility.

This stage often ends with the documentation of a plan and formal decisions to proceed on the proposals set out in the plan. It is the second point in the process when everyone should be clear about what will happen, why it will happen, and when it will happen.

Stage 7. Implementing change

When all the previous stages have been meticulously followed, implementation can begin. A key role for the change leader, supported by the team, is to keep track of progress. This means anticipating deadlines and chasing people before it is too late to take remedial action.

The leader and the team also need to keep their ears close to the ground as work progresses, to enable them to identify issues as they arise and deal with them before they become an impediment to the change programme. The change team should meet regularly to review progress and take remedial action when problems begin to emerge.

Prioritize quick wins

Change initiatives need to demonstrate results in order to maintain enthusiasm and momentum. If people work for months without seeing significant results, the whole project begins to lose credibility. People become available for meetings less often, will put in less effort and will focus on other matters.

Examples of quick wins include:

- A successful pilot for a new way of working
- A new service up and running
- A marked improvement in quality in one area
- A new performance report that captures information of the type required to work in new ways
- An old or disliked process or set of forms being scrapped.

Any initiative should aim to achieve a quick win within six months of the start; a smaller initiative should expect a quick win sooner than that. Once achieved, a quick win provides an ideal opportunity to communicate the success to all stakeholders and give the initiative new momentum.

Pilot extensively

The consequences of change are inevitably difficult to predict; it therefore makes sense to pilot anything that can be tested on a small scale before rolling out the proposals more widely. Opportunities for piloting might include:

- Piloting a new service in one area
- Testing a new process with a group of people who are keen to pursue the idea
- Trialling user-involvement initiatives in one part of the organization
- Reorganizing one part of a department to see if the new arrangements produce the desired results.

The disadvantage of piloting is that it may delay final implementation. However, the advantages are huge. Unanticipated problems can be identified and corrected at low cost and with less effort. Proposals can be further developed and refined with the benefit of practical experience. If the pilots begin to show signs of success, commitment to the proposed changes will grow in other parts of the organization as people not involved in the pilot come to see the positive results.

Supporting implementation

Change leaders can take a number of actions to support implementation:

- **Offer training**. A mini skills audit to determine whether individuals or groups of people have training needs may shed light on the requirement for training.
- **Adjust people's personal objectives and performance review targets**. A review of personal objectives will help to assimilate change at all levels of the organization.
- **Appoint new staff**. Making one or two key appointments can significantly increase the speed of change and implant new beliefs into the organization culture.
- **Encourage consistency**. Change leaders need to ask people to identify inconsistencies at the earliest opportunity and then attend to them before they become irritations.
- **Hold celebrations**. Change is always hard, so every opportunity should be taken to record progress with activities and events that mark progress.
- **Promote people who implement the initiative**. In the long term, promotions for people who embody the new behaviour and methods of working will do more to ensure long-term success of the change initiative than many other measures.

When implementation runs into problems, it is often because either a misjudgement was made at an earlier stage about the scale or scope of the initiative, a stage was carried out only superficially or one was completely missed out. In these circumstances, it may be necessary to go back a stage rather than pressing on against the odds.

Stage 8. Incorporate changes into the organization's culture

Ideally, change leaders want their initiatives to be long-lasting. Changes are irreversible only when they become fully embedded in the organization's culture.

Changing culture is undoubtedly the hardest part of change management; it takes the greatest time and requires the most consistent effort. Experience suggests that culture change happens as a consequence of actions and the results of change programmes, rather than as a consequence of attempts to change the culture directly.

Change leaders should recognize that the timescales over which culture change happens are long – usually measured in years rather than months. However, effective change leaders do speed up the process of change by judicious application of the most appropriate actions at the most appropriate times.

Ways of embedding changes into the different levels of an organization's culture include:

- Changing visible representations of culture:
  - develop a new performance report
  - introduce a new corporate image
  - rename the organization
  - reorganize office space
  - move to new offices.

- Changing behavioural norms:
  - create new management processes
  - reorganize the meeting's structure
  - develop new meeting agendas
  - improve or create new internal communication mechanisms
  - establish user groups to strengthen 'customer' orientation
  - hold joint board/management meetings to create a new strategy
  - celebrate specific achievements with a memorable event.

- Changing underlying beliefs:
  - recruit people who hold the new beliefs
  - promote people who show commitment to the new ways of working
  - demonstrate how new practices are improving results.

Ups and downs of change

Presenting major change as a sequence of eight stages makes the process appear as a sequence of events that always move forward. In practice, organizations going through significant change tend to take two steps forward, followed by one step back.

The critical point for the change leader is to anticipate that there will be ups and downs in the process and that it is difficult to predict when a down will come and what will cause it. Experienced change leaders are not disheartened. They know there will he setbacks, but they also have the confidence and commitment to adjust the process and ensure that they do not lose sight of the overall objective.

Managing change is an art.

The task of the change leader has been succinctly summarized as: 'effective leadership of change involves bringing together apparently contradictory qualities. Successful leaders shape the future *and* they adapt to the world as it is. They are clear about what they want to change *and* they are responsive to others' views and concerns. They are passionate about the direction in which they want the organization to go *and* they understand and value the current reality of the organization, why it has been successful and what its people are good at. They lead *and* they learn' (*Leaning into the Future*, Binney and Williams, 1995).

References

Ackerman, L. (1984) 'The flow state: a new view of organisations and managing', in J. Adams (ed.) *Transforming Work*. Alexandria, VA: Miles River Press.

Binney, G. and Williams, C. (1995) *Leaning into the Future: Changing the Way People Change Organisations*. London: Nicholas Brealey.

Influencing skills

Neil Thompson

Introduction

When we communicate with one another, it is, of course, not simply a matter of people conveying information to each other. What also happens is that people seek to influence each other – this is a common aspect of day-to-day interactions. This may be at a very simple level. For example, if we want someone to smile, we smile at them first. It may not always work, but it none the less remains the case that we are daily trying to influence the behaviour of others. And, of course, other people are seeking to influence us, to persuade us to do what they want us to do or to fit in with their plans. An example of this would be when someone reminds us of a deadline for a particular piece of work to be completed. Of course, they are not simply doing us a favour in reminding us, they are also trying to make sure that we meet that deadline. Influencing skills are basic components of working life (and, of course, of our private lives – interactions based on influencing do not end when the working day does!).

When it comes to interaction skills, then, we should bear in mind just how important influencing skills are in helping us achieve our objectives and make progress. Without them we would really struggle to get anywhere in the context of people work. Consequently, this chapter explores what is involved in one person seeking to influence one or more others in a particular direction and highlights a number of strategies that can be used to maximize our effectiveness.

This is an edited version of material first published as Chapter 14 in Thompson, N., *People Skills*. New York: Palgrave Macmillan.

Working in partnership

Before looking at what is involved in influencing other people, one important point we need to bear in mind is that people work is based on working in partnership – that is, my success depends on other people, and other people's success relies on mine. We are not isolated individuals who can just do as we please without consequences for ourselves and the people we work with. In view of this, before we go any further in exploring influencing skills, there is an important distinction to be drawn, namely that between influencing and manipulating.

The latter term implies that we are attempting to influence people in ways that will benefit *us* but disadvantage *them*, while the former (in the sense I am using it here at least) implies that we can benefit from what we are hoping they will do, but so can they – or, at least, they should not suffer as a result of it. For example, if I persuade a colleague to join me in a particular project because I know their involvement will be a significant benefit for me, is that influencing or manipulation? Well, it depends. If he or she also benefits from being involved in the project (or at the very least suffers no disadvantage from being involved in it), then I would regard that as influencing and thus as legitimate. However, if I persuade him or her to get involved, knowing that he or she will suffer problems or difficulties or otherwise be disadvantaged by being involved, then that amounts to manipulation – getting what I want at his or her expense.

The aim is to achieve a 'win–win' and not for one party to gain at the other's expense. Manipulation, then, is one form of influencing but one I would regard as not only unethical but also counter-productive, in so far as achieving our ends at other people's expense simply gives them grounds for trying to achieve their ends at our expense. Influencing skills in general are part and parcel of working in partnership and can be a fully legitimate part, as long as we do not stray into the territory of manipulation instead of staying on the firmer ground of seeking to influence others for mutual advantage.

Strategies for influencing

What, then, is involved in seeking to influence others? What can we actually do to make ourselves effective in this regard? Let us now look at some of the strategies or 'tools of the trade' that can be drawn upon. The following list is not exhaustive but should be sufficient to paint a picture of what is involved and how we can develop our skills.

Connection

This refers to the basic idea of 'connecting' or engaging with people. At its simplest level, this may simply be smiling, asking somebody how they are and so on. Now, while that may seem fairly obvious, it is amazing how often these basics are forgotten. If you deliberately look out for an example of this, it will not take long to find one (for example, somebody trying to sell something without making any effort to 'connect').

There are also more sophisticated levels of connection, but the basis of them all is having the ability to form a rapport with someone. Note, however, that this should not be tokenistic. 'Making the right noises' fools nobody. Making people feel at ease because you are taking a genuine interest in them, person to person, by contrast, is far more likely to produce a good working relationship in which your views will be listened to. In other words, a good rapport provides a sound platform from which to influence situations.

This idea of connection can also be broadened out to apply to such issues as connecting with someone from a different culture from your own. Being able to communicate across cultures is an important skill or set of skills, and its significance should not be underestimated if we are to take seriously the importance of valuing diversity.

Putting cards on the table

This refers to being open about what you are trying to achieve and encouraging the other person(s) to do likewise. This can then set the scene for being able to identify overlapping areas of interest. That is, even where there are significant areas of conflict between you and one or more people, it may still be possible for you to work together and for them to assist you in achieving your ends. Initially this may seem a strange idea as it means that you may be influencing (and being influenced by) someone with whom you have a significant conflict of interest. However, by 'putting your cards on the table', you may be able to reach a position where you can agree to disagree on some things but be able to support one another in other areas.

Another advantage to this approach is that it may actually reveal that some conflicts of interest are more apparent than real. That is, by attempting to find areas of common ground, you may come to realize that you have far more overlapping areas of interest than you had initially realized.

Give solutions not problems

'I've raised this with my boss several times but still nothing's been done' is a common refrain. One way round this is to offer your boss (or anyone else, for that matter) solutions rather than problems. That is, rather than identifying problems and then giving somebody else the problem of solving them and feeling frustrated when they do not do so, an alternative is to decide what you think the solution should be and then presenting both problem and solution together. For example, instead of saying: 'Here is Problem X, can you please solve it?', we could try: 'Here is Problem X, we think the solution is Y because Z. Is it OK if we try to get this sorted?' Experience suggests that this latter approach is far more likely to influence what the other person does. Put it this way, which would be more likely to influence you, if you were the person somebody was trying to influence by using this strategy – being presented with a problem or being presented with a proposed solution?

Giving feedback

One of the skills needed to be an effective staff supervisor is the ability to give feedback constructively and appropriately. However, this is applicable to not only the use of supervision, but also any situation where it is important for people to know where they stand in relation to one another – which basically means a very wide range of situations indeed.

Giving feedback can involve either positive or negative feedback. Positive feedback is where we praise someone or show our appreciation for something. This can be helpful in forming a positive rapport based on mutual respect. However, praising somebody just to influence them is likely to have very limited success – it does not take much for someone to see through this type of superficial approach. Negative feedback is where we express our concerns about someone or something. This is not simply a matter of criticizing someone, as that is hardly a skilled activity. What it involves is having the tact and subtlety to express negative feedback appropriately and constructively (see Gilbert and Thompson, 2002). This is not a simple matter or an easy set of skills to develop but, if you are able to do it, it can be very helpful in gaining respect – and being respected is a fundamental part of being able to influence others.

Speaking the same language

This can mean literally speaking the same language. If you are able to speak to someone in their first language, this is something they are likely to value, but again this is something that should not be done tokenistically. It must be part of a genuine commitment to forming a positive rapport, and not a cheap or empty gesture.

Speaking the same language can also refer to speaking the same type of language. It is important to match our 'register' to the situation – for example, to use a formal style of speech in formal situations, and an informal style in informal situations. The same approach can be taken in relation to matching the style of language to not only the formality or otherwise of the situation, but also to the preferred speech style of the person. For example, using a lot of jargon in a conversation with someone who is unfamiliar with such jargon or is averse to its use is not likely to help when it comes to seeking to influence that person. By contrast, using a sporting metaphor to get your message across to someone who is very keen on sport is likely to be a much more favourable strategy.

Dealing with objections

Lambert (1996) argues that it is important to handle objections when trying to influence people. That is, we have to recognize that there may be resistance to what we are trying to do or say. If so, then we should be clear about what the specific objections are, perhaps by making them explicit and then attempting to respond to them where we can. For example, if someone has anxieties about a particular aspect of what you are proposing, making this explicit will give you the opportunity to give them reassurances or to make changes to what you had in mind in order to accommodate their concerns.

This is clearly preferable to meeting objections or resistance and just trying to sweep them under the carpet, in the hope that they will go away. In fact, it could be argued that it is precisely in those situations where we meet objections that we are most going to need to be on our mettle when using our influencing skills. It is also perhaps in dealing skilfully and fairly with objections that we have major opportunities for gaining the respect and credibility we need to be effective influencers.

Listening and empathy

Active listening is an important part of effective communication. Being a good listener is also part of being a good influencer. That is, if we want people to listen to what we have to say, then we have to return the favour – we have to show that we too are prepared to listen.

However, it is not simply listening in a direct sense; we also have to be able to put ourselves in the other person's shoes, as it were. We have to have empathy, the ability to understand the other person's perspective, if we wish to develop a good working relationship in which we are respected and our views have credibility. Understanding where the other person is coming from (and where they are heading for) can give us a fuller understanding of the situation and make us much better equipped to deal with the situation in a way that is acceptable and advantageous to all concerned – a 'win–win' situation.

Conclusion

This chapter is not intended to turn you into one of those slimy, manipulative people that everybody gives a wide berth. As we have seen, influencing is one of the basic building blocks of social interaction. When people are together, the chances are that somebody is trying to influence somebody else or indeed that they are seeking to influence one another. These are basic skills that we develop as we grow up and learn the 'rules' of our society and culture. However, as with so many people skills, we learn the basics from our day-to-day social lives, but to use those skills at the advanced level required for effective people work, we need to work at them, learn more about them and develop them further. It is to be hoped that the discussions in this chapter will help you to do just that. By raising awareness of some of the issues and processes involved and exploring a range of strategies, this chapter can play a part in helping you improve your understanding and your effectiveness as a people worker. I hope I have managed to influence you enough to realize just how important influencing skills are, and therefore to appreciate the need to keep learning about them and developing them as far as you can.

References

Gilbert, P. and Thompson, N. (2002) *Supervision and Leadership Skills: A Training Resource Pack*. Wrexham: Learning Curve Publishing.
Lambert, T. (1996) *The Power of Influence: Intensive Influencing Skills at Work*. London: Nicholas Brealey.

15

'Getting better all the time': a case study of leading and managing change

Bryan Merton, Rob Hunter and Harriet Gore

Introduction

Services working with young people are facing some serious challenges as they seek to come to terms with a rapidly changing policy agenda. *Every Child Matters* (2003) and *Youth Matters* (2005) herald fundamental change in the way that youth work is likely to be managed and delivered in the future. Examples of change include the development of an integrated youth offer within broader Children and Young People's Services, the pooling of budgets and deployment of youth workers alongside other professional specialists in multi-agency teams, and the potential for local authorities to commission services from a range of providers. Leaders and managers of work with young people are increasingly required to have a vision of what they can offer to young people, to have a clear rationale for doing what they do, and need to be able to convince others that what they are providing for young people is effective and should be funded.

This chapter explores a case study of how change has been planned, led and managed in one particular context – Derbyshire Youth Service. The material on which it is based was generated through interviews with a range of staff in the service and through studying other sources of documentary evidence. It

This is an edited version of material first published as Merton, B., Hunter, R. and Gore, H., *Getting Better all the Time*. Leicester: National Youth Agency.

originally appeared as one of six case studies featured in a report published by the National Youth Agency (Merton et al., 2006). This aimed to share lessons that might be learnt from services that had brought about significant change in youth work provision and practice. Particular themes were selected that impact on quality outcomes for young people, including issues of curriculum development, quality assurance and collaborative work with partners. Derbyshire was chosen because of the way it made changes in the way that it approached analysing young people's needs and in how it allocated resources in response to this. It had also been identified by Ofsted as an effective youth service.

Issues highlighted in this case study include the importance of identifying and communicating the need for change; building a 'guiding coalition' of other people who will support change; establishing clear expectations and supporting staff, including with training; trying to create 'win–win' situations wherever possible, which in the Derbyshire example included improving administrative support for youth workers so that they could be released to do what they enjoyed and did best: work with young people; the importance of good communication, which includes listening not just telling; the need to establish effective partnerships as a support to change; monitoring and evaluating the impact of change; and perhaps above all, the importance of effective leadership in guiding and supporting the process of change.

We hope that this example of practice will help you to reflect on your own experiences of change, whether you have been seeking to create change, or trying to find ways of responding to it. We also hope that it helps you consider ways in which you might plan for future change, including in your practice with young people and in the organisation where you work.

Derbyshire – analysing needs and allocating resources

Identifying the need to change

Since 2002, there have been three major changes in the youth service in Derbyshire:

- A switch from historical to needs-led resourcing
- Maximising the use and value of existing resources
- Moving from 'planning for activity' to 'planning for learning'.

While there had been examples of good youth work taking place in the county before 2002, much of it lacked purpose and was in the wrong place at the wrong time. Opportunities across the county were haphazardly located and distributed. One external driver for change came in the form of Transforming Youth Work (DfEE, 2001) and its sharper focus on learning and youth work's role in the wider Connexions strategy. Another was the local authority's Best Value Review of 2002. This pointed up, among other things, that:

- Only 11 per cent of 13 to 19-year-olds were being reached by youth work; in fact, service managers believed the proportion was even smaller.
- A needs-led approach to funding was required in order to focus provision more on areas of multiple deprivation and groups of vulnerable young people.
- Existing resources would be better deployed by withdrawing from many of the underused buildings managed by the service.

Another catalyst for change had been the experience of three senior service managers attending a management development programme where they enjoyed sheltered time to debate strategy with staff from other services. More recently the Children Act compelled the service to address directly the five outcomes that had been identified as priorities in *Every Child Matters* (DfES, 2003). The five outcomes are: staying safe, being healthy, enjoying and achieving, making a positive contribution, and achieving economic wellbeing.

Making changes to methods of working

The first imperative was to develop a more rational **funding** system. This entailed:

- Developing a funding formula for each district based on the 13 to 19 population with additional weighting for areas of deprivation – the county council at first used quartiles as a means of identifying target areas and now is even more precisely using deciles.
- Beginning to dispose of surplus buildings. This has been time consuming because it needs substantial investigation to identify ownership, patterns of use and alternative facilities; and the politics of withdrawal are sometimes sensitive.

In **fieldwork** terms, the three main priority changes were:

- Designating and resourcing a single youth resource base in each district – an enhanced youth centre.

- Developing street-based youth work in the small towns and villages, both to increase contact with hard-to-reach young people and to encourage them to make use of the relevant base.
- Developing mobile provision to take resources to where the young people are as well as transport young people to the youth resource base.

A capital grant was secured to establish the fleet of mobiles and an additional revenue grant of £140,000 to fund two extra full-time youth worker posts and enhance the resource bases.

The service began to pilot the use of mobile provision and street work. With hindsight this was really important because it gave decision-makers the confidence that these approaches would be beneficial and demonstrated to frontline staff that they worked, might not be as daunting as they seemed at first, and might even give them greater job satisfaction. The process and impact of these changes took different forms in each of three districts.

District 1

There used to be no fewer than 27 youth projects in South East Derbyshire. These often had sessions where there were two or three youth workers with less than ten young people. They were usually located in village halls which were seldom suitable premises for youth work. The young people felt no ownership and often damaged the premises. Staff morale was low. We switched to one youth resource base (an enhanced youth centre) per district. We formed detached teams who would work with young people on the streets. When the work was established, we would negotiate taking them to the youth resource base in our own transport. Staffing the base would be those staff who were happier doing centre-based work – we had the often younger, more flexible workers in the street work teams. As the work developed and as we felt confident the young people could handle it, we would bring groups from two or even three villages to the base. The youth worker relationships plus the young people's involvement in influencing the programme at the base ensured that essentially there was no trouble between different village groups. After all, they spent the day at school with each other without fighting. The important principle was to respond to their needs and the consequence would be responsible behaviour.

On the few occasions we have had problems, we will go back to street work in the relevant village until stability has been restored and allows us to transport them to the base. It's taken some courage and meant taking risks. I had a team that trusted me as a leader. At times, I had to give them the right to go back to street-based if it got too hot to handle. At the start in particular we had a high ratio of staff to young people to make it work. This was not made possible through new money

(Continued)

(Continued)

but by using vacant posts sometimes to make contracts of part-time youth workers more substantial – doubling the time allocated from 6 to 12 hours a week.

Now the community in the individual villages has less hassle from young people who were either in a poor youth club and bored or on the streets, not attracted by it in the first place. We tried to ensure that those few who were attending those clubs that closed had somewhere to move on to. We had to explain the changes to the parish and district councillors but the case was quite easy to put across, and because we had the management information about the use of facilities to show them and alternatives to suggest; and because they meet together quite frequently across parishes the word soon got around.

The result is that the young people get a buzz. Numbers in the base are often around 70. They feel part of something. The base is better resourced. The staff are more energised because it is clearly working and what they came into the work for in the first place.

District 2

In High Peak the numbers contacted through outreach had been good but in centre-based youth work they had been diabolical. We went to the councillors and said that we understood the problems occurring at the bus station and we shared with them the numbers we have to reach and those we were currently working with. They recognised this could not continue and when we suggested street work, they thanked us for not abandoning them. We put the mobile in. On the first night there were ten and then about 25. Those who were on the streets are no longer intimidating as they had been. The young people say, 'you're coming to meet us on our turf and that's good.'

District 3

In North East Derbyshire changes could not happen overnight because of staffing patterns and vacancies. However, the service's vision allowed us to develop a strategy. I approached the district council's community safety officer and took him down to see the vehicle we had acquired. We talked about anti-social behaviour and about funding. He was enthusiastic and agreed to put in resources from the district's community safety partnership. In the end the county and the district paid half and half. This allowed us to buy a laptop, a WAP phone and some additional staff. The Best Value Review report was really helpful in this in backing up our professional judgment. If I get letters from communities I wave the Best Value recommendations at them. The youth work had been happening where the buildings were and the buildings were not in the right places. The outreach was initially in addition but we got an additional detached youth worker and merged existing vacant posts into a detached youth work team. The vehicles have been wonderful.

Assessing needs and deploying resources

The agencies working with young people in any particular disadvantaged area are getting together, discussing need, mapping and reviewing existing provision, and trying to make more accurate interventions.

> We are increasing our credibility by going to these meetings with a clear picture at our fingertips of who we are working with, how, for how long and with what outcomes.

By contrast, in more prosperous areas resources are being reduced. But the service is phasing its withdrawal. In other cases negotiations take place between the parish councils and the other stakeholders to take over the funding of the provision. The county council's statistics and the Bset Value Review have helped to do this. The staff in the voluntary and community sector provision continue to be supported by youth work training.

Decisions on the nature and range of open-access provision are based on:

- The youth workers' professional judgment; they know the profile of the area and they develop an understanding of the needs of young people through listening and observation.
- The young people's views on issues in their area and in their lives. The fact that 20,000 young people (over 30 per cent of the age group) vote in the local youth parliament elections shows they believe their voice is being heard.

Making better use of resources

As a result of these changes the service is now in contact with 27 per cent of 13 to 19-year-olds and participation levels are 16–17 per cent – both above the national benchmark. This has been achieved with a relatively small increase in the revenue budget. This increase in 'productivity' has different aspects.

During the Best Value Review staff diary sheets were examined and it became evident that full-time youth workers spent on average only 35 per cent of their time doing face-to-face interventions with young people. This was a waste of resources and it was tackled in four main ways:

Streamlining administrative tasks. By withdrawing from a lot of buildings tasks associated with premises management were reduced. The whole of the service's administrative system has been reorganised. There is now a principal administrative officer at headquarters who manages a senior administrative officer in each district who in turn manages a district administrative team. One particularly important development is improved management information. YouthBase is used because it helps with quality assurance and enables reports to be made on themes and expressed needs.

This administrative structure sits alongside the youth worker structure but, by having flexibility and 'a life of its own' – there is an annual administrative conference as well as regular district meetings – it seems to give a clearer sense of purpose and collective identity to the administrative role. Administrative resources at district level are deployed more flexibly rather than being tied to individual centres. Most of the administrative staff chose to do work specifically in the youth service and the new structure recognises that commitment and makes use of their skills. They are making constructive suggestions for how things can work better.

While improving the administrative structure, senior managers have tried to slim down the paperwork:

> We only ask youth workers to provide what we count and use.

One district worker commented:

> I am really grateful to be returned to the tasks I do best and which I came into youth work to do – work face-to-face with young people. The administrative staff do all the entering of information into Youth Base and support us in doing the remaining administrative tasks efficiently and not make a meal out of them.

Agreeing with the unions contractually at least 50 per cent contact work with young people. Even this was below what is often required but it gives everyone clarity about expectations and many workers do more.

Consolidating part-time hours into more substantial posts. New appointments are now to posts of ten hours or more and on an hourly not a session basis over a 52-week year. This gives flexibility and a greater level of investment in staff.

Releasing staff energy and creativity. The examples given above illustrate the increase in energy created in a youth resource base session with 100 young people who have been brought together on the basis of good youth work relationships. This has to be compared with the previous frustration of staffing unsuitable buildings with provision that had no clear purpose.

New staff knew no different so they were keen and happy. None of the established staff left out of protest. Some who were committed to 'their' young people did leave happily when they saw the young people were taken care of.

Managers sought to review and recognise the skills in other staff. For example, one member of staff was excellent at recording and at keeping finances right and now each project has an evidence file and a QA file.

Empowering managers

Senior managers took the decision to devolve resources with a clearer formula to district managers. The district managers now control the vacancies so the issues and the resources are locally owned. Part-time youth workers and administrative staff are appointed to districts not centres and so there is an important increase in flexibility. This was new. Everyone knows their job and trust has percolated through the system. Resourcing is fair and transparent.

This clarity gave managers greater confidence. Management information allowed managers to make better decisions. Where provision was clearly not providing value for money, managers were able to be more assertive, saying that it could not continue.

There are still inevitably tensions in trying to spread limited resources across numerous priorities. With 24 parishes in one district it is difficult to stay long in any one. However, the young people's interest and contact can be sustained by siting the mobile at lunch time in the secondary school. Alternatively, provision might not be withdrawn completely but can be made over alternate weeks for a while, or instead additional resources, such as the mobile climbing wall, can be called up to make any withdrawal more gradual.

These issues of resource deployment mean that planning and communication are crucial. Meetings are now different and planned well ahead. There is also management supervision and stocktaking with staff. Managers take on a logistical planning role and more business-like skills towards transport, premises and staff. The district managers are now engaged much more as full-time managers, operating as a kind of switchboard between the policies coming down nationally, from the county council and from the senior management, and the experience coming upwards from the young people and the youth workers.

Team meetings are vital, since all need to know what others are doing. Partnerships emerge at local level and demand a response but in doing so it is important to retain a corporate identity.

The culture change has had to come from the top. The senior management team has had to be clear, strategic and assertive but at the same time they have managed to bring staff along with them. The transparent funding allocations and devolution of responsibility to districts for effective use of these has released a lot of energy but fostered collaboration between district managers.

Investing in staff

There has been a lot of investment in training for the whole workforce, including district and senior managers. Within the service the consistency of the message has been key. These development sessions were taken round the county by management rather than using the cascading approach that had tended to dilute the message.

The service has also invested in training for the administrative staff both for YouthBase and in involving them in youth work meetings. Training for part-time youth workers is strong. In the 'compulsory' introduction, there is a session called 'Digging for Diamonds' which really engages them with the key descriptors in the Ofsted framework so from the outset they know what is expected of them and why. Quality assurance includes three internal inspections a year using a system which has now been going for four years and has earned the respect of all.

Working with partners

Perhaps the most dramatic change, as elsewhere in the country, has been the way the youth service is now working more with the police. Young people in the district and county youth forums were constantly raising the issues of Anti-social Behaviour Orders (ASBOs) and the conflict these caused. A meeting between the head of service and the chief constable revealed erroneous perceptions on both sides. As a result the head of the youth service went on to speak with each 'command' in the county and the chief constable walked the streets with county youth forum members and has locally got his inspectors involved in similar activity.

Youth workers in each district are now required to put on two initiatives a year with the police. In one district there has been a series of local meetings as a result of which there has been a shift of culture, from persistent antagonism now to the young people being given a shelter by the police. The only two professions working with young people on the streets at night are youth workers and the police. Although there are occasional differences there is much closer cooperation. They need to work together effectively. The police talk about sending in rapid response teams while the youth workers persist in explaining that if any issues are highlighted in advance, they will try to prevent the need for the rapid response team.

Other professions have seen the benefit of youth work skills and are trying to develop their staff to acquire the same. For example, school nurses and staff in sexual health clinics are among the more progressive professions.

Assessing the overall impact

Looking back on the four years, the head of service reflects:

> It's been about knowing your business and being confident and bold and taking control yourself and not waiting for others to invite you. We've had to invest in conversation with staff. We've had to work very hard over the last few years to break down the previous hierarchical approach.

The differences achieved amount to the following:

- Resources are more responsively distributed, in response to need more than according to precedent. They are used more wisely and efficiently.
- Youth work is taking place in locations and in forms better suited to the needs of young people.
- Young people have more say in shaping the kind of provision and services.
- Roles and responsibilities are more clearly specified and staff can play to their strengths. Youth workers are freed up to do more direct face-to-face youth work; administrators are deployed locally to support them; and managers are empowered to use their leadership and management skills.
- There has been a change in culture which has led to a greater transparency about how decisions are made and confidence has been shown in the professionalism of staff.
- The profile of youth work has been raised among other providers of public services.

As for the future, the service identifies two main priorities:

- Improving communications between young people on the street and young people at the county youth forum so that needs assessment is further improved. In the recent youth parliament elections there were 72 candidates for 16 places. It is hoped to persuade the unsuccessful candidates to help bridge this gap.

- Measuring impact to see if need has been met – and particularly across partnership working.

References

Department for Education and Employment (2001) *Transforming Youth Work*. London: DfEE.
Department for Education and Skills (2003) *Every Child Matters*. London: The Stationery Office.
Department for Education and Skills (2005) *Youth Matters*. London: The Stationery Office.
Merton, B., Hunter, R. and Gore, H. (2006) *Getting Better All The Time – Case Studies of Improving Youth Services*. Leicester: The National Youth Agency.

Partnership

In the current policy climate we could not have produced a book on leading work with young people without including a section on partnership. Working across agencies, across sectors and alongside community members whether they be young or old has become a central element of government policy and of local planning and implementation of practice within the social care environment. Although specific policy varies across the four nations, the general trends are the same – guided by the idea that services need to be more coordinated and focused on the needs of young people and communities rather than those of individual providers. This trajectory has taken most practitioners and policy makers into the territory of joint bidding and planning, shared resources and joint accountability.

There are undoubtedly benefits to be gained from partnership working – not least, discovering what matters to other people and how they think about and plan their lives and work. On occasions when the 'whole' really does turn out to be more than the 'parts', it is particularly rewarding. However, there are also downsides to partnerships, for example, the time they can take up and the potential for inequality within the partnership arrangements. The chapters within this section give a cross-section of views on these issues and some ideas as to how to progress the work to the benefit of young people and communities.

The chapter by Alison Gilchrist, 'Linking Partnerships and Networks', discusses the value of networking as a strategic tool within one's practice that will enable practitioners and the community to make more effective use of more formal partnerships. She alerts us to the benefits of an ethical networking approach and the need for a supporting infrastructure if its value is to be maximised. Alison reminds us that partnership working, whether strategic or operational, local or national is fundamentally about people and relationships and consequently needs to have an informal as well as a formal structural dimension.

Vipin Chauhan considers partnership working from the voluntary sector perspective and, in particular, addresses the relative difficulty that some organisations may experience when working with the 'big players'. He discusses the opportunities and risks associated with partnership working and finishes with some practical suggestions as to how to move towards more successful and inclusive practice.

In Chapter 18, 'Managing in Integrated Services', by Rob Hunter, with Dee Hammerson and Dee Treweek from the Doncaster Youth Service, takes a different approach. This takes the form of interview transcripts with two key managers within the local authority youth service as they move towards an integrated Children and Young People's Service. Their perspectives on how they experience this change give interesting insights as to how effective work with young people can evolve in response to changes in the policy environment.

16

Linking partnerships and networks

Alison Gilchrist

Introduction

Community participation has become part of the government's approach to decision-making and service delivery, involving 'joined-up' thinking and cross-sectoral working. Current policy needs partnerships and partnerships need people. This chapter will look at the implications for community development of the expectation that a range of public services and policies will increasingly be carried out by multi-agency coalitions.

The second half of the chapter looks at how networks and networking can be used in community development to develop and maintain partnerships, particularly supporting the involvement of community representatives. It argues that informal connections complement formal structures by allowing trust and mutual understanding to emerge, and that this web of personal relationships forms the basis of most successful partnerships.

Community involvement in practice

Although the desire for community involvement in partnership working is not new, there has been a welcome realisation that for this to become a reality, two things need to happen. Communities may need help to become organised, to develop the democratic and inclusive structures needed to support their representatives and to hold them accountable (Skinner, 1997). This capacity building often uses the methodology of community development but without a commitment to autonomous, 'bottom-up' organising, which enhances, but is independent of, state-sponsored partnerships. *The Community Development Challenge* report (DCLG, 2006b) identifies how the methods and values of community development can be used to empower disadvantaged sections of the population (such as young people) whilst helping public bodies to become more inclusive, responsive and accessible in their community engagement strategies. As the *Strategic Framework for Community Development* (SCCD, 2001: 5) states:

> Community development is about building active and sustainable communities based on social justice and mutual respect. It is about changing power structures to remove the barriers that prevent people from participating in the issues that affect their lives.

Essentially, community development aims to support community-inspired and led activities, which address issues arising from their direct experience, and articulated through processes of critical reflection and dialogue (Freire, 1972). By encouraging discussion and self-organised activities, community development workers help to create a sense of 'collective identity' and to enhance the confidence of communities to speak and act on their own behalf. This includes addressing some of the inequalities and divisions that make it difficult for communities to achieve a consensual view or to reconcile competing interests. In many deprived areas this work is a necessary precursor to establishing community participation in partnerships. Public authorities and the partnerships themselves need to be committed to removing obstacles to community empowerment. There has been a belated acknowledgement that the attitudes and organisational practices of the other partners (usually local authorities and business interests) may need to change in order to accommodate the less formal styles and needs of community representatives. Research has found that many community leaders on partnership bodies feel intimidated and frustrated by the management arrangements (Purdue et al., 2000; Skidmore et al., 2006), perceiving themselves to be excluded from the real policy-making arenas (Skelcher et al., 1996; Mayo and Taylor, 2001). Generally, they experienced levels of institutional discrimination that should be unacceptable in public bodies. The rhetoric of community empowerment and active citizenship evident in the recent *Strong and Prosperous Communities* White Paper (DCLG, 2006a) is not yet being reflected in the day-to-day reality of partnership working.

The benefits of partnership

Partnerships are usually formed in order to facilitate and manage joint ventures where there exists a common purpose (or at least compatible aims) amongst a number of different organisations. They represent a coalition of interests, identified on the basis of policy, but often assembled through networking between individuals and the relevant agencies. Partnerships were intended to replace competition with cooperation, unlocking resources, ideas and energy in the separate organisations and making them available for shared use (Taylor, 1997). Effective partnerships create 'collaborative advantage' (Huxham, 1996), by:

- Releasing synergy
- Exchanging information and ideas
- Improving decision-making
- Integrating provision across sectors and services
- Making more efficient use of facilities and staff time.

Partnerships allow agencies to develop a more holistic and strategic approach to their work by sharing resources and responsibility, and setting up at least a shell of common ownership and purpose. Different types of partnership have been identified, varying in their prime functions and formal structures (Clark, 1999). The strategic partnership aims to bring together key decision-makers in the relevant agencies in order to reach a consensual overview of a particular problem (for example, training provision for people leaving institutional care), but leaves the separate agencies to manage the actual delivery of services in a coordinated way.

Sometimes it is possible to provide access to services through a single 'one stop shop' arrangement, which eases referrals and generally makes more sense to the user. The focus of this might be a particular client group, such as homeless people, who can come for advice or care on a range of issues, such as drug use, housing, health care, benefits information, and so on. A partnership of appropriate agencies would jointly manage the building and possibly some shared staff, but would maintain 'Chinese walls' between their services for purposes of accountability and auditing. A more advanced version of this model might be the establishment of a new agency, with representation from the various stakeholders, but with its own identity, legal powers and separate status. This might be necessary to deliver services to 'hard to reach' sections of the population, whose needs are not being met within mainstream provision, or simply to improve area-based working.

One of the real benefits of partnership working is in opening up discussions about 'joined-up' provision of services and facilities to residents and communities of interest (Holman, 1999). In principle, users are acknowledged as both beneficiaries and contributors to programmes. Community representatives are invited to sit on partnership boards, and community consultation exercises seek out the views and energy of local people. Community development makes sure that communities are able to make informed decisions, and have the capacity to communicate and organise themselves in order to debate issues and arrive at a position which can be communicated to other members of the partnership. In theory, community representatives sit as equal partners on a partnership board and are expected to express considered opinions across a range of issues. Ideally this will be based on deliberation with other members of the community to reach a united view on what should be done. The reality rarely conforms with this ideal for a number of different reasons.

Managing community diversity

Although policy documents often refer to 'the community' as if it was homogenous and could speak with one voice, the term masks the complexity, diversity and sheer dynamism of the population living in a given area. There may exist communities of interest (for example, around faith or culture), communities based on 'social identity' derived from a collective experience of oppression, such as being disabled or having a particular sexual orientation (Rutherford, 1990) and communities which organise themselves around an earlier displacement or origin, such as Somali refugees or economic migration (the Portuguese in Somerset, for example). Communities of refugees and asylum seekers experience particular difficulties in being heard within partnership bodies, as do young people and children. These different experiences, perspectives and priorities do not easily form a coherent 'community view' which can be articulated by just one community representative. It is vital that community workers support different sections of the community to:

- Counter disadvantages
- Accommodate different needs and customs
- Actively encourage minority or dissenting views to surface in the discussion.

Community representatives are often selected from a relatively privileged set of people, namely those that have the time, the confidence and the charisma to gain leadership positions. They are not always the most appropriate or competent individuals to represent the complex mosaic of ideas and opinion within the area, and often they are not given adequate resources and support to carry out this task properly. Community development is one means of developing the infrastructure and capacity within communities to enable effective and democratic participation in cross-sectoral partnerships. In particular, they can help with establishing and maintaining the mechanisms and processes (including informal networks) that enable community leaders or representatives to be informed, supported and accountable.

The limitations of partnerships

Partnerships sometimes provide a façade for the same old practices and 'usual suspects' whereby delivery agencies decide 'what is best' for residents and users, and continue to work separately (and occasionally in competition with each other) to provide services according to conventional wisdom and budget limitations. The partnership exists on paper only, and community representation at meetings is tokenistic or non-existent through absence or silence (Geddes, 1998). This happens when there is lack of clarity and respect as to what communities can contribute, or when the power dynamics within the partnership are not sufficiently analysed so that inequalities can be acknowledged and reversed (Brownill and Darke, 1998; Byrne, 2001). In both instances, the more powerful partners will need to examine their own attitudes and procedures with a view to making them more accessible and relevant to people used to working in communities, rather than institutions.

It may also be necessary to consider how informal networking (behind the scenes wheeling and dealing) excludes some partners from decision-making (Hastings et al., 1996; Skelcher et al., 1996). Partnership working is neither straightforward nor always the most appropriate way of empowering communities. They can sometimes be wasteful of activists' (unpaid) time and effort, getting embroiled in apparent bureaucratic niceties or overly technical discussions that could be dealt with elsewhere. Partnerships tend to advance only on the basis of consensus and are reluctant to acknowledge that there may be conflicts of interest around the table. This renders them risk-averse and detracts from the potential synergy that such combinations of expertise and experience should generate.

Partnerships can be a cumbersome experience for all concerned and have been criticised as forcing communities to adopt a 'corporatist' approach to governance: masking contradictions, suppressing dissent and constraining the creativity of local enterprise and initiative (Meade and O'Donovan, 2002). Partnership working can be seen as a mechanism for managing, rather than resolving conflict, usually in favour of the majority or most powerful interests. Nevertheless, partnerships can be an effective means of enabling organisations in the different sectors to work together and to involve communities in the design, development and delivery of services (Chanan et al., 1999).

Partnerships in practice

So what works in reality? The evidence from experience and empirical research suggests that relationships between partners based on trust, respect and mutual understanding are essential to the sustainability and effectiveness of partnerships (see Geddes, 1998; Goss and Kent, 1995; Loughry, 2002; Means et al., 1997; Wilcox, 1994). Where individuals on the partnership see each other as 'rounded' people, and are aware of other aspects of their lives beyond the business of the partnership, this can lead to a greater willingness to see things from different perspectives, to compromise and to deal constructively with disagreements.

Opportunities for people to get to know each other outside the formal meetings are helpful, as are shared training events where participants learn from each other and tackle common problems. This enhances partners' negotiating and problem-solving skills, and can subtly shape the balance of power within the group (Newman and Geddes, 2001).

It is helpful to have a set of protocols or a compact that sets out how the partnership operates and to undertake early 'visioning' exercises to develop a shared goal or focus. This phase often takes longer than expected as people usually bring very different aspirations and needs to the partnership. For agencies it may be about meeting targets within a given timeframe. For communities, this could be a chance to get their voices heard at a strategic level, and they want to make sure that their ideas are listened to and given credence. Anecdotal evidence reports that communities feel that their participation is only welcomed when their views correspond with the preconceived plans of the other agencies. When they do not, their legitimacy as 'representatives' is questioned, or their suggestions are dismissed as unviable (Collins and Foster, 1999). Unless decision-making is seen as transparent and inclusive, this swiftly results in cynicism and withdrawal.

Developing community leadership

The most effective community leaders or representatives are usually key members of strong informal networks, which provide them with support and intelligence around cross-cutting issues (Purdue et al., 2000). They get to hear about local concerns, are involved in conversations about solutions and receive feedback on how the partnership is perceived. Over-reliance on personal connections can, however, distort the representative's judgement in favour of the views of like-minded people whereby minority or unpopular experiences are overlooked or suppressed. More formal democratic structures are needed which are open and accountable to all members of the relevant community. These might already exist in the form of tenants' forums, residents' associations, a youth council, cultural association or neighbourhood committee. However, they can be dominated by a particular clique and may need support (or pressure) to become genuinely representative. Where they do not exist or are not well linked, some kind of area-based forum is recommended where people can meet regularly, discuss a range of proposals emanating from the partnership body, and generally build a collective capacity to communicate and organise around shared issues (Collins and Lister, 1996).

The effectiveness of community involvement strategies cannot be taken for granted. It is useful to have objective monitoring and evaluation of the impact that communities have on the deliberations and actual programme delivery of partnerships. This has two aspects – processes and outcomes. How are communities able to influence decision-making and is this impact demonstrated in tangible changes which reflect the priorities and needs of local people? It is possible to assess the value (and the limitations) of community participation using a framework, such as that devised for Yorkshire Forward (the regional development agency) by COGS consultancy (COGS, 2000). This provides a useful set of questions, indicators and suggestions for good practice to encourage self-appraisal by the partnership body. The benchmarks, as they are known, enable the partners to reflect on four dimensions of their work: influence, inclusivity, communication and capacity, and to develop action plans for continuous improvement. Another approach is to audit the impact of community involvement by measuring both the processes of participation and how these are manifest in the decisions that are taken. It is clear from preliminary research and experience that in order to achieve genuine community participation, there has to be organisational development within the partner institutions as well as capacity building within communities (Burns et al., 2004; Burns and Taylor, 2000; Involve, 2006).

Networking the networks

Community development encompasses both these approaches. This means considering what needs to change in the formal organisations involved in the partnership, and in relation to the communities, which they serve. Managers of community development may have to face in more than one direction – helping their own organisation to adjust to more informal community-friendly styles of working, and supporting their practitioners in more nebulous work to extend and consolidate local networking. As indicated, partnerships have both a structural dimension and 'softer' features characterising the loose social networks in which they are embedded. These strands somehow have to be knitted together to form the partnership jigsaw.

Studies have shown that extensive networking within communities supports strong collective action (Marwell and Oliver, 1993) and renders effective participation in partnerships more robust and sustainable (Hastings et al., 1996; McCabe et al., 1997). A particularly important aspect of this seems to be boundary-spanning mechanisms, such as the linkages set up by multi-agency consortia and what are known as 'weak ties' between individuals (Granovetter, 1973). These are more than formalised inter-organisational liaison in which information is exchanged and activities coordinated. They are also about the conversations, the greetings, the favours and shared values that are communicated when people meet and talk outside of formal meetings. Face-to-face interactions convey the emotional or more risky aspects of people's thinking. It is said that around two-thirds of someone's thoughts are communicated non-verbally through gestures, body posture and facial expressions (Dunbar, 1996). Being able to interpret these signals is a useful skill within networks and partnerships because they create the basis for group loyalties and the identification of potential 'allies' and 'enemies'.

Informal networks thread within and between organisations, shaping our experience of communities. They link private, public and communal aspects of our lives in ways which are partly pragmatic, partly selective and partly proscribed by circumstances. The everyday encounters in local public spaces (on streets, at the school gates, places of worship, in the pubs and at community events) generate familiarity and a sense of 'community'. This is not always a positive experience. Divisions and prejudices within communities breed hostility, misunderstanding and resentment, as witnessed in periodic disturbances and inter-ethnic conflict in British cities. Community networking can be both skilled and strategic, nurturing the more difficult links between sections of the community (old and young, black and white, newcomers and long-term residents) in order to foster a degree of community cohesion (Blunkett, 2001; Gilchrist, 2004b).

Recent research reveals the hidden role played by community workers in maintaining the web of relationships within communities and between organisations, creating circumstances in which people who might otherwise find it hard to communicate can connect and share ideas (Gilchrist, 2001, 2004a). By asking practitioners about their tactics, their aptitudes and their personality traits, the study revealed the qualities, skills and strategies that are used in networking practice, and demonstrated that informal, and often invisible, links led to tangible outcomes in the wider world of policy and programme delivery. This was especially evident in the development of partnerships where people from different sectors and policy areas find themselves required to work together in unfamiliar and challenging surroundings.

These partnerships are frequently constructed around specific initiatives, with accompanying sets of targets and performance criteria. By facilitating more effective partnership working, networking contributes to achieving such directly measurable outputs. It is also the case that there is a subtle added value to networking. Evidence from social sciences indicates that people with robust and diverse personal networks are more resistant to disease, more likely to recover from emotional trauma, less prone to experience long-term unemployment and are less likely either to perpetrate or suffer from criminal activity (Pilisuk and Parks, 1986; Halpern, 2004). This in itself suggests that building social capital by strengthening formal and informal networks will achieve many of the objectives desired by various partnerships, irrespective of changes in service delivery (Putnam, 2000; Field, 2003). There are benefits to individuals, to organisations and to society as a whole. Networking is primarily concerned with interpersonal relationships rather than structures and procedures. By connecting the strengths and commitments of community and partnership members, networks create the conditions for the emergence of leadership and flexible forms of collective organisation (Gilchrist, 2000).

Valuing informal interaction

Formal organisations are governed through legal structures and responsibilities, whilst communities are much more informal, coordinating their arrangements and activities through relationships, local customs and *ad hoc* voluntary associations. Organisations rely on negotiated, often explicit, regulations and protocols. Members or staff operate according to rules, which designate the scope and limitations of their role. Lines of accountability operate through a hierarchical framework of job titles and fairly well-defined departmental responsibilities. Communities, on the other hand, function through interaction between individuals who have some level of acquaintance or recognised association. The flow of emotions through community networks depends on people's experiences of each other's behaviour, their values, attitudes and past associations. Usually these convey mutual loyalty, shared commitments and trust, but interactions are also likely to be based on antagonistic connections, reflecting prejudices, dislike, jealousy and fear.

Another difference between communities and formal organisations concerns representation versus participation as a means of influencing decisions. People participate in community activities because they want to. They are motivated by personal or altruistic reasons (or both) rather than because of notions of civic duty or citizenship. Consequently, the views and commitments expressed are usually individual, rather than organisational. As indicated earlier, one of the aims of community capacity building is to assist communities to engage in debate and negotiation, resulting in a shared perspective about what needs to be done to improve an area. A more coherent and collectively agreed approach is more likely to have an impact on planning and decision-making than a cacophony of divergent views and competing voices.

Supporting representation

One of the most frequent complaints made by community representatives is that they do not understand the material provided and therefore cannot contribute in an informed way to decision-making (Anastacio et al., 2000; Burton et al., 2004; Stewart, 1998). Experience tells us that good communication is a vital component of community development, making sure that information is provided in accessible formats and language, and that papers are circulated in good time for people properly to digest their content and consider any implications. Community representatives who are unused to technical reports or formal policy documents may need help in interpreting these, either from independent advisors or from officers of public authorities and institutions. It is well known that people are more willing to ask for such help or to pose questions constructively if they feel their contributions will be valued and understood. This can be difficult for those who are not accustomed to being accountable to lay people or tend to rely on jargon for their explanations. The mainstreaming of community development means that people throughout the organisation need to understand the implications for their own area of work and to be persuaded that the benefits of adapting to this new approach outweigh the initial disruptions and uncertainties.

It is important to ensure that individuals coming forward to represent communities are supported in this role and held accountable for their decisions. Resources and time need to be found for this and sometimes guidance in dealing with more powerful institutions (Duncan and Thomas, 2000). Community leaders and spokespeople are often self-appointed or selected by media or public officers. They may well speak with knowledge and wisdom on behalf of their community, but it is equally likely that their own interests or prejudices predominate.

Effective and ethical networking

A key purpose of networking is to develop trust and tolerance and it should be evaluated accordingly. Such intangible processes can be problematic for organisations accustomed to measuring progress in terms of specific outputs or performance criteria. The quality and diversity of connections within the practitioner's web are crucial, hence the importance of proper management of this aspect of community development. Staff should regularly evaluate their contacts and significant informal conversations and be encouraged to explain why they believe these might yield useful outcomes in the future. A manager should be confident that the worker is developing an array of connections, which are representative of the communities within the organisation's remit, and that they are using these to make progress towards agreed aims. It may not be appropriate, however, to define specific targets or milestones, as it is vital that workers are free to take advantage of chance encounters and unexpected linkages. Serendipity is often the key that unlocks successful and innovative community initiatives, but networking in community development should also be strategic in identifying possible collaborators and critical friends.

Managers need to monitor their staff's networking activity on a regular basis and to judge whether it is effective. They should encourage community development workers to be strategic in establishing links with key individuals and organisations across all sections of the community. Effective networking is far more than simply chatting and being helpful to others. Research suggests that good networkers are versatile, diplomatic and bold (Gilchrist, 2001). Community development workers need to be able to:

- Communicate in different ways
- Operate comfortably in informal settings
- Manage an array of relationships.

An important aspect of community development is assisting people to establish links with others that can then be sustained with minimal external support. The practitioner may set up or facilitate the initial connection (a process the author has elsewhere termed meta-networking: Gilchrist, 1998; 1999) but tries not to become the constant intermediary. Meta-networking involves introductions, referrals, keeping up-to-date contacts, providing information and identifying potentially useful connections. Arranging events and meetings, which bring people together across boundaries, is a more tangential aspect of meta-networking, and may involve organising community-based activities or ensuring the inclusiveness of local communication strategies. The resultant web of relationships provides a significant collective resource for the agency *and* community members, but the work involved is not always sufficiently resourced or recognised.

Networking works best through informal interaction – the conversations, favours and mutual support that occur outside of, or on the periphery of, formal occasions when people really begin to get to know each other, to discover shared interests and to build trust. It would be impossible to regulate or scrutinise this too closely, but there are issues which managers can help their workers to negotiate, or at least to be aware of. The first of these relates to role boundaries and accountability. Networking relies on people stepping partially out of role, developing authentic relationships with others and operating across normal boundaries. This can result in confusion and lapses of confidentiality where information is divulged, but not explicitly marked as 'confidential'. We know from experience that rumour, gossip and opinion are very useful for gaining a sense of the emotional and political aspects of situations, but tend to be distorted by the individuals concerned. They are not usually a sound basis for action without further corroboration. Judgement needs to be exercised in appraising the validity of information gleaned from networking, before they are allowed to influence formal decisions. Equal opportunities principles dictate that covert preferences and prejudices are removed as far as possible from organisational procedures and activities. The same applies to networking but is far more difficult to monitor.

Networking allows different perspectives and experiences to be drawn into the mainstream. Diversity is often accompanied by unacknowledged tensions and conflicting loyalties. Networking seems to thrive on intuition and imagination. There exists an underpinning expertise in perceiving the interpersonal dynamics of situations and identifying or creating new patterns of interaction. Managers should encourage those aptitudes and activities which make good networkers amongst their community development workers. Training opportunities and funding can be found to support everyone in developing more effective and ethical networking.

Conclusion

Networks and partnerships enhance cooperation and coordination, providing mechanisms for improved services and feedback from users. They allow (indeed require) the development of trust, respect and cohesion within communities, facilitating voluntary association and building social capital (Burt, 1997). Strengthening informal networks weaves and mends the social fabric, resulting in enhanced community initiative, collective action, shared problem-solving, consensus and conflict mediation. The lifeblood of communities flows through the capillaries of personal relationships and inter-organisational networks. Well-connected communities are vibrant, tolerant and relatively autonomous of government agendas (Gilchrist, 2004a). They are able to preserve traditions of protest and solidarity, as well as building alliances, which improve partnership working. Community development must adopt a delicate balancing act between partnership targets and encouraging genuinely independent community activity. In the long term these aims will coincide, but only if there is a shared sense that some of the many difficulties encountered can be overcome through sensitive and empowering community development work.

References

Anastacio, J., Gidley, B., Hart, L., Mayo, M. and Kowarzik, U. (eds) (2000) *Reflecting Realities: Participants' Perspectives on Integrated Communities and Sustainable Development*. Bristol: The Policy Press.

Blunkett, D. (2001) *Politics and Progress. Renewing Democracy and Civil Society*. London: DEMOS, Politico's Publishing.

Brownill, S. and Darke, J. (1998) *Rich Mix: Inclusive Strategies for Urban Regeneration*. Bristol: The Policy Press.

Burns, D. and Taylor, M. (2000) *Auditing Community Participation*. Bristol: The Policy Press.

Burns, D., Taylor, M., Wilde, P. and Wilson, M. (2004) *What Works in Assessing Community Participation*. Bristol: The Policy Press/Joseph Rowntree Foundation.

Burt, R. (1997) 'A note on social capital and network content', *Social Networks*, 19: 355–374.

Burton, P., Goodlad, R., Croft, J., Abbott, J., Haskings, A., Macdonald, E. and Slater, T. (2004) *What Works in Community Involvement in Area-Based Initiatives? A Systematic Review of the Literature*, London: the Home Office.

Byrne, D. (2001) 'Partnership – participation – power: the meaning of empowerment in post-industrial society' in S. Balloch and M. Taylor (eds) *Partnership Working: Policy and Practice*. Bristol: The Policy Press.

Chanan, G. and West, A. with Garratt, C. and Humm, J. (1999) *Regeneration and Sustainable Communities*. London: CDF Publications.

Clark, C. (1999) *Winning Partnerships: A Guide to Cross-Sectoral Regeneration Partnership*. London: Civic Trust.

COGS (2000) *Active Partners: Benchmarking Community Participation in Regeneration*. Leeds: Yorkshire Forward.

Collins, C. and Foster, J. (1999) 'Problems with partnership', *New Times*, 8: 25.

Collins, C. and Lister, J. (1996) 'Hands up or heads up? Community work, democracy and the language of "partnership" ' in I. Cooke and M. Shaw (eds) *Radical Community Work: Perspectives From Practice in Scotland*. Edinburgh: Moray House Institute of Education.

DCLG (2006a) *Strong and Prosperous Communities*, Local Government White Paper. London: Department for Communities and Local Government.

DCLG (2006b) *The Community Development Challenge*. London: Community Empowerment Division, Department for Communities and Local Government.

Dunbar, R. (1996) *Grooming, Gossip and the Evolution of Language*. London: Faber and Faber.

Duncan, P. and Thomas, S. (2000) *Neighbourhood Regeneration*. Bristol: The Policy Press.

Field, J. (2003) *Social Capital*. London: Routledge.

Freire, P. (1972) *Pedagogy of the Oppressed*. Harmondsworth: Penguin Books.

Geddes, M. (1998) *Local Partnership: A Successful Strategy for Social Cohesion*. Dublin: European Foundation for the Improvement of Living and Working Conditions.

Gilchrist, A. (1998) 'Connectors and catalysts', *SCCD News*, 18: 18–20.

Gilchrist, A. (1999) 'Serendipity and the snowflakes', *SCCD News*, 19: 7–10.

Gilchrist, A. (2000) 'The well-connected community: networking to the "edge of chaos"', *Community Development Journal*, 35: 264–275.

Gilchrist, A. (2001) Strength Through Diversity: Networking for Community Development. Unpublished PhD thesis, University of Bristol.

Gilchrist, A. (2004a) *The Well-connected Community: A Networking Approach to Community Development*. Bristol: The Policy Press.

Gilchrist, A. (2004b) *Community Development and Community Cohesion: Bridges or Barricade*. London: Community Development Foundation.

Goss, S. and Kent, C. (1995) *Health and Housing: Working Together? A Review of the Extent of Inter-agency Working*. Bristol: The Policy Press.

Granovetter, M. (1973) 'The strength of weak ties', *American Journal of Sociology*, 78: 1360–1380.

Halpern, D. (2004) *Social Capital*. Cambridge: Polity Press.

Hastings, A., McArthur, A., McGregor, A. (1996) *Less Than Equal: Community Organisations and Estate Regeneration Partnerships*. Bristol: The Policy Press.

Holman, K. (1999) *New Connections: Joined Up Access to Public Services*. London: CDF Publications.

Huxham, C. (ed.) (1996) *Creating Collaborative Advantage*. Bristol: The Policy Press.

Involve (2006) *People and Participation*. London, Involve, *www.involving.org*.

Loughry, R. (2002) 'Partnering the state at the local level: the experiences of one community worker', *Community Development Journal*, 37: 60–68.

Marwell, G. and Oliver, P. (1993) *The Critical Mass in Collective Action: A Micro-Social Theory*. Cambridge: Cambridge University Press.

Mayo, M. and Taylor, M. (2001) 'Partnership and power in community regeneration,' in S. Balloch and M. Taylor. *Partnership Working: Policy and Practice* (eds) Bristol: The Policy Press.

McCabe, A., Lowndes, V. and Skelcher, C. (1997) *Partnerships and Networks*. York: Joseph Rowntree Foundation.

Meade, R. and O'Donovan, O. (2002) 'Corporatism and the ongoing debate about the relationship between the state and community development', *Community Development Journal*, 37: 1–9.

Means, R., Brenton, M., Harrison, L., and Heywood, F. (1997) *Making Partnerships Work in Community Care: A Guide for Practitioners in Housing, Health and Social Services*. Bristol: The Policy Press.

Newman, I. and Geddes, M. (2001) *Developing Local Strategies for Social Inclusion*. Paper presented to Local Authorities and Social Exclusion Programme, the Local Government Centre, Warwick University, March.

Pilisuk, M. and Parks, S. H. (1986) *The Healing Web: Social Networks and Human Survival.* Hanover, NE: University Press of New England.

Purdue, D., Razzaque, K., Hambleton, R. and Stewart, M. (2000) *Community Leadership in Urban Regeneration.* Bristol: The Policy Press.

Putnam, R. D. (2000) *Bowling Alone: The Collapse and Revival of American Community.* New York: Simon Schuster.

Rutherford, J. (ed.) (1990) *Identity: Community, Culture, Difference.* London: Lawrence and Wishart.

SCCD (2001) *Strategic Framework for Community Development.* Sheffield: Standing Conference for Community Development.

Skelcher, C., McCabe, A., and Lowndes, V. with Nanton, P. (1996) *Community Networks in Urban Regeneration.* Bristol: The Policy Press.

Skidmore, P., Bound, K. and Lownsborough, H. (2006) *Community Participation: Who Benefits?* York: Joseph Rowntree Foundation.

Skinner, S. (1997) *Building Community Strengths: A Resource Book on Capacity Building.* London: Community Development Foundation.

Stewart, M. (1998) 'Accountability in community contributions to sustainable development,' in D. Warburton (ed.), *Community and Sustainable Development: Participation in the Future.* London: Earthscan.

Taylor, M. (1997) *The Best of Both Worlds: The Voluntary Sector and Local Government.* York: Joseph Rowntree Foundation.

Wilcox, D. (1994) *The Guide to Effective Participation.* Brighton: Partnership Books.

Partnership working in the voluntary and community sector

Vipin Chauhan

Introduction

The purpose of this chapter is to explore some of the policy and contextual issues behind partnership working, what it means in practice and why increasingly this is becoming an important area of social policy and service delivery. I will examine whether partnership working is a negative development for the voluntary and community sector (VCS) or if it offers opportunities for growth, expansion and sustainability. Finally, I will propose some simple guidelines for successful partnership working built on principles which are compatible with the values of the VCS and the public sector and the notion of active citizenship and community empowerment.

The content of the chapter has been shaped by my own professional experiences as well as my experiences as a board member of several voluntary organisations over the years. In my role as a consultant I am often involved in working with various types of strategic as well as delivery partnerships and I am able to see, feel and experience partnership working from a number of perspectives. Apart from working with partnership bodies to help them achieve their aims and objectives, I am involved in the in-service, qualifying and continuous professional development programmes for youth workers, community development workers, VCS managers and volunteers where the theme of partnership working is an evergreen topic.

Policy context

Government policy which seeks to promote the benefits of partnership arrangements in achieving greater efficiency in the delivery of public services runs across departmental boundaries. This extract is taken from a Home Office document and relates specifically to VCS organisations:

> The voluntary and community sector has a vital role in society as the nation's 'third sector', working alongside the state and the market … This Compact is aimed at creating a new approach to partnership between Government and the voluntary and community sector … Government and voluntary and community organisations share many aspirations – the pursuit of inclusiveness, dedication to public life, and support for the development of healthy communities. The Compact is the starting point for developing our partnership, based on shared values and mutual respect. (Home Office, 1998: Foreword)

Much use is made of the term 'partnership working' to suggest that many of the issues that challenge our society could be dealt with better if only there was greater and better co-operation between key agencies including VCS organisations. The lack of effective partnership working is seen to contribute to poor service delivery, inefficient use of limited resources, lack of effective engagement with local communities as well as an inability to tackle many of the social issues that we face (e.g. crime, street violence, healthy living, domestic violence, and so on).

Increasingly, voluntary, community and public sector organisations are caught up in this frenzy about 'partnership', 'multi-agency', 'inter-professional' and 'inter-agency' working. Such terms are used almost daily without paying much attention to what they mean in reality and whether or not these ways of working will result in any substantial, tangible benefits for local communities. Indeed, these days, it is nearly impossible to meet anyone from the VCS whose organisation, directly or indirectly, does not receive any partnership funding, is not represented on a partnership and/or has not been consulted about partnership development. The following is an extract from the job description of a recently advertised post for an Area Youth and Community Worker:

> Working in partnership with other organisations and agencies, including the voluntary sector, access external funding opportunities in support of the development and delivery of youth and community work. (Dudley Metropolitan Borough Council, 2006)

Partnership working is not new and arguably is as old as humanity itself if you consider how fundamental the coming together of people, systems and organisations is to human social interaction. One needs only to look at the history of the VCS in this country to see that it would not have developed to the extent that it has were it not for the willingness of people to come together and work in partnership, e.g. the Girl Guide movement or the International Red Cross. Historically, such acts of coming together were not confined just to individuals but also underpinned joint arrangements between the state (central, local and more recently, regional), the VCS and the private sectors, e.g. the establishment of the National Heath Service or the welfare state.

The expectation that key planners, commissioners and deliverers should work together in partnership is not confined to rhetoric and now underpins the policy, decision-making and resource allocation processes at local, regional and national levels. It forms part of the government's modernisation agenda and manifests itself in the form of Local Area Agreements, Local Strategic Partnerships, local and national Compacts, Best Value, the ChangeUp infrastructure investment programme, regeneration, the community cohesion policy agenda, and so on. These initiatives have not only reinforced the 'partnership buzz' at local levels but represent tangible arrangements by which key decisions are made, funding allocated and services delivered.

In relation to health for instance, the Department of Health's Public Health White Paper *Choosing Health: Making Healthy Choices Easier* (DoH, 2004) is underpinned by a number of key principles. First, the need for key agencies to work together and progress towards targets being dependent upon effective partnerships across communities, including local government, the National Health Service, business, advertisers, retailers, the voluntary sector, communities, the media and faith organisations. Second, the need for greater leadership, co-ordination and promotion of partnerships and partnership working by government. Third and finally, the expectation that the general population can be encouraged to take their health and the health of their families seriously and create willingness for them to engage constructively in shared efforts.

The Children Act (DfES, 2004: 5) which forms the basis of the reform of children and young people's services in England wants to establish:

> a duty on Local Authorities to make arrangements to promote co-operation between agencies and other appropriate bodies (such as voluntary and community organisations) in order to improve children's well-being (where well-being is defined by reference to the five outcomes), and a duty on key partners to take part in the co-operation arrangements.

Such a mixed economy approach to social welfare is central to the government's modernisation agenda and its attempts to reconstruct public services through greater 'joined up' working:

> Working with other agencies is crucial to addressing the multifaceted needs of drug users ... Collaborative working between agencies which seeks to combine and co-ordinate all the services required to meet the assessed needs of the individual involves drug treatment services, generic and specialist health services, training programmes, educational sector and employment services, criminal justice services, housing services and childcare organisations among others. (Effective Interventions Unit, 2003)

The Audit Commission's report *A Fruitful Partnership* (1998) identified five main reasons for the increasing trend towards partnership working. First, the need and desire to move towards greater co-ordination in the delivery of services so that duplication was minimised and there was a better overview about what was being delivered, by whom and how. Second, it was believed that partnership working was a logical and more effective way of tackling the more 'wicked' social issues such as crime and education. Third, it was believed that partnership working could help to reduce the impact of organisational fragmentation and a lack of co-ordination in the delivery of key services. Fourth, partnership working had the potential of helping to maximise the use of resources and also provide access to new or different resources. Finally, as can be seen from the above example of the introduction of the Children Act, partnership working is a legal expectation in many cases and therefore a means to meeting statutory requirements.

For the VCS, with the rise of new public management (often referred to as 'new managerialism'), there has been the added pressure to adopt private sector styles of management and service delivery. This has contributed to a pronounced pressure on VCS organisations to develop relationships and work in partnership with external agencies. There is often the expectation that relationships will be built with agencies which some VCS organisations might have been reluctant to work with previously and/or with whom they had a limited contact or trust, e.g. the police, the health sector, places of worship, and so on.

Despite the seemingly strong ethical, policy and economic case for partnership working, the Audit Commission's report recognises that building partnerships is only *one* way of working jointly with other agencies. Other methods of working jointly which also had a crucial and complementary role to play included networking, commissioning, contracting, consultation and community participation.

What do we mean by partnership working?

> Partnerships are formal structures of relationships among individuals or groups, all of which are banded together for a common purpose. It is the commitment to a cause – frequently purposive change – that characterises these partnerships, whether the partners are organisations or individuals, voluntary confederations of independent

agencies or community assemblies developing multipurpose and long-term alliances. (El Ansari et al. cited by: Orme et al., 2003: 61)

We only need to scan the internet or look through professional journals to see the numerous references to various partnerships at local, regional or national levels. The chances are that if you volunteer for, are employed by and/or involved in the management of VCS organisations, elements of your work and/or the funding you receive will have come through some form of a partnership arrangement. If you were to list the types of partnerships that exist in your local area you are likely to come across some of the following, albeit by different names:

- Local Area Agreement
- Local Strategic Partnership
- Crime and Disorder Partnership
- Partnership for Health
- Health Action Zone
- Sure Start
- Early Years Partnership
- New Deal for Communities
- Public Private Partnership.

The above are examples of more formalised partnerships where agencies come together and/or are required to work together (say, because of funding or legal obligations), to plan, co-ordinate, contract and/or deliver local services. In such cases, agencies would come together and agree the broad terms of reference for the partnership including its powers, authority, role and composition. In some cases, (e.g. economic regeneration) such partnership arrangements could become more formalised through the creation of a separate legal identity such as a company limited by guarantee and the adoption of a formal 'Memorandum and Articles of Association'.

A number of different partnership models have been developed. For example, Orme et al. (2003) (Table 17.1) have suggested a typology of five approaches to partnership working.

Often, when partnerships are established, substantial energy is devoted to arguments about who sits on them, how often they will meet, how they will be serviced, who will resource them, and so on. Though these basic mechanics are important for ensuring that partnerships are well resourced and functional, the tendency is to spend less time and energy on the principles of partnership working and how, for example, issues affecting marginalised and excluded groups and communities will be tackled.

Table 17.1   Approaches to partnership working

Approaches	Description	Illustration
Isolationist	No identifiable partnership exists.	A self-help parent–toddler group based in a rural location which meets at different parents' houses on a rotating basis and which has no obvious links with external bodies.
Encountering	Some inter-agency and inter-professional contact is maintained.	A residents' association that is based in an area of high crime and there is sporadic contact with external bodies such as the police and community wardens.
Communicative	A limited amount of joint working is undertaken, often just for the interest of individual agencies.	A luncheon club for Asian elderly which is based in a gurudwara and which is contracted by the local social services department to provide this service. The contact between the two agencies is infrequent and largely defined by their contractual relationship.
Collaboration	Separate organisations work together, recognising each other's strengths and contributions.	A consortium of voluntary and community sector infrastructure organisations coming together to apply for funding, to work in greater harmony and to minimise duplication.
Integrationist	A high level of collaboration takes place, sometimes leading to the creation of a unitary organisation.	The creation of a legal entity in the form of, for example, a regeneration company whose board members comprise people from private, public and voluntary sector organisations.

The point is that partnership working is more than just about the setting up of formal structures – it is as much about an ethos and a way of working. The VCS is used to working in partnership with other agencies in order to provide a holistic service to local communities and so the concept is nothing new. Partnership working involving the VCS has to acknowledge this and accept that effective partnership arrangements are not possible without a commitment to the spirit of sharing, being open and a willingness to work co-operatively. Indeed, study of the government's *Every Child Matters: Change for Children* (DfES, 2003), which aims to shape the services for children and young people, shows the term 'co-operatively' used repeatedly throughout the document.

Risks in partnership working

As we have seen, there is an overwhelming pressure for the public, voluntary and community sectors to move towards greater and more formalised partnership working. The assumption is that partnership working is a 'good thing' and that it can 'reach the parts that individual organisations by themselves cannot reach'. One of the key arguments for partnership working is that it can result in greater effectiveness and efficiency in the design and delivery of local services.

On the surface, the argument is plausible and difficult to challenge especially given the fact that the history and culture of the VCS is steeped in partnership working of one sort or another. However the actual proof for this is contentious and scarce. There are accusations that public funds have been used to host showcase events to put a positive spin on community activities but which do not lead to any measurable improvement in the lives of local people. Of course, different partnerships will work in different ways and even within a given area there will be differences between the effectiveness of different partnerships and so as volunteers, workers, managers, funders and policy makers involved in the VCS, it is important also to consider some of the limitations of partnership working.

Many would argue that partnership working is an unworkable and ambitious solution to many of the issues that we face and that it has been used as an instrument to cut public services, undermine local democracy and administer government policies. From my experiences of working with the VCS and other local organisations, partnership working often can be an inefficient and ineffective tool for tackling social issues and not necessarily the best fit solution to local issues – more a case of trying to 'fit square pegs into round holes'.

For example, in one West Midlands outer estate where crime and vandalism were a big issue for local communities, attempts were made to get together local residents, councillors, the police, the youth workers, the church and local authority representatives. The involvement of local people and key agencies operating within the community was seen to be crucial in tackling crime and vandalism. In this example, crime and vandalism were reduced for a short period of time while the partnership was working but once the key agencies pulled out because of shifts in funding priorities, the residents were unable to sustain the work by themselves and the whole initiative folded.

Many small VCS organisations including self-help groups and bodies that rely solely on volunteers do not feature prominently on the radar of local partnerships. Although their contributions to community life are acknowledged, engaging smaller organisations in partnership working is seen to be a laborious, resource intensive process. In a way this is not surprising as one of the key assumptions behind partnership working is that all sections of the VCS are well resourced and staffed to engage in effective partnership working on par with the bigger and better resourced public and statutory sectors.

For example, one of the most frequent complaints made by smaller VCS organisations regarding partnership working is that meetings are held during the daytime which make it difficult for organisations that are reliant on volunteers to attend. In any case, it is argued that it is easier for a local authority to release one of its hundreds of staff to attend partnership meetings than it is for an organisation that is reliant wholly on volunteers or a handful of paid staff that are overstretched anyway. The truth is that the VCS is under-staffed, under resourced and reliant on the goodwill of ever decreasing numbers of committed volunteers.

It is thus important to recognise that it takes resources and sustained efforts to establish, develop and maintain partnerships, whether these resources are in the form of money, time, skills, facilities or equipment. For all organisations any time and effort that is spent on partnership working is time and money away from frontline service delivery. For smaller VCS organisations which are under funded and under staffed, a disproportionate amount of their resources can end up being absorbed into partnership working without seem-ingly enhancing frontline services and benefiting local people. This then raises the question of how partnership working can be funded properly so that smaller organisations and the VCS overall does not have to bear a dispropor-tionate cost of partnership working compared with some of the bigger, better funded and staffed public and statutory sector bodies.

The VCS also needs to get its own house in order. There are inequalities within the sector which mean that larger and more established organisations tend to be at an advantage and have a greater capacity for partnership working. Often, the same organisations are better recognised by statutory and public sector partners because of their past track record resulting in the exclusion or neglect of smaller and or less well established organisations. An off the cuff remark by a local authority officer highlights this issue:

> How possible is it for a Chief Officer of a local voluntary organisation earning say £25,000 and running an organisation of two staff with an annual budget of £75,000 to sit as an equal at a partnership table with the Chief Officer of a local authority earning £100,000+, managing hundreds of staff and a budget of millions?

Such structural and embedded differences between organisations of different sizes can result in the partnership treating some partners more equally than others. In most cases, the VCS tends to be in a minority on many partnerships and so this raises two fundamental questions: first, how can one organisation be truly representative of the VCS which might comprise hundreds of organi-sations in a given area, and second, how can this 'representative' organisation be effective in partnerships comprising more powerful and better resourced organisations? A possible net effect of such inequalities at partnership levels is that instead of promoting a 'feel good' factor between key organisations, it could result in greater competitiveness and rivalry. Instead of co-operation and coherence there could be unhealthy competition and fragmentation.

The VCS is seen often by statutory and public sector bodies as a conduit into local communities and an advocate for local people especially sections of our society that are deemed to be 'hard to reach'. Indeed, the sector often sells itself as the voice of the people and argues that it is in closer proximity to the client base of local providers including local authorities. The sector also prides itself on being based on community development and empowerment principles, enabling local groups and individuals to articulate their needs and aspirations.

For instance, the governance of voluntary and community organisations by local people who sit on management committees and boards is seen to be a concrete demonstration of how local people work in partnership with others to start initiatives, establish projects and manage organisations. However, the VCS faces an uphill and constant struggle to recruit and retain trustees and management committee members, perhaps illustrating that the VCS does not always find it easy to verify its claims of being representative of or working in partnership with local communities.

Partnership working as an opportunity

Historically, the VCS has been funded and resourced poorly and without the goodwill, donations and public funding, the sector could not have survived. One of the most fundamental issues that continues to plague the VCS is funding and the longer-term sustainability of individual organisations given the demise of grant giving in many local authority areas. Even recent moves towards the creation of income generation or trading arms in the form of social enterprises do not address the structural issue of insufficient funding for the sector and the constant uncertainty that faces individual organisations.

Despite such contextual difficulties, a number of opportunities do exist. Partnership working has the potential of opening more or different funding streams for the VCS and in turn exposing and showcasing the work of the sector to a wider range of funders. Partnership working can open up opportunities for the sector to share its knowledge, skills and experiences of local communities with other partner agencies.

Often, the VCS or significant parts of it are excluded from key decision-making processes affecting local service delivery, funding and commissioning arrangements. Partnership working is a key opportunity for the VCS to assert its own case to people and partners who are external to the sector and may not appreciate what the sector does or how important it is in the lives of local communities.

Partnership working can offer local planners and decision makers an opportunity to explore alternative and perhaps more innovative ways of solving local issues especially when it comes to tackling social exclusion and inequality. However, such an approach requires the strengths of individual agencies to be drawn upon, an expectation that there will be mutual respect among key partners and an acknowledgement that what is at stake is local democracy not just the financial interests of individual organisations.

Improving partnership working with the VCS

For partnership working to improve and for this to benefit local communities, a number of factors need to be addressed. At a fundamental level, there is the need to acknowledge the contribution of the VCS to the life and development of this country. The VCS is a tremendous asset to this country but its true worth is not always recognised and acknowledged.

Partnership working, advocacy and representation work comes at a price. Not only is there a direct cost in terms of time and money but there is also the 'loss of earnings' resulting from not delivering direct services in the time that you are doing partnership work. Additionally, not all organisations have the capacity or the skills to work in partnership, therefore there is a need for an investment programme if partnership working is to become a more effective and sustainable way of co-ordinating ad delivering services in the long run.

The VCS comprises different types of organisations working with different communities in different environments: self-help groups established by recently arrived refugees and asylum seekers, long established national voluntary organisations, regional support agencies, homelessness charities, community and social enterprises, and so on.

Partnership working has to acknowledge these differences but also in the spirit of wanting to address equal opportunities ensure that the perspectives of a range of organisations are represented, advocated for and are able to access and influence decision-making structures. One of the greatest challenges facing agencies involved in partnership working is ensuring that the needs, experiences and expectations of marginalised communities are represented and heard.

At local, regional and national levels the VCS is served by specialist and generalist infrastructure support organisations such as the National Council for Voluntary Organisations (NCVO), The Council for Ethnic Minority Voluntary Organisations (CEMVO), local Councils for Voluntary Services (CVSs), and so on. These bodies need to ensure that not only do they serve the interests of the whole VCS but that they do so with equality. Often many infrastructure bodies are seen to be competing for the same resources as their clients and/or member organisations and because they are seen to be closer to local decision makers, it is argued that they have an unfair advantage over frontline organisations.

Overall, it is imperative that every partnership regularly reviews its effectiveness and whether or not its work has contributed to increased effectiveness, efficiency and an improvement in public services as experienced by local communities. The following guidelines have been compiled from a number of sources including the Audit Commission's (1998) report on partnership working and offers some basic pointers for developing good practice in partnership working.

Guidelines for successful partnership working

Culture

Create and communicate openness, transparency and honesty.

Vision

Work through, agree and deliver to a shared vision.

Co-ordination

Allocate responsibilities, clarify lines of accountability and ensure effective co-ordination and administration.

Mutuality

Work to individual strengths and explicitly acknowledge what individual organisations are investing in and will get out of the partnership.

Resourcing

Secure sufficient resources for the partnership to carry out its functions and for individual partners to participate equally.

Equality and diversity

Recognise existing inequalities in partnership arrangements and the diverse needs and expectations of different partners and their constituencies.

Joint solutions

Work co-operatively to strive for joint and mutually agreeable solutions.

Reward

Celebrate the contributions of and enable all partners to reap the benefits of partnership working.

(Continued)

(Continued)

Evaluation

Implement periodic reviews and evaluations to ensure that the work of the partnership remains focused and is fulfilling its overall mission not just output targets.

Exit

Adopt an exit strategy and answer honestly the question, is the partnership still as beneficial as it was when it was thought of and in whose interests?

Conclusion

Partnership working is seen to be an important way of delivering local services and improving working relationships between the public, voluntary, community and private sectors and local communities. Though a much used phrase and much accepted way of working, little evidence exists to confirm how effective partnership working truly is and to what extent it makes a real difference to local service delivery. There is little doubt that increased and improved partnership working can lead to greater awareness by agencies of each other's work. On current form though, it could be argued that existing partnership models are ill-conceived and tend to favour the bigger organisations thus strengthening the already strong and further marginalising the weak or the excluded.

For the VCS, partnership working can open up opportunities but this would depend on whether or not a VCS organisation was in the right place at the right time. The major pitfall with partnership working for the VCS is its treatment as a junior partner thus undermining its credibility and limiting its full potential. However, the VCS has to draw upon its history and one of its strengths is that it has been one of the first to engage in partnership working as a way of maximising resources and drawing in other key stakeholders including the private sector. This ethos of benefiting the end user has to be the central plank and perhaps the only plank bridging different agencies under the guise of partnership working.

At a more practical level, the essence of partnership working is about making the most of the limited resources that might exist, to minimise duplication and to play to the strengths of key partners and allocate tasks and responsibilities accordingly. Ultimately though, partnership working will be only as good as the intent and the genuineness of different partners wishing to work together for the betterment of local communities, regardless of self-interest, funding or policy imperatives.

References

DfES (2003) *Every Child Matters: Change for Children*. London: The Stationery Office.
DfES (2004) *The Child Act*. London: The Stationery Office.
DoH (2004) *Choosing Health: Making Healthy Choices Easier*. London: The Stationery Office.
Effective Interventions Unit (2003) *A Guide to Working in Partnership: Employability Provision for Drug Users*. http://www.scotland.gov.uk/Publications/2003/03/16641/19341
Home Office (1998) *Compact on Relations between Government and the Voluntary and Community Sector in England*. London: Home Office.
Orme, J., Powell, J., Taylor, P., Harrison, T. and Grey, M. (eds) (2003) *Public Health for the 21st Century: New Perspectives on Policy, Participation and Practice*. Maidenhead: OUP.
The Audit Commission (1998) *A Fruitful Partnership: Effective Partnership Working*. London: The Audit Commission.

18

Managing in integrated services

Rob Hunter with Dee Hammerson and Dee Treweek

Introduction

Local authority youth services are moving from the periphery of local authority provision to a position which is both more structurally integrated with, and potentially more influential in, council services. Some see this as an opportunity to be seized. Others are more wary. Will it be 'the death of the youth service'? Will it change the nature of youth work? The reality is that significant change is taking place in the provision of services for young people and inevitably this will have implications for youth workers and those leading and managing youth work. In this chapter we explore some of the issues raised in semi-structured interviews with two managers in one youth service which is still in the early days of reorganisation. Every organisation will have its own distinctive style, purpose, structure and political context. We hope to highlight, however, some of the common themes that leaders and managers of youth work are likely to have to address as they negotiate the developing agenda of integrated working.

The youth service and structures

For much of their 60-year history prior to the millennium, the organisational location of youth services in English local authorities' structures was not a major issue. Decisions about where services sat in departmental structures were made locally by individual authorities. Youth services were usually based in education departments. A small number of authorities, including Cambridgeshire, Leicestershire and Coventry, developed youth work within a broader community education model, with youth work taking place alongside adult education and provision managed and delivered through schools and community colleges.

Occasionally there were concerns regarding the location of youth work. In the local government reorganisation of 1974, for example, a number of services fought to stay within local authority education departments, fearing that the educational basis of their work would be at risk if they moved. In services that did move, however – to Leisure Services in the cases of Avon and Nottinghamshire – there is little evidence that the educational basis was diluted. And again, in another local government reorganisation in 1997, with many newly created unitary authorities taking on responsibility for youth work for the very first time, some youth services had to work particularly hard with politicians to promote an awareness of the conditions under which youth work could best be supported.

At the interface with young people, did it matter where youth workers were physically or organisationally located? A school-based location might alienate some young people from engaging but it made youth work more accessible for others. Being located alongside recreation might lead to an emphasis on the need to attract large numbers and provide entertainment rather than education but there could be advantages to being part of a broader range of community services.

On the whole youth services across England saw themselves, and were seen as being, on the margins of local authority structures and activities, on the outside looking in. Youth workers, while traditionally complaining about a lack of professional recognition, often relished their freedom and the greater degree of autonomy they had to determine their work compared with other professionals and local authority staff. This marginalisation made youth services particularly vulnerable at times of reduction in public spending. In the later Thatcher and early Major governments, for example, a number of services suffered swingeing cuts.

The election of a new Labour government in 1997 brought new hope to those working with young people and communities. The work of the Social Exclusion Unit, and its report *Bridging the Gap* (SEU, 1999), highlighted the difficulties of 160,000 socially excluded young people aged 16–17 and the need for more 'joined up thinking' in work with young people. Interest in the youth service's contribution to social policy objectives revived. Youth work was formally placed at the heart of the Connexions Strategy (DfEE, 2001) though the models of joint working between youth services and Connexions saw a wide range of local variation. In some areas of the country, Connexions services developed a high degree of integration between the youth work and careers functions and structures. In other areas, the two services were much more separate, both organisationally and culturally.

The 'best value' mantra of involving consumers in the design, delivery and evaluation of services, as well as democratic deficit and active citizenship imperatives were among the forces luring youth services into what some would see as a Faustian pact: the government promised enhanced resources in exchange for youth service's contribution to meeting targets for cutting teenage pregnancy rates, reducing drugs and alcohol misuse, and raising educational attainment. Some criticised the selling out of youth work principles in the face of government money and influence. *Every Child Matters* (DfES, 2003) was followed closely by *Youth Matters* (DfES, 2005). Both heralded major change in the way that services for young people would be managed and delivered, including the creation of Children's Trust and proposals for 'the development of an integrated youth support service, with integrated governance, processes and frontline delivery'. (DfES, 2005: para 76). It was clear that statutory youth services had little if any alternative to engaging with integration. The only question was the nature of that integration.

Approaches to integration

Local authorities have responded to the integrated services agenda in different ways. One approach has been to create integrated structures, bringing together a number of services and different professionals working with young people within a larger Children's Services department. Another approach has been to adopt a neighbourhood management model, drawing together the management of all council services in a particular geographical area. Both approaches may result in youth workers working in integrated teams with staff from other professional backgrounds and not necessarily being managed by staff with youth work experience and training. An alternative approach has been to adopt a strategy of 'virtual reorganisation', focused on integrating strategies and improving joint working across different professions and departments working with children and young people, before deciding whether to consolidate change through major restructuring.

Different models of integration also involve different budgetary arrangements. In some areas, youth service budgets are being pooled within larger Children's Services budgets. Other youth services still retain control of their own discrete budgets. Central government has emphasised the devolution of funding within Local Area Agreements and the importance of local collaboration in delivering these.

Many youth workers have viewed these policy developments with deep concern, worried by what they see as a threat to a distinctive professional identity based on youth work values and principles. Smith (2005), for example, writing about 'the tyranny of joined up thinking' attacks proposals for information sharing that threaten young people's space 'away from the constant surveillance of families, schools and the state', denying a fresh start for some young people, and potentially leading to 'a depersonalised approach that emphasises the management of cases rather than working with young people's accounts of situations and experiences.' But is the picture necessarily so negative and what can be learned from experience so far?

Integration in practice: reflections from Doncaster Council Youth Service

Maximising the advantages and minimising the problems of working in integrated services are likely to be a key part of the job of those leading and managing work with young people in this new era – issues we explored with senior staff from Doncaster Youth Service. Doncaster was chosen for a number of reasons. At the time of writing it already had 15 months' experience of involvement in a new integrated structure, in advance of many other youth services. A report (Ofsted, 2003) also indicated that Doncaster Youth Service was a 'very good' youth service, providing young people with, 'a wide range of activities and programmes of a very good quality'. This judgement suggested that reflection on the early processes of integration would be less likely to be contaminated by the difficulties of trying to manage an underperforming youth service, with a poor reputation in the authority and with other agencies. A bonus was the fact that after arrangements were made for interviews on which the rest of this chapter is based, the 2006 Ofsted report was published which classified the service as 'outstanding' across all key aspects, identifying 'a service that delivers well above minimum requirements for users' (Ofsted, 2006a).

The Doncaster context

Doncaster Metropolitan Borough Council has a population of 286,866, a quarter of whom live in Doncaster and its immediate suburbs. There is significant deprivation. Over 40 per cent of residents live in neighbourhoods which are among the 10 per cent most disadvantaged in England. BME families number about 9,000 or 3 per cent. The number of Traveller and asylum-seeking families has increased over the past four years.

Doncaster Council Youth Service provides work through 16 youth centres, a number of outreach and targeted projects, one information, advice and support centre and through three mobile units. The service is managed by a Youth Service Manager and six youth officers. Eighteen full-time youth workers and 97 part-time youth workers deliver the service. The budget of the service is £2,348,350 and 29 per cent of 13–19-year-olds are reached annually.

The report of the 2006 Ofsted inspection, (Ofsted, 2006a: section 3) which formed part of a joint area review, stated:

> Doncaster Youth Service is an outstanding service. It has ... significant strengths and few weaknesses. The outcomes for young people are very good and in some cases excellent ... Young people are at the heart of service development. Leadership and management are excellent and create the environment within which youth work can flourish and youth workers can provide first-rate support for young people that enables them to make considerable progress.

This inspection took place four months after a major reorganisation of council services. Doncaster MBC decided that in order to put residents at the heart of its services it would adopt a neighbourhood management structure, dividing the borough into five geographical areas. Each area was subdivided into three neighbourhoods, making 15 neighbourhoods in all across the authority. Line management of the youth service is now through five Area Youth Officer posts, which are each line managed by an Area Manager. Youth Officers remain accountable to the Youth Service Manager in relation to professional and strategic youth work issues. The Youth Services Manager reports to the Director of Children's Services in the council's Directorate (consisting of the Directors of Services and the five Area Managers).

The remainder of this chapter is based on interviews with two senior youth service officers, Dee Hammerson and Dee Treweek, and explores their experiences of managing in an integrated structure from its inception in July 2005 till October 2006. Dee Hammerson had been Youth Service Manager in Doncaster from 1995. On reorganisation she maintained this role and took on an additional role as one of 15 Neighbourhood Managers in the authority. Dee Treweek had been the youth service's Quality Assurance lead officer. She is now a Youth Officer in one of the authority's five areas and she has maintained her Quality Assurance role across the youth service.

Dee Hammerson's role now has a very wide range of responsibilities which make interesting reading. As well as being Youth Service Manager, she has other borough-wide responsibilities for the Music Service, the Ethnic

Minority and Traveller Service, School Admissions, and Pupil Support and Transport. As an Area Manager, she also has responsibility for all services to children and young people in a fifth of the borough, and, as one of the 15 neighbourhood managers, she manages the delivery of all council services in an area of approximately 20,000 people.

The McKinsey 7S Framework

We have examined the two managers' experiences of integration over the last 15 months using McKinsey's 7S Framework (Figure 18.1). On one level this is simply a sophisticated checklist for examining the main elements of an organisation – or reorganisation. On another level, the framework can help leaders and managers to develop strategic approaches to complex issues, based not just on their understanding of individual elements within a particular organisation or situation, but also on an understanding of how individual elements interact with and impact on each other.

The significance of shared values to integration

Shared Values are at the heart of the 7S Framework. Since it was originally developed in 1982 there has been a resurgence of interest in the importance of values in driving and holding organisations together. As Collins (1999), a respected management writer observes: 'In the long run, individual leaders do not hold an organisation together; core values and purposes do'.

Doncaster MBC reorganised its structures in order to put residents at the heart of its service delivery. This resident-centred value chimes well with the Youth Service's values and approaches, with their focus on young people-centred services and commitment to young people having a voice in decision making. Dee Hammerson believes that the development of integrated teams is enabling Youth Officers to transmit youth work values across each area team. She also believes that this is having a positive impact on the way that young people are viewed by different professionals, who previously might only have seen young people in terms of youth nuisance and diversionary activities. Other important youth work values, including a strong commitment to equality are values shared across other Council departments.

Structural change is also providing an opportunity for other professionals to see evidence of the value of youth work.

> I think it's becoming clear to all those involved that when young people, as happened recently, are asked by the Teenage Pregnancy Unit to do a mystery shopper exercise for

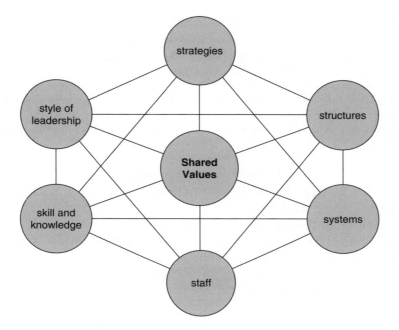

Figure 18.1   The McKinsey 7S Framework (Pascale and Athos, 1981)

> the Borough's eleven sexual health units, and they then present the sometimes critical findings in a very sensitive way to an audience of 50 adult professionals – this is not only valuing their voice and opinion but it's so obvious that they are developing confidence and skill and learning from the process and that this too is part of what we're about. (Dee Treweek)

So the congruence of Youth Service and some broader council values may well have helped the process of integration. Developing more young people-centred approaches has also enabled other services to demonstrate they are working to the council's resident-centred agenda.

> It hasn't always been rosy. There's been occasional resistance. Some local community members and council officers are happy with 'resident-centred' but don't appreciate that young people are also residents. But the growing reputation of the Youth Council helps with this. (Dee Hammerson)

The significance of structure to integration

In the context of the 7S Framework, Structure refers to the way the organisation is configured and ways in which group decisions are taken. Dee Hammerson believes that structural change has already led to a greater sense of joint responsibility, indeed a shared sense of pride, amongst staff who had previously worked quite separately in different departments of the council.

> I thought 'pride' seemed initially over-the-top. But there **is** a pride and it does develop. It grows on you, that feeling of ownership ... We attended various workshops in the run up to the restructuring but it wasn't that which did it. It was the doing it. It grew inside you. A lot of people feel this. It's a sort of collective responsibility. It's wonderful.

Dee Hammerson highlights the relationship between structure, shared values and style. She believes that new opportunities for promoting young people's issues across the council have helped to create an environment in which youth workers' values and skills are now being valued within different integrated teams. Youth workers have structured contact with other professionals through neighbourhood team meetings, as well as lots of opportunities for informal contact. Young people also have opportunities for dialogue and different ways of making their voice heard within the structure, again reflecting shared values.

> The views of children and young people are taken very seriously by the council and its partners. A very good range of opportunities for young people of all ages, from diverse backgrounds and from vulnerable groups, enables them to contribute to decision-making and shape the provision of services. Their views have influenced policy, plans and practice, at strategic and at local level, most notably through the very effective youth council and its representation on strategic boards ... A significant number of young people are involved with the youth service and take part in checks on the quality of the work of services. (Ofsted, 2006b: para 60)

Dee Hammerson admits that there have been significant challenges.

> There was a lot of talk that the restructuring was going to be the end of the youth service as we knew it. Well, it was, but it's evolved into something else. It's all neighbourhood based.

The new structure includes a new Principal Youth Officer post, managed by the Youth Service Manager, with responsibility for overseeing key aspects of youth work, including quality assurance, training, youth engagement, awards and accreditation. She sees this as a crucial post:

> People can so easily become wrapped up in their areas rather than looking at things strategically.

Appointment to the post, however, was delayed for budgetary reasons, which she admits has put the situation under some strain.

I'm relieved that the appointment will now be made to start from April 2007. In the meanwhile we've managed to stop the separation into silos because people had the will to ensure it didn't happen.

Change has also had an impact on how the Youth Officer group operates, with individuals taking on additional responsibilities. They now meet less often – fortnightly, rather than weekly – though they still have monthly individual supervision with the Youth Service Manager. They are also now located in different areas, rather than in a central Youth Service base, which potentially makes informal contact and communication more difficult. Again though, staff are aware of the importance of good communication and have a commitment to ensuring that this is maintained.

The significance of strategy for integration

Doncaster's overarching community strategy reflects the government's strategy for neighbourhood renewal: that within 10–20 years, no one should be seriously disadvantaged because of where they live. Sixty per cent of youth service participants are classified as 'disadvantaged' and work with young people reflects a neighbourhood agenda, working to create area and neighbourhood cohesiveness.

> It's like a jigsaw with all of us playing parts within this frame. (Dee Hammerson)

Youth work fits within Doncaster's Children's and Young People's Strategy which in turn reflects the five outcomes of *Every Child Matters* (DfES, 2003).

> The (youth) service makes a very strong contribution to (ECM) outcomes in a number of areas. Established and well thought through projects based on young people's needs are the key to the service's strengths in this area … A very good range of programmes are available and nearly 1 in 3 young people in the 13–19 age group voluntarily take part in youth service activities each year. (Ofsted, 2006a: para 5).

So it seems the service is aligned with statutory and local policy strategic requirements in terms of priority groupings, reach and range, and delivers effectively on these. It aims to put young people at the heart of its own internal service strategies and bring that thinking into integrated structures.

> Part of our strategy is to communicate the positive aspects of youth work and what youth work can bring to a neighbourhood and an area. Young people are a fantastic force for good and can be so productive and be that force for good in a neighbourhood. They cannot be ignored. If they are ignored, they have the energy to cause problems. The government's respect agenda distorts the word. It's the mutual respect that young people crave. (Dee Hammerson)

The significance of staff to integration

The 7S Framework highlights how issues relating to staff, including numbers of staff and their levels of experience and qualifications, influence the effectiveness of an organisation. All posts in the Doncaster Youth Service were retained in the reorganisation. The job descriptions of field staff were not affected. Officers' posts have changed significantly.

> In addition to retaining my responsibility for quality assurance across the service, I have taken on the Area Youth Officer role which entails responsibility for staff and programmes in a fifth of the authority. My two officer colleagues – there were five of us in the former service but two took Voluntary Early Retirement after reorganisation – are currently in charge of two area youth work teams each. This has several effects. We have to work hard at keeping a strategic perspective and not only looking inwards into the needs of our areas. We also need to work hard at communication with each other to ensure consistency. An unexpected positive for me wearing my QA (quality assurance) hat has been that if I see the need to change certain systems to sharpen QA, I can pilot changes with the team in my area and learn from them before working with colleagues to roll them out across the service. (Dee Treweek)

The influence of systems on the task of integration

The move to integration in Doncaster was helped by the fact that the Youth Service had well established and effective systems, including for quality assurance, that it was able to transfer into the new structure. It was a service that was used to having to provide evidence of its work.

> These allowed us to know pretty much what was going on in our projects and centres and be able to speak confidently about our offer and our plans for improvement. (Dee Treweek)

She believes that having clear systems including an established system of supervision was important in helping to support staff in the new structure. She also is very aware that systems need to be owned, rather than just being imposed on staff.

> Take, for example, that around recorded and accredited outcomes. Our first go at this had been rather top-down and there was substantial resistance. So we decided we needed to start again and opened up with staff the feelings level surrounding this, giving time and space to explore their anxieties about how these might distort their work and the anger about what they saw as imposition. Handling these feelings allowed us to get into a more rational dialogue on the issue, understand that what we all wanted was the best for young people and release energy for testing out what were seen as more manageable approaches with young people ... In all this, I thought I was

being sensitive but I realised that occasionally I had lost sight of the workload for youth workers ... Being responsible for QA I needed to get the maximum amount of information for the minimum of effort and I also needed something people would comply with – it's no use having a system which many ignore or you have to spend ages chasing things up ... Staff saw the system which emerged as reasonable and that we had been responsive to their concerns.

This thinking has underpinned systems the service has developed in the new organisation, including a form for sharing information from meetings which she has developed with Youth Work Coordinators.

It's only a simple set of headings – a personal note made every time they go to a meeting. It gives them a focus for noting the meeting and allows others to pick up quickly on what went on ... My two Area Youth Work Co-ordinators also now do monthly account, review and projection reports; these give a brief account of how they've spent their time, review this against plans and outcomes, and look forward over the next month. These go to neighbourhood and area managers and allow them to pick up issues and communicate them across their team.

As well as meeting with the Youth Work Co-ordinators she also has a monthly youth work team meeting involving full- and part-time youth workers, cleaners and administrative workers, who are all paid to attend.

The purpose is team-building, ensuring strong support for youth workers, and trying to ensure consistency of quality across the area. It's a big investment of time and money and we may have to make the meetings less frequent after this first year but I think this sort of team development is really important in an integrated service. We have a social event every six weeks in which no-one is allowed to discuss work. Even an employee of the month award! All of this is reflected in our contribution to the youth service newsletter which is developed by the Curriculum Worker for the whole service monthly and which goes to all Area and Neighbourhood Managers, to the police, to libraries – another system to promote our work internally and externally.

The influence of style on integration

In the 7S Framework, style refers to leadership style. Dee Hammerson reflects on her leadership style and how she has tried to lead and position the youth service in the new structure, advocating and interpreting on its behalf and on behalf of young people.

My leadership style is very hands-on. I do try and walk the talk. But I've had gradually to let go and empowered my officers to take more responsibility – I think they've enjoyed the extra responsibility. My leadership role in relation to youth workers has, I think, been helping them feel positive about the opportunities of the restructuring and encouraging workers to be proactive in their areas, heighten their awareness. I think you've got to keep listening to young people and to your staff. Don't let things fester. You've got to go head-on to some things and tackle others in a more round-about way. Trust your officers.

I've tried to value and respect the work of other agencies. I've been shadowing staff in those services which are new to me and getting out and about with them. It's the doing of things together – the joint meetings about how best to support a particular family – and joint action we take as a result of our discussions … We're all in this together.

It hasn't all been easy. At first I felt it was quite an alien environment I was going into, in some quarters there was a lot of negativity about young people – which is not surprising as many professions only come up against young people whose behaviour is causing difficulties. I wondered what I could contribute. I had management skills but in the particular area of youth work. But I should have realised you can widen out. I do believe in transferable skills but had lost sight of the fact that I might have them!

Dee Treweek reflects on the way she approaches her role as a leader and how this has developed with time and experience.

I used to be a protector and defender of young people and to hell with the consequences … Now I work on the basis that if I want to meet the needs of young people, there's more than one way, and there are advantages of taking routes which involve colleagues from other agencies. It may take more time but it's often a better long term solution than if I had done things on my own – I appreciate what we can do together – and now I find myself quite liking those other professionals I work with! I am so excited because initially I did have serious doubts about, for example, who would be managing our service.

I think professional empathy has been important. We are doing a lot of things well in our own eyes and in Ofsted's but we haven't the monopoly on good practice or on advocacy for young people. There's lots of good work out there by colleagues in other professions and we need to learn from them. I'm constantly looking for how colleagues perceive the youth service and how we can present our work even better.

We've been through some tough times. After a few months in the area there were things coming at me from all directions and we hadn't got the capacity or the resources to meet the demands of people who were using us as a dustbin – 'it's a problem with young people, let the youth service sort it out'. We had to get the difficult balance between holding our boundaries without being unwilling; of saying when we hadn't the time in the short term but nevertheless offering what we could do by when. There were some clashes with people who saw us as the containment service who wanted simply to stop the noise and nuisance calls.

Now several Area Managers and Neighbourhood Managers are making great efforts to get alongside young people. They often come to evenings on which we are celebrating awards to young people and these make a deep impression. One Area Manager has been out on patrol with the police but, with our support, got into good dialogue with young people when it might have been confrontational. A Neighbourhood Manager asked to spend three sessions with a youth work project so that she could get the feel of the young people and understand better what the youth workers were trying to do. She got a lot from it and now she uses that experience in the wide variety of meetings she goes to.

The influence of skills on integration

'Skills' in the 7S Framework means the collective skills of people working within an organisation.

Dee Treweek reflects on how youth workers have had to develop new skills in integrated working, building on the skills they already had in working with young people and with those they managed.

> Youth workers across Doncaster have got much smarter at promoting young people in a positive light whilst acknowledging that some young people do create a nuisance some of the time ... Youth workers are increasingly seeing meetings as opportunities rather than chores taking them away from 'the real work'. They are being proactive, taking an advocate role, promoting young people and asking, 'What can we do as a group?' ... Good youth work has always been about engaging young people in conversation, listening – and taking action where necessary. This style is transferable to work with professional colleagues.

Some final reflections

It is early days in Doncaster's new structure. For the youth service, in Tuckman's (1965) terms it would seem that 15 months after the initial forming period and some inevitable storming, constructive new norms are developing and staff are performing and developing high quality learning opportunities with young people. There will inevitably be new storms ahead, new norms to negotiate – but the groundwork seems in place to continue and grow youth service influence.

This is of course just one picture of the experience of reorganisation in Doncaster. Others including youth workers, staff in other organisations, and young people are likely to have different perspectives – particularly in relation to whether outcomes for young people have improved. As Dee Treweek concludes:

> It may be too early to tell. The processes leading to outcomes would seem to be on track. Our new colleagues from other agencies say they have a clearer understanding of young people's needs and the issues they are having. They know more about what youth workers can contribute and the process of referrals is clearer.

Our purpose here has been simply to explore and record the perspectives of two managers with successful experience of managing at different levels within a youth service, as they reflect on their own initial experience of managing within integrated services. We recognise that there are likely to be challenging times ahead for youth services as they negotiate the new terrain of integrated services and integrated ways of working. Some services will not be entering this new arena with as strong an identity, or with the same track record of effective work with young people, as has been the case in Doncaster. We are mindful of the reservation expressed by one commentator reflecting on the potential dangers for youth work's distinct identity within new integrated structures.

> Youth work, by its very nature and definition, though not oblivious to wider public and political considerations, builds primarily from the needs, issues and concerns of young people. It gives priority to young people. It operates at the interface between the aspirations and perspectives of young people, and the expectations of public policy. If it is to retain that distinct identity – and thus a credibility with young people that is lacking with some other agencies that have more top down imperatives – it must avoid being subsumed with either children's agendas or practice specifically identified with a single thread of public policy (such as crime or health or schooling). (Williamson, 2006: 12)

There seems, however, to be interesting progress in Doncaster.

References

Collins, J. (1999) 'And the walls came tumbling down', in Drucker, P.F. (ed.), *Leading Beyond the Walls*. New York: Peter Drucker Foundation.

Department for Education and Employment (2001) *Transforming Youth Work*. Nottingham: DfEE Publications.

Department for Education and Skills (2003) *Every Child Matters*. London: The Stationery Office.

Department for Education and Skills (2005) *Youth Matters*. London: The Stationery Office.

Ofsted (2003) *Inspection of Doncaster Youth Service*. London: Ofsted.

Ofsted (2006a) *Doncaster Youth Service Report*. London: Ofsted.

Ofsted (2006b) *Joint Area Review–Doncaster Children's Service's Authority, Review of Services for Children and Young People*. London: Ofsted.

Pascale, R.T. and Athos, A. (1981) *The Art of Japanese Management*. New York, Simon and Schuster.

SEU (1999) *Bridging the Gap – New Opportunities for 16–18-year-olds not in Education, Employment and Training*. London: Social Exclusion Unit.

Smith, M. (2005) *Youth Matters – The Green Paper on Services for Youth*. http://www.infed.org/youthwork/green_paper_2005.htm 29.08.2005

Tuckman, B. (1965) 'Developmental sequence in small groups', *Psychological Bulletin*, 63(6): 384–99.

Williamson. H. (2006) *Youth Work and the Changing Policy Environment for Young People*. Leicester: National Youth Agency.

Evaluation

This section looks at the ways in which we operate as practitioners with young people on a day-to-day basis, and at how we monitor and evaluate the impact of our work. The last few years has seen increasing pressure to demonstrate the worth of work with young people to a range of external stakeholders, including to those who are making decisions about funding and resources. This external accountability and the accompanying requirement to measure specific outputs, outcomes and impact raises questions about how we plan our work, how we record and share what we do, and how we define learning and change among young people and communities.

The writers within this section aim to demonstrate how these activities can be integrated into our everyday practice so that they enrich our work with young people rather than detracting from it. They discuss the need to consider how we use information gathered to inform our own practice so that we can provide better activities and services for young people and develop as reflective practitioners. While doing this we need to pay attention to the values and principles of work with young people so that we address these elements of practice in an inclusive and participative way. This will enable young people and practitioners to feel ownership and pride in the results of their endeavours. These chapters demonstrate how thoughtful consideration of such issues can take us to the heart of good practice.

Mark Smith and Tony Jeffs demonstrate how individual workers can analyse and therefore prioritise their day-to-day work, thus ensuring that they are getting the most out of each area of activity. They suggest that this approach will help practitioners to more easily understand the broader principles behind what they are trying to achieve and the value of their work.

Bryan Merton et al. write about an impact study carried out in 2003–2004. They discuss the importance, benefits and difficulties of measurement, making it clear that the first priority is to provide good services for young people. They highlight the ambivalence that some workers feel when asked to measure impact and demonstrate that when given the tools for the job, even the most sceptical begin to see the value of this approach.

Finally, Gersh Subhra considers evaluation. He outlines the history of evaluation as we understand it today and suggests the ingredients for a practical strategy that will embed evaluation as a central focus within an organisation's planning and review process.

19

Organizing the daily round

Mark K. Smith and Tony Jeffs

How does all this translate itself into our activities on Monday morning or Tuesday night? The starting point is that informal educators need to find and foster environments in which people can talk. We have two basic options. Either we go to places where people congregate, or we create a setting that will attract them to where we are located. In youth work these approaches have been traditionally separated as detached and centre-based work. To some extent there has also been a similar split between community organization and development, and community centre work. Such divisions are reflected in almost every area of welfare and have set up false dichotomies – prison versus probation, residential versus community care, and so on. One of the advantages of thinking about informal education in the way we have been here is that it takes us beyond such simplistic splits.

Informal educators undertake six basic kinds of work. According to Smith (1994) these can be labeled as follows:

- **Being around** involves activities such as walking round the area, visiting local drinking places and going into the school. In centres 'being around' translates into the time spent sitting round the bar, and coffee lounge. The aim, generally, is to be seen, to make and maintain contact with people, and to intervene where appropriate. This is a positive activity requiring planning and reflection. It is neither a 'filler' nor something undertaken randomly.
- **Being there** involves informal educators setting time aside for responding to situations and crises. 'Being there' is a holding operation. It can

This is an edited version of a chapter first published in Smith, M. and Jeffs, T., *Informal Education: Conversation, Democracy and Learning, third edition*. Nottingham: Educational Heretics Press.

involve some practical assistance. It might mean, for example, going with someone to a rights project. The other key aspect is being a 'shoulder to cry on' in times of crisis. It involves taking steps to be contactable and in a position to respond.

- **Working with individuals and groups** describes more 'formal' encounters. It is linked into ideas about the depth of work undertaken. It entails moving beyond the making and maintenance of contact, or the holding operation that often takes place when 'being there'. 'Working with' involves building an environment in which people can entertain feelings, reflect on their experiences, think about things and make plans. It entails working to deepen conversation and to further democracy. With groups, for example, our task is, on the one hand, to work for democratic mutual aid. On the other hand, it is to help people to realize their purpose.

- **Doing projects** varies from one-off pieces of work, through regular sessions over a three-month or ten-month period (for instance, with a girls' group) to activities like residentials or study visits. It may involve short courses, for example, for carers or around childcare. Frequently, it takes the form of a particular activity such as developing a newsletter. Such projects are planned in advance, time-limited, focused on learning, and largely arise out of the work, rather than being imported as 'good ideas'. While 'working with' is conversation-based, projects tend to have a curriculum or output focus.

- **Doing 'admin' and research**. Informal educators usually have various administrative tasks to complete. These can range from simple returns dealing with pay and attendance through ordering and accounts to longer-term planning and fund raising. We may also have to do small research tasks. These can be to do with the places and neighbourhoods in which we work and the problems and issues we encounter. Classically, workers can get overrun by administrative work – especially if they work in organizations and programmes that require detailed reporting. There is also the temptation for some to do more and more administrative work as an escape from the demands of face-to-face work or as a way of gaining status.

- **Reflecting on practice** allows us to develop as workers, and to work for the best interests of clients and the community. Recording our work is a key element here – as is exploring practice with others. As a team we may talk about what happened in a session, as individuals we may sit down with a supervisor or collegue and examine what happened and our feelings about it.

Successful practice depends on there being a good mix of these ways of working. A measure of confidence in doing them is essential for all informal

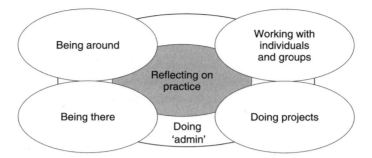

Figure 19.1   Six basic modes of work

educators. None are optional extras because each feeds off the other. Figure 19.1 tries to show how these come together.

Some basic considerations

When planning our work we, thus, need to ensure that we attend to some basic points.

We work where our target groups can be found

We cannot expect people magically to come to us. For those working with young people this may mean overcoming a number of prejudices. For example, many of the places where young people can be found have not been part of the traditional youth work pattern: schools and colleges, homes and commercial leisure operations. This also involves developing new ways of getting access. Often those who manage such sites are resistant to the presence of informal educators. Our style of working can be seen as strange and threatening, not least because of the subjects we are handling. Health educators may find it difficult to work in schools and colleges, for example. These institutions often fear their presence will be interpreted as an admission that they have a problem with drugs or promiscuity. We may also want to organize new settings where we can make contact, such as drop-ins, clubs and cafes.

We make ourselves and our work known

Informal educators have to work mostly in settings that are not overtly educational. As a result, we need to establish our role and be clear about what we can offer. This entails 'cold' contact work, that is to say, approaching people we have not previously met: on the street, door-to-door, or in social areas in schools and churches. Consequently, care has to be taken regarding style and manner. We have to be sensitive to the right of others to privacy, and to our own safety. We also need various 'props' to allow us to make contact: leaflets, programmes, calling cards. However, such props should reflect our priorities. Consider, for example, if we have made a decision to work with older people in an area, then leaflets must be designed and prepared in a way that is sensitive to their concerns and interests.

We have a range of more organized activities into which people can feed

Informal educators need a number of projects on the go at any given time. This can help us to communicate our identity as well as offering a range of new or wanted opportunities to those we are working with. Projects can also deepen the work and give it an overt focus. For many workers it is vital they have something more to offer than conversation, and themselves. In making contact with people who are homeless it is important that they are able to offer various services, e.g. help in accessing temporary accommodation and obtaining benefits.

We have space to respond to situations

One of our key strengths is the ability to respond quickly to what people are bringing. We need to 'catch the moment'. It is important, therefore, that we do not over-programme our time. We must leave plenty of time to 'be around'. This is time that is flexible. Where crises emerge or, say, we need to spend time talking something through with a group then we can convert 'being around' to 'being there' for someone, or to 'working with'. For example, we may be working with a group of women who use a family centre drop-in. It is likely that we will have to spend time with particular individuals as issues arise around, for example, relationships with partners and ex-partners, income support and the educational needs of their children.

We attend to administration

Informal education is demanding and sophisticated. We can find ourselves dealing with very difficult problems, we have to work in settings that are not at all straightforward and we have continually to think on our feet. To be clear about what we are doing we need to talk to others. We also must not underestimate the benefits of recordings, sound paper work and organization. Colleagues need to be able to cover for us if we are ill or dealing with an emergency. Activities generally involve a lot of preparation; for work to be financed applications have to be made and reports written. These areas have tended to be under-recognized. Full-time workers should be sensitive to those working part time who are often expected to do these things unpaid and to the needs of those working on a voluntary basis.

Records and recordings are vital. However, we must ask 'what are they for?' Time spent recording is time denied from face-to-face work. Recordings have to be judged in terms of their value to practice. Three direct benefits arise. They provide us with a means to reflect on our daily practice. Through writing things down we can often see issues more clearly. For example, we may jot things down in a journal, or write a more detailed recording of an event or experience. Second, recordings allow us to plan. By looking back at what we have done – in the previous week or month – we can in turn look at what we hope to achieve. This might take the form of a list of tasks, or the concerns we face. Third, records provide for continuity. They allow us to communicate with other workers. These may be colleagues, or workers who take our place. We must always ask ourselves what would happen if we were not able to be in work tomorrow or next week? Could what we are doing be picked up, or would those we work with be left in the lurch? Records are a way of preventing us letting others down. Each may involve different types of recording, although there may be some overlap. We may keep a personal journal, recordings of specific events or experiences, and logs of work (i.e. what has happened in particular groups). The former may be more about our development, the latter may be more administrative (keeping other educators in touch with the work).

We look to our own development

If we are not learning and developing, then we are unlikely to be any good as educators. In conversation we have to be ready to change our thinking as we listen to what is said. We have to be open to the other, otherwise we are unlikely to be engaging with people in a good spirit. We must value what they have to say. Furthermore, if we are to continue to have something worthwhile to say, then we have to keep reflecting on situations and deepening our knowledge. Being wise is not a static state.

Reflection on practice is of little use unless it is informed by good theory and with a growing knowledge of the world. Reading and the exploring of

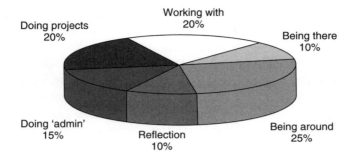

Figure 19.2   Time allocation

ideas with others often fall by the wayside. Having trained, many rely on professional magazines and briefings in order to keep up with things.
Unfortunately, these can only give a taste of policy issues and practice; they
rarely give an insight into why things may be happening or into the processes
involved. Educators need to put time aside for reading and engaging with other
practitioners around the issues and questions that arise around their work.

However, if this work becomes the sole focus then narrowness can creep
in. Informal educators often have enthusiasms – particular activities or interests that fascinate them. They can both bring personal satisfaction and growth,
and be great assets in the work. They may be enthusiasms that could spark
some of those we work with and so become tools of the work, for example, a
passion for the theatre or sports. As part of the people we are they can certainly
provide hooks for people to connect to us. Jokes can be made and questions
asked. Our greatest resource as informal educators is 'ourselves' and we must
be aware of the need to ensure we attend to maintaining the fabric of our personality and mind as much as we would a building.

Using modes as building blocks

The six modes of working provide us with the basic blocks to structure our
work. In planning what we may do over a period of time we can begin by working out some rough percentages. We might even try drawing a pie chart with
the various modes represented (Figure 19.2).

Just how we split up these elements depends on the work we are doing.
Some jobs may involve more administration, others may have a different balance between project work and being around. For example, some community

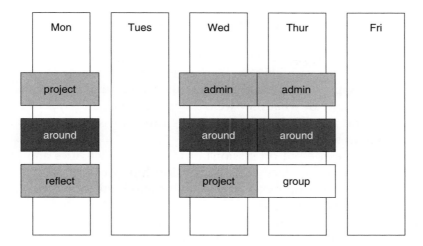

Figure 19.3   An informal educator's planner

development work can involve a substantial amount of letter and report writing, and keeping up with policy changes. Elements can shade into one another when planning. We often do not know in advance when we will be needed to 'be there' for someone. Similarly, we may set time aside for working with people and they do not turn up so we can then use this space for doing paperwork.

The work split featured is for a student support worker in a further education college who works half time. She plans her week so that she spends about four hours around the student areas – the canteen, the 'common room', etc. Here she wanders around making contact with people, stopping to chat here and there. Once a week she sets up a stall with leaflets and various guides such as welfare rights handbooks. She also has some set office hours when people can come to see her privately (three hours). There is a fairly constant flow of people during this time – although when things are slack she can update her recordings and catch up on her 'admin'. She also has some other fairly regular pieces of project work – training for students running clubs and groups; a group for young women of colour, and so on. There are also some working sessions with student union officers. The fixed spots on her planner are as in Figure 19.3. She is mainly 'around' at lunch time (black boxes). She has two office sessions for more private work with people plus a session with the student officers ('working with' – grey boxes). Lastly there are two main 'project' sessions. She then fits in other pieces of work around these.

Thinking about intensity

As we have already noted, aspects of the work involve differing degrees of depth. Sometimes we are making new contacts and maintaining relationships. Here we may simply greet people, ask how they are getting on, or talk about some TV programme or what they were doing last night. In terms of evaluating our work and reporting it to managers we can discuss this in terms of the number of contacts we make.

At other times we put on sessions or take part in activities and groups. This involves a more intense working relationship. We are looking to the processes in the group or the exchange; thinking about the subject matter; and trying to foster opportunities that can help people to gain better understandings, develop skills and to explore their values and feelings. We can think about these situations in terms of participants in sessions.

Last, there are times when we are dealing with sensitive questions – perhaps one-to-one or in a small group. We could describe this as counselling but we prefer 'working with'. This is because we take counselling to be a specialist activity drawing heavily on psycho-dynamic insights. Educational approaches make some use of such insights but draw mainly from other, developmental, traditions. Examples here may be working with individuals around their family relationships or their strategies when dealing with social security officials. Here we may think of people as 'clients' and describe it as 'casework'. This term may indicate a long-term approach that seeks to explore how individuals can handle problem relationships and situations (Masterson, 1982).

From this we can see that the work of the same person may fall into different categories at various moments. To do casework we have to be known and to have contacts. The need for particular projects may emerge out of casework or from casual conversation. Each is dependent on the other. Again we are brought back to the false separation of informal and formal approaches.

Numbers

This now leads us on to the tricky question of numbers. We may complain about having to keep details of the numbers of people we work with and of the emphasis put upon this area of work by some managers. However, there is a real point to such figures. We want to make sure that we are spending our time in the best way possible.

In thinking about numbers it is important to make some judgements about the intensity of the relationship. We make a lot of contacts, a smaller

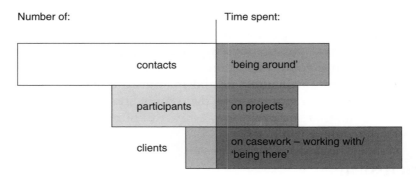

Figure 19.4   Numbers and time

number of whom participate more intensely in groups and projects, and an even smaller number are involved as clients in casework relationships. If we then plot the amount of time involved (in this case from our student support worker) then a more complex picture emerges. We can see this in Figure 19.4. We may spend more time on casework (represented by the right-hand block) but have fewer 'clients'.

The $64,000 question is how many people and to what intensity should we be working in any particular setting? In answering this we have to consider, for example:

- The number of hours working time we have to play with.
- Our qualities, strengths and weaknesses as workers.
- The wishes and needs of the people we are engaging with.
- The constraints of the settings we operate in.
- The aims and policies of our agency.

Two part-time informal educators working with young people in a small village, for example, will have a limited number of people they can work with, but it may take some time to contact them (because of physical distance). We might also expect them to place an emphasis on doing projects – partly because of the limited numbers of young people, partly because of the relative lack of local opportunities. They might organize trips, for example, or undertake various arts and cultural activities.

An informal educator with a focus on community development may spend a substantial amount of time on projects (for example, linked to various campaigns) and on the associated administration. They are also likely to devote a good deal of time to working with local groups so that they may better achieve their goals. The classic bind here is that 'being around' – knocking on doors, meeting parents at the school gate, etc. can be neglected.

Further, to make comparisons we really need to think in terms of the agency, club or unit. While a focus on individual workloads is needed when planning, questions about numbers and intensity are best approached as a whole. This allows us to properly value the contribution of workers – voluntary, part-time and full-time.

Conclusion

Several things come out from this. First, each area of work has a different shape and balance. The ease of making contact with large numbers of people within colleges and schools, and access to facilities, for example, provides informal educators in those settings with a flying start. Second, there is something of a case to combine different approaches. For example, rather than thinking of workers being attached to a particular centre or club, we should think of them being attached to an area or neighbourhood.

Many of the old distinctions, for example, between building-based and detached work; working with young people and adults; and between play work, youth work and community work, are overblown. The real questions concern the extent to which we think of ourselves as educators, our comfort in working in less overtly structured settings, and our ease in conversation.

References

Masterson, A. (1982) *A Place of My Own. Young People Leaving Home – A Youth Work Approach*. Manchester: Greater Manchester Youth Association/National Association of Youth Clubs.
Smith, M.K. (1994) *Local Education. Community Conversation, Praxis*. Buckingham: Open University Press.

20

Recognising and recording the impact of youth work

Bryan Merton, Hilary Comfort and Malcolm Payne

Introduction

This chapter is an edited extract from a National Youth Agency publication that is designed to inform and stimulate debate and action about the impact of youth work and the importance of recognising and recording this impact. It is a development from the findings of an 18-month study carried out in 2003–04 that evaluated the impact of youth work in England, referred to as the Impact Study (Merton, Payne and Smith, 2004).

The importance of impact and the need to demonstrate it

Impact of service provision and its assessment are important themes in current discussion of public policy. Education, health, social care and youth justice services are all engaged in processes of capturing different kinds of evidence of the difference they make to people's lives and the social dividends they produce for the money invested. There are at least three reasons why they should be given serious consideration with regard to youth work.

This is an edited version of material first published as Merton, B., Comfort, H. and Payne, M., *Recognising and Recording the Impact of Youth Work*, Leicester: The National Youth Agency.

Benefits for young people

Young people deserve good services: they want, expect and generally obtain respect and trust in the relationships they have with youth workers. As the Impact Study showed, this provides the wellspring of confidence that leads to their enhanced motivation and achievement; it brings them a greater sense of 'agency' and control in their lives. The young people and the state both gain from this public investment because the work makes a significant contribution to building human capital and social capital, and to the achievement of the public policy goals of personal and social development and the social inclusion of young people.

Service providers are expected to show that youth work has impact on the achievement and development of young people. For example, in providing activities outside the formal structures of school and college through which young people can develop new relationships, skills and knowledge, youth work can show that it is making a significant contribution to 'enjoyment and achievement', one of the five outcomes specified in *Every Child Matters* (DfES, 2003).

Service improvement

Youth workers want to make the best possible provision for young people and are continuously seeking to improve their practice. They need to be able to assess and evaluate their interventions so they can judge which work and which do not, in which circumstances and with which groups of young people. By analysing their work in this way, they are better placed to decide how to use resources and plan programmes so that their interventions are effective.

Moreover, youth services and organisations are expected to have in place tools and processes for checking on the quality of their programmes and projects for purposes of self-assessment and external inspection. A common factor among those services that fail to meet the standards expected by Ofsted is the inadequacy of quality assurance procedures. It makes sense to devise and refine arrangements for recognising and recording the impact of youth work, so that adjustments and improvements can be made wherever impact and outcomes do not meet the expected standards. It makes sense for these arrangements to be fit for purpose since there is no single system that necessarily suits the different types of youth work reported on in the Impact Study – (a) short-term project work with specified outcomes; (b) open-access or generic building-based provision; and (c) detached or street-based youth work.

Public accountability

Government is interested in impact because it needs to know whether the service is providing value for (the taxpayers') money and making a contribution to improvements in people's active citizenship and quality of life in keeping with public policy objectives.

At local level, a similar process is in play. Services and organisations that directly provide youth work have to be able to demonstrate reliably to stakeholders that their interventions have impact and contribute to the same kinds of policy objectives. There are a number of services and organisations that work with young people who may be making claims on the same finite pool of resources. Those who command the budgets for these services require reliable management information about service results – about the impact and outcomes the different services achieve – when making decisions about how to allocate resources, in response to needs.

The assessment of impact is important because it testifies to the benefits acquired by young people, encourages professional workers to improve the quality of the service provided and makes the results of service provision more transparent so their value can be judged.

Recognition, recording and the challenge of measurement

The purposes for recognising and recording impact are linked to but different from those for measuring it. In the case of the first, the principal purpose is for the young person to reflect upon a youth work experience and extract the meaning, in particular the social and learning gain from it. It also helps the service-provider to explain how the outcomes can contribute to policy objectives. These explanations are particularly of interest to policy-makers and funders of services for young people.

The purposes for measuring impact – both a conceptually and technically fraught exercise as we discuss below – are to enable service providers continuously to improve by comparing their results year by year or with those of other providers. Impact measurement could also enable those who make policy and fund service providers to have some statistical benchmarks as a basis for comparing and contrasting performance, giving them outcome measures to set aside input and output measures when deciding on the allocation of resources.

Measuring achievement of the 'soft' or 'intermediate' outcomes of youth work is conceptually, methodologically, technically and professionally complex. It might allow the simplistic counting or weighing of evidence but scarcely does justice to the nuanced changes in attitude, behaviour and relationships that come with effective youth work that are described in the Impact Study. Moreover, measurement gives spurious objectivity to an exercise that is essentially subjective, relying as it does on judgment and interpretation. Numbers may afford a questionable scientific status to something that owes more to alchemy than arithmetic.

Impact and outcomes

There is often confusion about the ways in which the terms outcomes and impact are used to describe the changes brought about by an intervention. In this chapter we refer to terms drawn from a guide published by the National Council of Voluntary Organisations (Wainwright, undated).

In this model, *outcomes* refers to the benefits to the intended beneficiaries. In the youth work situation, these are usually focused on development in young people. However, they may also benefit the communities in which young people live, and other services working with them. Outcomes are usually planned for and set out in an organisation's purpose or objectives. *Impact* encompasses all the changes resulting from activities or projects. It includes effects that are intended as well as unintended, negative as well as positive, long-term as well as short-term. It may include changes that were not included in the programme objectives (for example, increases in confidence as well as achievements that were planned for; benefits for groups additional to the intended individual beneficiaries).

Impact, as defined in this way, embraces outcomes. The main distinction is whether or not they are contained within the objectives of the programme or project. Where the detailed intentions or objectives of a piece of youth work are not set out – and this is often the case in more open-access forms of youth work – it can be difficult to distinguish outcomes from impact. Sometimes, then, it is necessary to refer to outcomes and impact together in describing the total difference that youth work makes.

It is also important to be clear that youth work can have *impact beyond* that which happens to the young people who engage with it. For example, while the primary focus of youth work should be the young people who are the intended beneficiaries, youth work often has impact on others. Youth workers may decide to change their practice and work with young people on the streets in a neighbourhood to minimise risk to the young people and the local community by engaging them in more creative and purposeful activities. If the purpose of this intervention is seen to be 'getting them off the streets' because they are seen to be creating a nuisance to local people, then the local residents, not the young people, are the intended beneficiaries. However, if the reason that the young people are on the streets is that there are no other attractive resources available to them and the result of the youth work is the provision of new opportunities – for example, the opening of a youth club on two nights a week – then there has been an out-come (change in situation or condition) that brings benefit to the young people and also to the wider community.

Youth work can influence the procedures, behaviours and attitudes of staff in other services that work with young people, such as schools and colleges, health and social services, police and youth offending teams. Youth work organisations can help partner agencies make their own services more effective in the work they do with young people. Here the impact on young people is *indirect*, mediated by the other services. In this way youth work can *multiply its impact*, with the other agencies enhancing the impact of youth work beyond the resources of youth work itself.

Youth work can also have impact on young people not engaged by youth work but who may be in contact with young people who are. This is a second form of *indirect impact*. An example may be anti-racist work which may lead young people to change their attitudes resulting in reduced tension and improved community cohesion.

Youth work can have *consequential impact* in the sense that groups of the population may derive benefit from youth work even if they are not directly involved in it. Diversionary activities in school holidays, for example, may result in reductions in youth crime that may improve the quality of life for local residents, including the young people themselves.

Policy drivers

Public policy has provided the impetus for attention being paid to he impact and outcomes of youth work and associated services for young people. This trend is likely to be intensified with the creation of Children's Trusts that will be commissioning services for young people across a local authority area.

When in 2001 the government introduced its *Transforming Youth Work* (DfEE, 2001) policy and followed this in 2002 with *Resourcing Excellent Youth Services* (REYS) (DfES, 2002) it became clear that in return for greater public investment it expected to see higher standards of youth work and local services better placed to be able to demonstrate their conformance to them. For the first time, government specified sets of standards and benchmarks it expected of all local youth services. It required each service to produce its own plan for achieving them, identifying precisely how it would use the resources made available.

Building on the performance measures earlier specified in *REYS*, the minister set out in a letter in December 2003 clear benchmarks for local services to aim for with regard to *reach* or *contact, participation, recorded outcomes* and *accredited outcomes*. The National Youth Agency produced guidance designed to interpret and clarify the meaning of the benchmarks so that services could create arrangements locally for collecting the data that would inform them how well they were doing in relation to these benchmarks (NYA, 2004).

In 2004, Ofsted (Ofsted, 2004) produced a revised inspection framework which emphasised the standards of young people's achievement and the quality of youth work practice, the steps that services take to assess needs, deploy resources and devise a curriculum in response to them, and provide programmes that young people respond to and that give good value. The focus on young people's achievements makes clear that through youth work, young people are expected to acquire knowledge, skills and understanding, attitudes, values and self-confidence; that youth work should foster young people's ability to function socially and politically, make choices and decisions, become more tolerant and sensitive to others and enjoy good relationships.

During this period, senior representatives of the youth service together with government ministers and officials addressed youth work's role in a public policy that urged services to adopt more joined-up approaches to meeting the needs of children and young people. The youth service had always claimed that it had a distinctive contribution to make and now sought to show it could do what it said it could. Government wanted all services for young people to support its policy initiative in establishing the new Connexions service, designed to provide high quality information, guidance and support to all young people between the age of 13 and 19, in particular those deemed to be at risk. The youth service sought to demonstrate how its specialist skills, techniques and processes could enrich and extend the offer made.

The result has been greater pressure on service leaders and managers to 'modernise' their approaches, to become efficient and effective both strategically and operationally (mirrored again in the 2004 inspection framework), manage effectively the performance of their staff and systems and better account for impact and outcomes. This has led youth services to seek more reliable ways of accounting for the results of their work. As the provisions of the Children Act 2004 take effect, they need to be in a position to show convincingly that youth work programmes and projects do make a difference, lead to outcomes and impact that enhance opportunity and achievement, and contribute conspicuously to the five outcomes of *Every Child Matters*.

Benefits of recognising and recording impact

Recognising and recording the difference made by youth work has therefore become a policy imperative for youth services and organisations. Even if it were not, there are inherent benefits in doing so.

First there is a direct relationship between planning for, recognising and recording impact and the quality of youth work. Youth work is essentially an educational activity concerned with young people's personal and social development and their social inclusion in their transition to adult roles and responsibilities. However, there is no national curriculum setting out how this is to be achieved; rather, it is up to each local authority youth service, in consultation with its partners, to devise its own curriculum framework, in the light of local needs and the interests, aspirations and circumstances of young people; and of the resources made available. Any curriculum framework is meant to contain or specify the kinds of outcomes that are to be achieved and the content areas, styles of youth work and forms of assessment that should underpin them.

By planning for outcomes and impact, youth workers are more likely to help young people achieve them. That does not mean that every thought and action has to be geared towards a pre-determined objective. As Merton and Wylie (2002) comment in their NYA publication on the youth work curriculum:

> Another objection to the idea of a curriculum for youth work is that some of the best youth work is done 'on the wing', that it is improvised from the day-to-day situations in which youth workers and young people interact. This is an essential tool of the youth worker's trade. Of course this kind of work often has enormous validity and potency. Learning is as often emergent as it is planned for and just as valuable for being so. But that is not sufficient reason for dispensing with the idea and application of curriculum. A curriculum does not preclude spontaneity.

This process of making explicit what is intended from a youth work intervention or programme helps to demystify youth work, making interventions transparent to young people and other stakeholders.

To those who hold fast to youth work principles and values, the explication of intended outcomes and impact should hold no fears. It should be regarded less as a technical exercise that youth workers have to go through and more as an opportunity to reaffirm the purposes and benefits of the youth work; of emphasising what it is there to do and the values that underpin it; that it is an activity through which people learn and achieve, framed by a curriculum and influenced principally by relationships.

The Impact Study provided some case study examples of how different types of interventions by projects working with specified groups of young people in particular settings produced evidence of impact. In one town where there had been conflict between young people from different ethnic groups, interventions were designed to recognise the importance of social learning and community development, rather than to pathologise the individuals involved. This helped to develop the young people's voice and influence in framing and resolving the problems they encountered with a resultant shift in relationships, perceptions and behaviours.

> I didn't mix that much with different people. They're not that bad. I want to do more.

In another town, young people who had given up on school were encouraged to shape their own education in a community-based project run by local staff known to the young people. The key to successful interventions was negotiation.

> We talk and discuss. Everything is discussed. There's a lot of responsibility on the young people. If there's a fight it's resolved before we leave the building. Not tomorrow, but sorted now.

The young people explained the benefits of the project:

> It stopped me getting into trouble ... got me off the streets, made me a better person and stopped me go out pinching ... I'm not so violent anymore ... get on better with people, don't steal any more ... made me more friendly, I'm staying out of trouble, less violent, don't cause trouble any more.

Further case studies revealed the wide range of interventions made and outcomes and impact achieved. These included a project in a general hospital where youth workers support young people some of whom have serious medical problems and others who are self-harming. The purpose is to give the young patients a greater voice in the way they are treated by medical staff leading to a greater sense of control over their situation so they can take greater responsibility for themselves. In a county-wide service, youth workers over an extended period support young adults who have left the care of the local authority and are seeking to live independently. In contrast to these which operate closer to the social work end of the youth work spectrum of interventions, another project deployed youth workers to work alongside groups of young skateboarders in a city centre whose social and recreational needs were being ignored by the authorities. What began as a concern for community safety turned out to be an intervention that strengthened the young people's voice and influenced leisure provision for themselves and other young people in the city.

The Impact Study has shown that, whatever its origins and achievements, most youth work is oriented towards at least one of five policy dimensions:

- Active citizenship
- Aspiration and achievement
- Enabling young people to actively engage with their social world and be protected from its dangers
- Prevention and diversion from risk
- The reintegration of those who are excluded.

The observations of young people, youth workers and professionals in other services testified to the benefits, providing a rich seam of qualitative evidence of impact. Until recently, youth services have not tended to collect information about outcomes and therefore it is more rare to find examples of the kind of quantitative data that tend to impress policy-makers and funders.

There is a close relationship between the assessment of impact and the evaluation of the quality of the youth work; knowing about the factors that contribute to effective youth work helps to explain the level of impact. A pre-condition of evaluation is the recording of outcomes and the collection of both qualitative and quantitative data to inform the professional judgments made. Moreover, a pre-condition of recording outcomes is some reflection on the activities in which the young people take part in order to identify the social and learning gains achieved. It is important that this becomes an integral part of the youth work process.

Difficulties in recognising and recording impact

The drive for measurement comes principally from one of two sources. First the providers themselves who believe they are more likely to secure funding for the provision if they can demonstrate that it leads to perceptible development in young people. Second the policy-makers and funders who want to compare the performance of providers, sometimes as a means of deciding on the allocation of resources, and believe that this can best be done by measuring the achievements of young people.

There is little evidence that the young people are asking for their performance in soft skills to be measured or scored in some way. They are more content to know whether or not they can do certain things and to have that skill or competence recorded or accredited so they can demonstrate they possess it to others (employers, teachers, other gate-keepers of opportunities, families and peers).

There are various conceptual and technical difficulties involved in seeking to demonstrate progress or distance travelled in the territory of what are sometimes called the soft skills or intermediate outcomes that characterise the purposes of youth work – personal and social development and social inclusion. These kinds of outcomes usually refer to attitudes, behaviours and attributes that are fluid or capable of change; these are harder to nail and therefore grade or differentiate by level. Examples include tolerance, sensitivity and confidence, the latter being the most commonly expressed benefit or outcome for young people as they themselves reported in the Impact Study.

The presence or absence of these characteristics is a matter of subjective perception and judgment rather than objective measurement. While it may be possible to observe whether somebody is displaying compassion, it is something quite different to quantify or give it weight. There can also be difficulties associated with establishing some benchmark against which to assess or measure, referring either to some kind of norm – usually other people's achievement/ performance – or some kind of criteria or standards that have to be specified.

Achievement and progress entail taking account of two different sorts of context. The first relates to the *learner* – their starting-point and prior levels of attainment in the skill, the circumstances and conditions of the learner's life which predispose them to have or not have a baseline level of the particular skill. This means that what may be considered a minor achievement by one young person – such as getting to an activity on time – may be regarded as very challenging and highly significant for another. The second relates to the *situation* in which the skill is being applied. It is not unusual to perform the same task well or poorly according to how well we know the people we are working with and how much confidence we have in knowing that they will help us if we get into difficulty.

There is also the matter of *transferability*. Being able to demonstrate a satisfactory level of performance on one occasion does not necessarily mean that the young person can do so on another when the conditions and circumstances may be very different. For example, confidence is often included in the basket of soft skills sought by employers. Experience tells us that this is an elusive quality, that waxes and wanes according to a whole set of contributory factors, some which we are more conscious of than others, and over which we have more or less control at specific times or in particular circumstances.

There tend to be many more variables at play in contexts for demonstrating soft skills that are often influenced by the interplay of psychological and social factors than there are in other contexts for demonstrating knowledge or more technical skills.

A further complication is posed by the question as to whether youth workers can be wholly *objective* in their assessment of the impact of their interventions. They are key actors in the process as it is their relationships with the young people that influence the outcomes of any intervention. The young people's assessment of impact may be similarly compromised by their involvement in the process. So caution has to be exercised in both making the judgments and in reading and interpreting them.

Recognising and recording impact is also troubled by questions of *causality*. It is hard to ascribe effects to particular causes, especially when they concern people's attitudes and behaviour. While youth work activities and interventions may contribute to particular outcomes or a result, it may be only one of several factors.

Many young people refer to the long-term impact of being involved in youth work. It is quite often the case that as a consequence of sustained attendance at a youth centre or project and continuous contact with youth workers that a young person begins to recognise there are alternative ways of seeing the world and acting in it, that they acquire a wider repertoire of insights, skills and relationships through which they gain the confidence to explore new experiences and opportunities. But this may take a matter of years, not weeks or months. It is also quite common for young people, once grown into more mature adults, to look back on their involvement in a youth work project and trace its influence on their direction and development. This has been well documented in one of the few longitudinal studies of people who had been in contact with youth work when they were young (Williamson, 2004).

Furthermore, there are some serious obstacles within the youth work profession. Some youth workers resist attempts made to encourage them to recognise and record impact because they believe that the process of youth work is as important as its outcomes. They argue that youth work is about relationships of trust and reciprocity, initially at individual or small group level, and then in larger groups and networks. As the Impact Study shows, at its best youth work builds social capital, bridging differences between cultural groups or generations, and strengthens communities by encouraging relationships of mutual benefit and regard. These qualities contribute to the social good and are inherently of public value; they are neither reducible nor amenable to precise measurement and grading.

It is certainly difficult to find reliable ways of calculating the benefits of the social capital built by a youth work programme, particularly of ascribing to it any numerical value so that its impact can be calculated and compared. It is possible to acquire anecdotal evidence and qualitative data of the difference made by a particular youth work initiative; some of this is powerful and often regarded as sufficient. But this may not be fit for the purpose of 'compare and contrast'.

There are more practical barriers to the recording of impact, principally concerned with who is to do the recording and how. One of the problems is that for recording to be of value, it should contain analytical as well as descriptive information. Reflection is a condition of analysis, but there is sometimes resistance to reflection in youth workers, for whom actions are deemed to speak louder than words.

Doubtless there are occasions when young people do not want to discuss things they have done together, but young people are often willing to reflect and talk about their experiences and what they have gained and learned from them.

> Young people love it and happily respond to it. They like one to one time. They like people talking to them about what they've done ... young people like giving their opinions – let's face it, young people are not usually asked – and others interested in them asking their views helps them.

This applies equally to young people in groups.

Much depends on the questions that are asked and the techniques used to prompt reflection. The following are examples of questions and prompts that seem to work:

- Let's explore ...
- How can we change ... ?
- How can we look at this differently . . . ?
- Let's take a step back ...
- Where were you in this situation ...in the middle or on the edge ... ?
- Because ... ? ... how come ...?
- What does this remind you of ... ?
- Can you say a little more about this .... ?
- I am not sure I understand ...why not tell me again ... ?
- What are the pros and cons? Tell me why ... ?

Some front-line workers are very gifted at befriending and building relationships with young people who are hard to engage. They may be 'natural' youth workers, well versed in the ways and concerns of local young people and able to make good use of their experience and intuition. Being asked to conceptualise what has happened in a relationship or activity may be something they find more challenging.

As the Impact Study shows, the front-line youth workers who are in some form of contact with those who are hard to reach are often the least qualified and trained. Furthermore, street-wise youth workers do not come from a culture of paperwork and writing things down, which is the usual medium for recording. They may consider that monitoring and evaluation processes distract from contact work – although they could and perhaps should be contained within it – and their time is limited. It becomes a problem for managers to persuade front-line workers to comply with such a requirement.

> There is a general resistance to writing anything down – there's the view that we need all the hours to do the work with young people rather than spend it justifying this to others.

> Workers perceive they do not have the time to do this.

For other youth workers, it is more a question of ensuring that the conditions are right for the more reflective work to be done.

> I want to be unhurried and unrushed and dig a bit deeper. They'd turn round tomorrow and say it was great – but I want to know what they get out of it – maybe what things they look at differently. I'm a perfectionist. I want to get it right! I want to make sure I give it our best shot.

Another difficulty lies in the organisational constraints that youth services may, often unwittingly, impose. While we would argue that reflection on and processing experience so that young people can learn from it is an integral part of youth work, optimum conditions may not be secured for it. The focus on activities sometimes occurs at the expense of calm and considered reflection.

Finally, there has been a shortage of appropriate tools and processes in the service. Checklists and evaluation proformas abound and many of these lead to a long succession of box-ticking activities for youth workers who believe their time would be spent better working directly with young people. The challenge is to find, develop and use tools and processes that form a central strand woven into the everyday patterns of effective youth work and that youth workers believe will improve the service they provide.

The need for some tools and processes

We have found that when presented with tools and process for capturing evidence of learning and achievement through youth work, young people and youth workers respond positively.

> When I read the interview results it reminded me of why I came into the job. It's about time someone realises what we do. Here we have a chance to practice it – workers get positive reinforcement and increased motivation in celebrating young people's achievements. Workers will get the evidence and can share the impact of what we've done – what lies behind the certificates.

> It's about helping you do better youth work and it will show you the good work you are doing.

They do so as long as the tools and processes they are invited to use conform to certain working principles that are set out below. We propose that if they do so and are integrated into youth work practice, they enhance the quality of the intervention and are less likely to be seen as an additional burden imposed by managers.

The tools and processes should:

- Be part of a process of ongoing dialogue between young people and youth workers
- Comprise activities that have inherent value and are attractive and enjoyable
- Capture and give expression to change, growth and development in the young people
- Recognise and record outcomes that contribute to personal and social development and are derived from some form of curriculum framework
- Be adaptable in response to changing contexts and needs and flexible so they can be used in different situations and settings in keeping with the style of informal learning
- Be fit for key purposes: enabling reflection and thus completing the Kolb Learning Cycle, providing a basis for planning further interventions, accounting to stakeholders.

References

Department for Education and Employment (2001) *Transforming Youth Work*, London: DfEE.
Department for Education and Skills (2002) *Transforming Youth Work – Resourcing Excellent Youth Services*, London: DfES.
Department for Education and Skills (2003) *Every Child Matters*, London: The Stationery Office.
Merton, B. and Wylie, T. (2002) *Towards a Contemporary Curriculum for Youth Work*, Leicester: National Youth Agency.
National Youth Agency (2004, updated December 2005) *Credit Where It's Due: Guidance on Youth Service Benchmarks*, Leicester: National Youth Agency.
Ofsted, (2004) *Local Authority Youth Services: A Framework for Inspection*, London: Ofsted.
Wainwright, S. (undated) *Measuring Impact, A Guide to Resources*, London: National Council for Voluntary Organisations.
Williamson, H. (2004) *The Milltown Boys Revisited*, Oxford: Berg.
Merton, B., Payne, M. and Smith, D. (2004) *An Evaluation of the Impact of Youth Work in England*, Youth Affairs Unit, De Montfort University/Department for Education and Skills Research Report 606.

Reclaiming the evaluation agenda

Gersh Subhra

Key points

1. Evaluation has to take into account the context of practice. De-contextualisation of practice can result in taking a blinkered approach that ignores the dynamics of funding, legislation, policies and the tensions of inequality within British society.
2. Community work often generates more questions than answers and highlights needs rather than meeting or resolving them. This may not be what funders want to hear but highlighting of further needs should be seen to be an acceptable outcome of evaluation.
3. A core part of community work is adversarial and often a challenge to institutions, policy makers, employers and funders and this often limits the openness with which information is presented.
4. The evaluation agenda can be reclaimed if there is a persistent assertion of the centrality of qualitative data, life experiences and values in community work.
5. Evaluation takes time! If funders or employers want evaluation material then resources need to be made available to generate this.

Introduction

In recent years the evaluation material required from practitioners operating in community work and related sectors has been directed not by those carrying

This is an edited version of material first published in Factor, F., Chauhan, V., and Pitts, J., *The RHP Companion to Working with Young People*. Lyme Regis: Russell House Publishing.

out this work but by external stakeholders such as funders. This has led to a change in the type, amount, scale and emphasis of evaluation material being generated. Everitt and Hardiker (1996) identify the origins of this to be the increasing influence of 'New Public Management', which is shaped by elements of scientific management. This technocratic approach is seen to offer an 'objective' and value free approach to evaluation and supposedly provides funders and managers with data to make sufficient judgements about efficiency, effectiveness and value for money.

In this chapter, it will be argued that these requirements ought to emerge from a shared agenda if practitioners are to 're-claim' the evaluation agenda. This also means that practitioners need to assert and demonstrate the impact and value of the work that they are doing and not just leave it to funders and managers, who often only make their own case. This chapter aims to provide workers in community work and related sectors with a strategic framework for evaluation which involves generating evaluation materials that correlate more closely to:

- The value base, philosophy and methods of working in these sectors
- The ability and capacity of the agency to undertake evaluation
- The level of funding provided for the work
- The nature of the work being funded
- The informal educational purpose of this work.

Such a framework offers a more flexible and appropriate strategy for individuals and organisations to begin the process of reclaiming the evaluation agenda for the community work sector.

Historical developments

Evaluation as an activity has been influenced and utilised by many disciplines with much borrowing of ideas between them. It is now confusingly, yet fascinatingly, multi-faceted, resulting in a number of contrasting perceptions about evaluation as an activity:

- That is normally undertaken by 'outsiders' ('external stakeholders'), checking up and assessing other people's work practices.
- That overemphasises quantitative and mechanistic performance indicators, inputs, outputs and outcomes.
- That searches for accountability rather than allowing processes to develop organically by workers and communities as part of their good practice.

- That is largely summative, 'objective' and takes place once a project is complete, contrasting with formative evaluations which consider developments as they occur and feed into the decisions and practices of agencies (Dale, 1998).
- That is based on concepts informed by a medical (treatment) model rather than a social (empowering) model (Everitt and Hardiker, 1996).

Thus, many practitioners currently view evaluation as: one of the increasing array of strategies of managerialism and control of policy, practice and professionalism, in and across social welfare organisations legitimising managerial and top-down decisions (Weiss, 1986).

In order to change evaluation from being a tool of control to one that will contribute to the development of good practice, the evaluation agenda has to be reclaimed by community work and other related fields. This should not be interpreted as a plea for reducing accountability to funders or employers, or lessening the priority of evaluation as an activity. On the contrary, it is an argument which aims to encourage the increased production of evaluation data, that more accurately reflects the real impact of community work and also encourages a higher profile for evaluation within organisations by integrating it even more closely into routine activities such as supervision and planning.

House (1986) examines the origins of evaluation by comparing the delivery of social programmes by social services and the voluntary sector to the metaphors of industrial production. In this analysis he points to the transfer of ideas and ideologies from the commercial sector to produce a mechanistic and quantitative series of concepts. These include many that are currently in wide use, such as inputs, outputs, and operational indicators of success, such as cost efficiency and unit costs.

The dominance of scientific objectivity or, in sociological terms, formal rationality and positivism have supplemented this influence. This underpinning logic emphasises the importance of tried and tested, objective procedures that result in predictable measured outcomes and frameworks. This approach, it is argued by Dale (1998), reflected the training as well as the needs of scientists, economists and engineers who dominated industrial production. The fallibility of this approach is further discussed by Dale and alternatives such as 'substantive rationality' and latterly, 'life-world rationality' by Dixon and Sindell (1994) are put forward as intellectual and practical challenges. The latter two approaches essentially argue for more emphasis to be placed upon the role of values and interests of the key players within an evaluation that is much more 'naturalistic'. To exclude the subjective dynamics of communities, and interpersonal relations and aspirations is to have an incomplete analysis.

This tension between science and social science goes to the heart of the tension that relates to the shaping and re-shaping of the evaluation agenda.

The historical influence of formal rationality on evaluation has been reinforced by recent developments in thinking about the welfare state and public policy. Everitt and Hardiker (1996), in examining the place of evaluation within the New Right's political economy of social welfare of the 1980s and 1990s, argue that it has been placed near the top of the agenda because of restraints on public expenditure, the need for greater accountability, inspection and quality control. This, they argue, has created a form of 'managerial evaluation' which they fear serves as a mechanism for social control by primarily meeting the informational needs of public sector management. The repercussions of this trend for community work and related sectors, which deal principally with issues of inequality, exclusion and disadvantage, are that the full value of the work is lost in the attempts to measure it.

As Taylor (1995) says in citing a resident called Julie Fawcett from a housing estate undergoing regeneration, 'working on the intangible is the most tangible thing we can do'. Taylor goes onto argue that 'evaluation needs to be built in from the start of any initiative and to be based on residents' views of what outcomes they want from the intervention in terms of both tasks and processes'.

When work being evaluated is about assisting someone who has been the victim of domestic violence by raising their self-esteem, do quantitative outputs really crystallise the processes more accurately than the qualitative impacts that occur diffusely and over an indefinite time period? As Everitt and Hardiker (1996) state:

> Increasingly evaluation of a technical kind is being imposed on projects and on practice for reasons of policy and budgetary control.

Coombe (1997) substantiates this by stating that:

> Expert evaluators quantitatively separate, measure, and score variables to scientifically test an a priori hypothesis derived from outside the community. Although the scientific method works best for measuring only a few variables under controlled conditions and with a comparison group for interpreting results, it continues to be viewed as the 'gold standard' for producing knowledge.

The use of quantitative methods to evaluate, may, at times, contradict with the goals of community work which are to work primarily with individuals and groups that may be disempowered by literacy, lack of self-esteem or confidence or specific skills. Subhra and Chauhan (1999) suggest that to resort to detailed and technical questionnaires, which try to encapsulate a community's experience into statistics may actually add to their feeling of being marginalised:

work by Black staff that attempts to change the way long established white organisations have delivered services and begins to recover this deficit, is essential groundwork but very difficult to measure. If an evaluation framework does not contain the means by which this work can be highlighted and acknowledged then clearly it has deficiencies. For Black workers such a trend has meant that much of the strategic anti-racist work they inevitably end up doing in white organisations goes unrecorded, unappreciated and unrewarded.

A historical tracking of approaches to evaluation can be represented by a generational analysis and it is widely recognised that there are four broad 'generations' (Guba and Lincoln, 1989).

Wadsworth, cited in Russell (1998), critically summarises the first three generations and their emphasis on technical, scientific or managerial disciplines:

> the 'first generation' which was preoccupied with measuring test results; 'second generation' objectives-based and outcome-oriented evaluation; and 'third generation' judgement and decision-oriented evaluation, on the grounds of their tendencies to disempower legitimate parties to the evaluation, their failure to accommodate other values, and their over-commitment to old paradigm science.

In a review of literature in this area, Estrella and Gaventa (1998) conclude that the major criticisms of conventional evaluation approaches are that they are costly, ineffective and have failed to actively involve project beneficiaries. The activity of evaluation has become increasingly specialised and removed from the actual work of communities. It ignores qualitative information which could help provide a much fuller understanding of project outcomes, processes and changes within communities. They go on to point out that evaluation practices 'remain externally oriented and attempt to produce information that is necessarily "objective" and "value-free" and "quantifiable": terms that are all being challenged'.

The fourth generation of approaches to evaluation argues for a radical departure from these historical traditions and attempts to locate evaluation within the methodology and value base of the practitioners' approach such as community work. The key features of this approach as summarised by Russell (1998), include:

- Qualitative data (narratives, stories, case-studies and so on)
- A belief in multiple realities
- Valuing subjective perspectives
- Seeing understanding as something different from measurement
- Embracing paradox and acknowledging uncertainties and ambiguities
- Acknowledging that values inevitably impinge on the evaluative process.

The challenge that is provided by the above analysis is that it questions the credibility of the historical approach to evaluation as being the 'right' way of assessing the value or effectiveness of community work. It is clear that such approaches have several shortcomings if they have:

- De-contextualised the work from the socio-political context
- Ignored the values and dynamics between different communities
- Excluded the telling of personal stories because they are subjective
- Ignored how intrusive, disempowering and exclusive quantitative methods can be.

Alongside this quantitative and qualitative schism is an equally contentious but related debate about who evaluation is primarily for. Russell argues that evaluation serves two purposes: first accountability to external stakeholders and second, promoting learning and development within the organisation. Whilst it is inevitable that this debate cannot crystallise into an either/or, the question that should be raised is which of the two purposes has priority and whose needs dominate the evaluation agenda? The political and economic climate facing the sector, as described earlier, means that the need for evaluation to take place and for funders to show that they are securing accountability and value for money takes precedence over the benefit to the organisation or the clients.

Armstrong and Key (1979) present an analysis of the two competing demands for evaluation, and describe an optimistic view of evaluation as learning being in tension, with a pessimistic view of evaluation as control. They go on to describe these as two ideal types, i.e. 'the learning practitioner' and the 'controlling sponsor'. The purpose of these concepts should be to clarify for a prospective evaluator, the political context and real purpose of the evaluation exercise to be undertaken. They suggest that prospective evaluators should not be naïve about the above tension, that sponsors shouldn't expect too much conclusive analysis from the evaluation and that managers will be pulled in both directions!

This imbalance towards evaluation being about control perhaps lies at the core of this whole debate. It is argued that until the benefits of evaluation activity accrue more directly to the community work sectors, this situation will not change.

The debate needs to consider how workers, projects and communities can try to demonstrate the impact, value and significance of what they achieve without compromising their need to demonstrate reasonable accountability and value for money. Recent developments in the community work and health promotion fields indicate that a move towards this reclaiming process has begun with the production of innovative frameworks and documentation on evaluation. Examples include the Achieving Better Community Development (ABCD) evaluation framework developed by Barr et al. (1996), the *Evaluation Resource for Healthy Living Centres* by Meyrick and Sinkler (1999) and Dale's (1998) and Rubin's (1995) work in the arena of international development. All of the above, plus the work of agencies such as the Charities Evaluation Services is symptomatic of an alternative approach to evaluation being developed, that can validate accurately the impact and contributions of community work.

A strategy for reclaiming the evaluation agenda

What follows will hopefully assist organisations and individuals to reframe evaluation into an activity that is initiated as a learning and educational process and is linked to future planning. Although the framework is presented in stages, it should be considered concurrently.

Stage one: formulate a manifesto

A manifesto which begins to locate your organisation's approach and thinking on evaluation within a policy framework can be a useful way of developing a clear consensus amongst staff, managers, management committees and so on. The following are assertions that organisations may want to consider as part of their evaluation manifesto:

1. A recognition that subjectivity has validity and that there are different perspectives, depending on your location, relationship to the issue and the type of agency that is carrying out the work.
2. Evaluation does not have to be carried out because others impose it.
3. Evaluation ought to be integrated into the fabric of an organisation as an invaluable planning tool to help validate work, acknowledge effort, shape priorities and generate material for a variety of uses.
4. There should be a recognition that in trying to establish the 'full picture', the square peg of quantitative evaluation and its need to demonstrate value for money seldom fits into the round hole of the qualitative impacts made by community workers.
5. There needs to be a corresponding recognition that qualitative evaluation methods do not aspire to tell the whole story either.
6. Not all of what workers and agencies do can be actually measured or easily presented.

7. Evaluation can and should empower communities and community organisations and not just enable external stakeholders to make judgements about value for money.
8. Communities with whom work is undertaken need to participate in evaluation processes.
9. At the outset, the level of capacity and resourcing needed to carry out effective evaluation has to be a key part of negotiations with funders.
10. The theoretical and philosophical value base that underpins the work of your agency has also to be extended to the approaches you use in your evaluation.

Once the above manifesto is written, consideration needs to be given to how it can be incorporated into the organisation's policy structures as well as how to publicise it to the community and funders alike.

Stage two: assessing the capacity for evaluation

It is essential to carry out an assessment of the organisational capacity and resources to undertake evaluation-related activities by considering the approach, interest, capacity and skills of stakeholders such as the workers, volunteers, management committee members, managers and service users. This includes examining the following:

- Historically who has had the responsibility for evaluation?
  (i.e. was it seen as a managerial task and primarily located with one person or a particular level of the organisation, e.g. a management committee?)
- How can evaluation become a more democratic activity?
  Can there be greater involvement of the staff team, management committee, other volunteers and community members?
- What is the predominant attitude to evaluation within the staff team and management committee?
  Achieving consensus within an agency is a key strategy if the evaluation agenda is to be reclaimed and staff and other key stakeholders need to agree about the model of evaluation that they want to adopt.
- What is the level of interest amongst the staff team in this area of work?
  If evaluation is essentially seen as a defensive activity that is imposed, then a strategy of training and staff development may be necessary.

Part of this could be incorporated into a participative or consultative approach to drawing up the organisation's new evaluation manifesto.

- How does evaluation as an activity integrate with the community work methods being used by the staff team?
  Coombe (1997) in his description of the 'Empowerment' model of evaluation encourages the involvement of oppressed people in identifying problems and designing and finding solutions to them.
  This approach puts people at the centre of the evaluation agenda and is entirely consistent with the philosophy and methodology of community work practice.
- What resources does the agency want to commit to evaluation?
  For example, are evaluation costs and time being built into new funding proposals as well as into the priorities of existing staff? What part does the management committee play in monitoring and evaluation activities? Is there any utilisation of student, volunteer and/or secondment placements or indeed partnerships with universities and research assistants as examples of ways of increasing evaluation capacity?

Stage three: the integration of evaluation

It is important to assess how closely evaluation priorities and activities integrate into the various functions of an organisation's routine operations. Examples include planning, policy making, recruitment and selection, supervision and appraisal systems, equal opportunities policies and systems, staff development and training, public relations, fund-raising strategies and so on. Each of these areas offer opportunities for evaluation to feature significantly and an audit may uncover some useful ways in which the profile of evaluation could be raised.

As an example, let us consider supervision and appraisal policies. This is slightly contentious because evaluation has often been thought of as a mechanism for checking up on workers. However it is being suggested here that supervision, as a regular organisational activity, should be seen as an active mechanism by which workers can actively generate, contribute and store evaluation data with their managers. This could include, for example, case studies that demonstrate attitudinal change in individuals being worked with or impacts on deep-seated community issues. This sort of material is regularly discussed in supervision, but is it called or seen as a source of evaluation data? Appraisals may involve workers providing accounts of impacts that they have made in the preceding year and could include case studies, summaries and progress reports that could easily be adapted into evaluation material.

Stage four: negotiating evaluation requirements

This is a critical part of the 'reclaiming of the agenda' process and may probably take some funders by surprise! Whilst it is recognised that many funders and other external 'stakeholders' have pre-identified evaluation requirements and pro-formas, it is worth putting this up for renegotiation. Van Der Eyken (1993) suggests checking what the sponsor wants the evaluation information for. Is it, for instance:

- To try to calculate value for money?
- For the sponsor's public relations purposes?
- To encourage an agency to learn and develop clarity about the work being undertaken?
- Just an administrative exercise that allows the agency to demonstrate accountability to the funder?
- That they have resorted to a relatively mechanistic evaluation framework because they are unfamiliar with the type of qualitative data to ask for?

The format, approach and type of 'data' required will vary, depending on which of the above is shaping the sponsor's thinking. The key issue is whether your agency has been assertive in trying to clarify this or has passively accepted the sponsors' demands. The strategy suggested is one which involves a presentation of your manifesto and the type and quantity of data that can be collected in relation to your capacity.

An example that illustrates this need to flag up the intangible aspects of community work could be the substantial amount of time that some agencies and workers have to spend in building relationships of trust with, say, young people whose life experiences have led them to mistrust authority, adults and organisations. No one can argue that this aspect of work is not essential and a pre-requisite for further work or that it takes time, but how do you:

- Recognise and acknowledge within an evaluation framework, the complexity of skills demonstrated by the worker in engaging with a young person showing extremely challenging, perhaps aggressive behaviour?
- Measure it?
- Identify what its outcomes are?
- Remember the importance of this groundwork when, say, three months later the focus is on the more tangible things that your agency is doing with that young person?

The time spent on this type of intangible work needs to be negotiated into the evaluation requirements by acknowledging its importance, the benefits of building trust and that nothing tangible may come from the work immediately. The young person may return to the project six months after the initial contact, in order to do something that is quantifiable for the purposes of an evalution exercise.

Stage five: monitoring and data collection tools

Monitoring and data collection is inextricably linked with evaluation. The quality of the data collection critically determines the quality of the analysis presented within the eventual evaluation reports. Questions to consider include:

- Will a range of data collection tools or templates be used?
- Have time and resources been invested into training staff and volunteers to generate evaluation data?
- What is the quality of monitoring systems, information recording and retrieval systems?
- Is there scope to establish an evaluation portfolio system, into which a wide variety of material can be located?
- What data are being lost?
- Are there systems within your agency that allow the value of this type of work to be retrospectively acknowledged? For example, are there annual reviews that give time and space to this reflection? Are there wider spin-offs, changes or benefits that have occurred within the organisation or indeed wider community as a result of a specific project?

Examples of data collection tools (from Estrella and Gaventa, 1998) include:

- Diagramming: a visual means, for example, one by which illiterate farmers in 'developing' countries could describe soil and ground changes, or the use of diaries and journals
- Audio-visual techniques: video, story-telling, popular theatre, songs and photographs
- Oral testimonies
- Case studies
- Tape recordings
- Time-lines or chronologies of progress.

A variety of tools should also be used when 'he results of the evaluation are to be disseminated. Edmonds (1999) writing in the context of health promotion work with young people, suggests presenting the findings through:

- A poster, leaflet flyer or booklet
- A comic or photo-story
- An article, journal article or report
- A workshop or seminar
- A video or audio-tape
- A health stall in a shopping centre, street theatre or public meeting
- A web-site or by e-mail
- Radio or TV.

Stage six: matching evaluation activities to evolving objectives

Evaluation is commonly thought of as an analysis of how much progress has been made against the original objectives of the project. Objectives however are not static or limited in number and are usually added to, formally or informally, by the variety of stakeholders involved in funding or implementing the work. What starts out as a single objective can change into a multiplicity of objectives that may actually be competing with each other. This, in essence, represents the fluidity of community work that is constantly and cyclically involved in:

- Assessing needs of community members and groups.
- Re-negotiating how groups respond to policy changes of, for example, the local authority.
- Having to re-prioritise because of changes in the composition and skills capacity of community group(s).
- Dealing with conflicts within the group that may prevent or delay the achievement of the original objectives.
- Responding to unforeseen funding opportunities.

Indeed it could be argued that a community work initiative that does not generate new objectives is perhaps being inflexible and dogmatic in its approach. It is therefore important for organisations to consider:

- How is this complexity of multi-level objectives represented within the mechanisms that your agency has for collecting data?

- Is the agency's portfolio system for collecting evaluation data flexible enough to accommodate these changing objectives?
- Is the evaluation work being undertaken actually reflective of the actual objectives or does it relate to out-dated ones?

Key questions

1. How can you demonstrate the impact, value and significance of what you achieve without compromising the need to demonstrate reasonable accountability and value for money?
2. Are you clear about whom you are evaluating for?
3. Is your evaluation process democratic?
4. Are the costs of evaluation built into the project proposals at the outset?
5. How can you reclaim the evaluation agenda and sell it to your numerous stakeholders?

Conclusion

It is essential that the re-claiming of the evaluation agenda is considered at a number of levels within an organisation, including at the level of the community that it works with as well as other key stakeholders. A dialogue with funders is essential if changes in the evaluation culture are to be stimulated. There needs to be a raising in profile of the rich variety of evaluation approaches that have been written about and practised so that the field of community work has at its disposal a range of powerful tools with which to begin re-claiming the evaluation agenda.

References

Armstrong, J., and Key, M. (1979) 'Evaluation, change and community work', *Community Development Journal*, 14: 3.

Barr, A., Hashagen, S., and Purcell, R. (1996) *Monitoring and Evaluating Community Development in Northern Ireland*. N. Ireland: Voluntary Action Unit, Dept. of Social Services.

Coombe, C.M. (1997) 'Using empowerment evaluation in community organising and community-based health initiatives, in M. Minker (ed.), *Community Organising and Community Building for Health*. New Jersey: Rutgers University Press.

Dale, R. (1998) *Evaluation Frameworks for Development Programmes and Projects*. New Delhi: Sage.

Dixon, J., and Sindell, C. (1994) 'Applying logics of change to the evaluation of community development in health promotion, *Health Promotion International*, 9: 4.

Edmonds, J. (ed.) (1999) *Health Promotion with Young People: An Introductory Guide to Evaluation*. London: Health Education Authority.

Estrella, M., and Gaventa, J. (1998) *Who Counts Reality? Participatory Monitoring and Evaluation: A Literature Review*. IDS working paper no. 70. Brighton: IDS.

Everitt, A., and Hardiker, P. (1996) *Evaluating for Good Practice*. London: Macmillan.

Guba, E., and Lincoln, Y.S. (1989) *Fourth Generation Evaluation*. London: Sage.

House, E.R. (ed.) (1986) *New Directions in Educational Evaluation*. London: Falmer.

Meyrick, J., and Sinkler, P. (1999) *An Evaluation Resource for Healthy Living Centres*. London: Health Education Authority.

Rubin, F. (1995) *A Basic Guide to Evaluation for Development Workers*. Oxford: Oxfam.

Russell, J. (1998) *The Purpose of Evaluation. Different Ways of Seeing Evaluation. Self-evaluation Involving Users in Evaluation. Performance Indicators: Use and Misuse. Using Evaluation to Explore Policy*. Discussion papers. London: Charities Evaluation Service.

Subhra, G., and Chauhan, V. (1999) *Developing Black Services*. London: Alcohol Concern.

Taylor, M. (1995) *Unleashing the Potential: Bringing Residents to the Centre of Regeneration*. York: Joseph Rowntree Foundation.

Van Der Eyken, W. (1993) *Managing Evaluation*. London: Charities Evaluation Service.

Weiss, C.H. (ed.) (1986) 'The stakeholder approach to evaluation: origins and promise, in E. House, (ed.), *New Directions in Educational Evaluation*. London: Falmer.

Index